Picture - Perfect
STEM
Lessons, Grade 2

Using Children's Books for Three-Dimensional Learning

EXPANDED EDITION
Grade 2

by Karen Ansberry and Emily Morgan

nsta Press
National Science Teaching Association
Arlington, Virginia

Cathy Iammartino, Director of Publications and Digital Initiatives

PRINTING AND PRODUCTION
Colton Gigot, Senior Production Manager

ART AND DESIGN
Linda Olliver, Cover, Interior Design, Illustrations

PRODUCTION AND PROJECT MANAGEMENT
KTD+ Education Group

NATIONAL SCIENCE TEACHING ASSOCIATION
Erika C. Shugart, PhD, Executive Director
1840 Wilson Blvd., Arlington, VA 22201
www.nsta.org/store
For customer service inquiries, please call 800-277-5300.

NSTA is committed to publishing material that promotes the best in inquiry-based science education. However, conditions of actual use may vary, and the safety procedures and practices described in this book are intended to serve only as a guide. Additional precautionary measures may be required. NSTA and the authors do not warrant or represent that the procedures and practices in this book meet any safety code or standard of federal, state, or local regulations. NSTA and the authors disclaim any liability for personal injury or damage to property arising out of or relating to the use of this book, including any of the recommendations, instructions, or materials contained therein.

Library of Congress Cataloging-in-Publication Data
Names: Ansberry, Karen Rohrich, 1966- author. | Morgan, Emily R. (Emily Rachel), 1973- author.
Title: Picture-perfect STEM lessons, grade 2 : using children's books for three-dimensional learning / by Karen Ansberry and Emily Morgan.
Description: Expanded edition. | Arlington, VA : National Science Teaching Association, [2023] | Includes bibliographical references and index.
Summary: "There's a lot to love about this newly expanded book in the Picture-Perfect Science series. You can combine STEM and reading through lively lessons that are just right for your second-grade students. Also, reading-comprehension strategies are embedded in all 12 of the to read and read to learn while engaging in activities that blend science, technology, engineering, and mathematics"-- Provided by publisher.
Identifiers: LCCN 2022043069 (print) | LCCN 2022043070 (ebook) | ISBN 9781681408491 (paperback) | ISBN 9781681409993 (pdf)
Subjects: LCSH: Science--Study and teaching (Elementary) | Technology--Study and teaching (Elementary) | Children's books. | Picture books for children--Educational aspects. | Reading comprehension--Study and teaching (Elementary)
Classification: LCC LB1585 .A585 2023 (print) | LCC LB1585 (ebook) | DDC 372.35/044--dc23/eng/20220917
LC record available at *https://lccn.loc.gov/2022043069*
LC ebook record available at *https://lccn.loc.gov/2022043070*

Contents

Preface

A class of second-grade students listens as their teacher reads *The Day the Crayons Came Home*, the clever story of a group of wayward crayons left in various places by a boy named Duncan. The crayons are sending postcards to Duncan, each with a woeful tale to tell and a plea to return to the crayon box. One postcard reads,

"Duncan!

It's us…Yellow and Orange. We know we used to argue over which of us was the color of the Sun…but guess what? NEITHER of us wants to be the color of the Sun anymore. Not since we were left outside and the sun melted us…TOGETHER! You know the real color of the Sun?? HOT. That's what. We're sorry for arguing. You can make GREEN the Sun for all we care, just BRING US HOME!

Your not-so-sunny friends,

Yellow & Orange"

The second-grade students giggle at the silly postcards sent by the desperate crayons, and after the read-aloud, they recount some of the ways the crayons were changed in the book: broken, melted by the Sun, chewed by a dog, sharpened, melted in the dryer, etc. This leads them into an exploration of crayon properties (including measurements), an investigation of ways their physical properties can be changed, and learning how they are manufactured by reading a nonfiction book and watching a video of crayons being made in a factory. Students discover that there is a surprising amount of engineering and technology behind the design and production of this classroom staple, and they apply the steps of the engineering design process to come up with a way to recycle crayons into new and interesting shapes. This activity addresses the engineering core idea that a situation that people want to change or create can be solved through engineering. Finally, students incorporate English language arts standards by writing their own postcard from an adventurous crayon who has been through a number of changes, demonstrating their understanding of the physical science core idea that heating or cooling a substance may cause changes that can be observed, and sometimes these changes are reversible. Through this engaging lesson, students learn about the interdependence of science, technology, engineering, and mathematics in the crayon-manufacturing industry—all within the context of an amusing fictional story.

What Is Picture-Perfect STEM?

The Picture-Perfect Science program was developed to help elementary teachers integrate science and reading in an engaging, child-friendly way. Since the debut of the first book in the Picture-Perfect Science Lessons series in 2005, teachers across the country have been using the lessons to integrate science and literacy. Following the first series of Picture-Perfect books, *Picture-Perfect STEM Lessons: Using Children's Books to Inspire STEM Learning* was published, adding an emphasis on the intersection of science, technology, engineering, and mathematics in the real world. Both books (K–2 and 3–5) in the Picture-Perfect STEM series contain 15 lessons, with embedded reading-comprehension strategies to help children learn to read and read to learn while engaged in STEM activities.

What's New?

Teachers love teaching Picture-Perfect lessons, but many have asked us for a more flexible and economical purchasing option. That led to the publication of Picture-Perfect Science Lessons by Grade Level, a series of compilations spanning grades K–5. Each book in the series is geared for a single grade level and is closely aligned to the *Next Generation Science Standards* (*NGSS*; NGSS Lead States 2013). The book you are holding is an expanded version of the original grade-level series second-grade book with 11 updated lessons AND one brand-new lesson.

Why did we write this new book, and what is different about it? Much has happened in science education since we wrote our first Picture-Perfect Science book back in 2005. Since the introduction of the *NGSS* in 2013, science education has been changing for the better. These standards are based on current understanding of how children learn—and how science teaching can reflect the way scientists and engineers do their work. Students are no longer just memorizing facts or learning about how other people have done science. Instead, students are engaged in investigations in order to make sense of *phenomena*—observable events that occur in the universe and that we can use our science knowledge to explain or predict. In this way, the focus of science learning in the classroom has shifted from simply learning about a topic to one that more closely reflects the work of real scientists: figuring out why or how something happens.

Another significant change in science education is the elevation of engineering to the same level as scientific inquiry. Engineering involves designing solutions to problems that arise from phenomena and using explanations of phenomena to design solutions. So, phenomena are the context for the work of both the scientist and the engineer. Most lessons in this book contain design challenges, and many have a focus on the role of technology in science and engineering.

A key idea laid out in the *NGSS* is that science learning should be three-dimensional, meaning that instruction will integrate these three dimensions: (1) the science and engineering practices, or SEPs, through which scientists and engineers do their work (what students *do*); (2) the core ideas of the disciplines, or disciplinary core ideas (DCIs; what students *learn*); and (3) the crosscutting concepts, or CCCs, that apply across all science disciplines (how students *think*). The lessons in this book emphasize teaching and learning in these three dimensions. Boxes throughout the lessons indicate the SEPs and the CCCs that are being addressed in each part of the lesson. In addition, the phenomenon or design challenge that drives each lesson is clearly identified in the description using bold print, and we identify questions, writing activities, and discussions that help encourage student sensemaking of STEM concepts.

The following list summarizes these and other new features of the lessons in this book:

- Engaging phenomena that students find interesting and relevant to their everyday or family experiences

- More questioning strategies to help drive student sensemaking

- All three dimensions (SEPs, DCIs, and CCCs) clearly identified, as well as prompts and activities designed to more fully reflect teaching and learning in all three dimensions

- Learning progressions for each DCI reflecting increasing sophistication of student thinking across elementary school grade levels

- Updated reading strategies, including prompts for modeling how good readers monitor their comprehension

- QR codes to make recommended websites more readily accessible

In addition, Spanish language translations of all student pages and STEM Everywhere pages can now be purchased. Locate your state's NSTA Regional Product Representative for more information here: *www.nsta.org/nsta-regional-product-representatives*.

Use This Book Within Your Curriculum

We wrote *Picture-Perfect STEM Lessons, Grade 2, Expanded Edition* and the other books in the Picture-Perfect STEM series to supplement, not replace, your school's existing science or STEM program. Although each lesson stands alone as a carefully planned learning cycle based on clearly defined objectives, the lessons are intended to be integrated into a complete curriculum in which concepts can be more fully developed. The lessons are not designed to be taught sequentially. We want you to use this book where appropriate within your school's current STEM program to support, enrich, and extend it. We also want you to adapt the lessons to fit your school's curriculum, your students' needs, and your own teaching style.

Special Features of This Book

Ready-to-Use Lessons with Assessments

Each lesson contains engagement activities, hands-on explorations, student pages, suggestions for student and teacher explanations, elaboration activities, assessment suggestions, opportunities for STEM education at home, and annotated bibliographies of more books to read on the topic. Assessments include poster sessions, writing assignments, design challenges, and presentations.

Time Needed

The information in this section helps you pace each lesson. We estimate a second-grade class "session" to be about 40 minutes.

Background for Teachers

This section provides easy-to-understand background information for teachers to review before facilitating the lesson. Some information in the background section goes beyond the assessment

boundary for students, but it is provided to give teachers a deeper understanding of the content presented in the lesson.

Reading-Comprehension Strategies

Reading-comprehension strategies based on the book *Strategies That Work* (Harvey and Goudvis 2017) and specific activities to enhance comprehension are embedded throughout the lessons and clearly marked with an icon: 📖. Chapter 2 describes how to model these strategies while reading aloud to students.

Standards-Based Objectives

All lesson objectives are aligned to the *NGSS* (NGSS Lead States 2013). The lessons also incorporate the *Common Core State Standards for English Language Arts and Mathematics* (NGAC and CCSSO 2010). In a box titled "Connecting to the Common Core," you will find the Common Core subject a specific activity addresses as well as the standard number. You will see that writing assignments are labeled with a pencil icon: ✏️.

STEM Everywhere

Each lesson also provides an extension activity that is intended to be done outside school with family or other communities (under adult supervision). Students share what they learned and what questions they have about the topic. Then, together with their family, they complete the activity to apply and extend the learning. The activities in this section also work well as in-class extensions.

Opportunities for Differentiated Instruction

Students are engaged in three-dimensional learning in a guided manner throughout the lessons. We encourage you to provide opportunities for differentiation and more student-directed learning. At the end of each lesson, an "Opportunities for Differentiated Instruction" box is provided to help your students further investigate the core ideas from the lesson, use the science and engineering practices more independently, and think about how

STEM concepts connect to one another. This box lists questions and challenges related to the lesson that students may select to research, investigate, or innovate. Students may also use the questions as examples to help them generate their own questions.

References

Harvey, S., and A. Goudvis. 2017. *Strategies that work: Teaching comprehension for understanding, engagement, and building knowledge, grades K–8*. 3rd ed. Portland, ME: Stenhouse Publishers.

National Governors Association Center for Best Practices and Council of Chief State School Officers (NGAC and CCSSO). 2010. *Common core state standards*. Washington, DC: NGAC and CCSSO.

NGSS Lead States. 2013. *Next Generation Science Standards: For states, by states*. Washington, DC: National Academies Press. *www.nextgenscience.org/next-generation-science-standards*.

Children's Book Cited

Daywalt, D. 2015. The day the crayons came home. New York: Philomel Books.

Publisher's Note

The Picture-Perfect STEM series builds on the texts of children's picture books to teach STEM. Some of these picture books feature objects that have been anthropomorphized, such as crayons that pack their bags and travel the world. Although we recognize that many scientists and educators believe that personification, teleology, animism, and anthropomorphism promote misconceptions among young children, others believe that removing these elements would leave children's literature severely underpopulated. Furthermore, backers of these techniques not only see little harm in their use but also argue that they facilitate learning. Because the Picture-Perfect STEM series specifically and carefully supports science and engineering practices, we feel the question remains open.

Acknowledgments

We dedicate this book series to all the primary teachers who are working to make STEM an important part of their students' lives, both in and out of the classroom. We thank Kim Stilwell and Rick Bounds for their dedication to making this grade-level series a reality. We appreciate the care and attention to detail given to this project by our editor, Katherine Hall. We also gratefully acknowledge the contributions of the reviewers and the NSTA Sensemaking Review Cadre.

About the Authors

Karen Ansberry is a teacher, writer, and mom to four young readers. She has a bachelor of science in biology from Xavier University in Cincinnati, Ohio, and a master of arts in teaching from Miami University in Oxford, Ohio. She is a former elementary science curriculum leader and fifth- and sixth-grade science teacher at Mason City Schools in Mason, Ohio. In addition to coauthoring the Picture-Perfect STEM series and *Teaching Science Through Trade Books,* she is the author of *Nature Did It First: Engineering Through Biomimicry.* Karen lives in Ohio with her husband, sons, daughters, and dogs.

Emily Morgan is a teacher, writer, and mom. She has a bachelor of science in elementary education from Wright State University in Dayton, Ohio, and a master of science in education from the University of Dayton. She is a former elementary science lab teacher for Mason City Schools in Mason, Ohio, and seventh-grade science teacher at Northridge Local Schools in Dayton, Ohio. She served as a science consultant for the Hamilton County Educational Service Center and as a science leader for the High AIMS Consortium. In addition to coauthoring the Picture-Perfect STEM series and *Teaching Science Through Trade Books,* she is the author of the Next Time You See series and *Never Stop Wondering,* all from NSTA Press. Emily lives in Ohio with her husband, son, and an assortment of animals.

About the Picture-Perfect STEM Program

The Picture-Perfect Science program originated from Karen Ansberry's and Emily Morgan's shared interest in using children's literature to make science more engaging. In Emily's 2001 master's thesis study involving 350 of her third-grade science lab students at Western Row Elementary in Mason, Ohio, she found that students who used science picture books instead of the textbook scored significantly higher on district science performance assessments than students who used the textbook. Convinced of the benefits of using picture books to engage students in science inquiry and to increase science understanding, Emily and Karen began collaborating with Sue Livingston, Mason City School District's elementary language arts curriculum leader, in an effort to integrate literacy strategies into inquiry-based science lessons. They received grants from the Ohio Department of Education (2001) and Toyota Tapestry (2002) to train all third- through sixth-grade science teachers, and in 2003 they also trained seventh- and eighth-grade science teachers with district support. This led to the publication of *Picture-Perfect Science Lessons, More Picture-Perfect Science Lessons, Even More Picture-Perfect Science Lessons,* and, in 2017, the first *Picture-Perfect STEM Lessons* books. The program has been presented at elementary schools, conferences, and universities nationwide. For more information on Picture-Perfect STEM teacher workshops, go to *www.pictureperfectscience.com*. For more information on Picture-Perfect books and materials, please visit *www.nsta.org/book-series/picture-perfect-science*.

Websites

 Picture-Perfect Science Workshops
www.pictureperfectscience.com

 Picture-Perfect Books and Materials
*www.nsta.org/book-series/
picture-perfect-science*

Safety Practices for Science Activities

With hands-on, process- and inquiry-based science/STEM activities, the teaching and learning of science today can be both effective and exciting. The challenge to securing this success needs to be met by addressing potential safety issues relative to engineering controls (ventilation, eyewash station, etc.), administrative procedures and safety operating procedures, and use of appropriate personal protective equipment (indirectly vented chemical splash goggles meeting ANSI Z87.1 standard, chemical resistant aprons and non-latex gloves, etc.). Teachers can make it safer for students and themselves by adopting, implementing, and enforcing legal safety standards and better professional safety practices in the science/STEM classroom and laboratory. Throughout this book, the safety notes provided for science/STEM activities should be adopted and enforced to create a safer learning and teaching experience. Teachers should also review and follow local policies and protocols used in their school district and/or school (e.g., employer OSHA Hazard Communication Safety Plan and Board of Education safety policies).

Additional applicable standard operating procedures can be found in the National Science Teaching Association's "Elementary Science Safety Acknowledgment Form" (see "Websites"). Students should be required to review the document or one similar to it for elementary-level students under the direction of the teacher. It is important to also include safety information about working at home or other community spaces for the "STEM Everywhere" activities. Both the student and the parent or guardian should then sign the document acknowledging procedures that must be followed for a safer working and learning experience in the classroom, laboratory, or field. The Council of State Science Supervisors also has a safety resource for elementary science activities titled "Science and Safety: It's Elementary!" (see "Websites").

Please note that the safety precautions for each activity are based, in part, on use of the recommended materials and instructions, legal safety standards, and better professional practices. Selection of alternative materials or procedures for these activities may jeopardize the level of safety and therefore is at the user's own risk. For more safety resources, visit NSTA's "Safety Resources" web page (see "Websites").

Websites

 Council of State Science Supervisors' "Science and Safety: It's Elementary!" resource
https://portal.ct.gov/-/media/SDE/Science/Safety/scisaf_cal.pdf

 NSTA's "Elementary Science Safety Acknowledgment Form"
https://static.nsta.org/pdfs/SafetyAcknowledgmentForm-ElementarySchool.pdf

 NSTA's "COVID-19 Pandemic Safer Science/STEM Online and Face-to-Face Learning Environments Instruction Disclaimer Statement"
www.nsta.org/covid-19-pandemic-safer-science

 NSTA's "Safety Resources" web page
www.nsta.org/topics/safety

Why Use Picture Books to Teach STEM?

Think about a book you loved as a child. Maybe you remember the zany characters and rhyming text of Dr. Seuss classics such as *Green Eggs and Ham*, or maybe you were inspired to write your own poetry after reading Langston Hughes's *The First Book of Rhythms*. Perhaps you enjoyed the page-turning suspense of Jon Stone's *The Monster at the End of This Book* or the powerful lessons in Shel Silverstein's *The Giving Tree*. Maybe your curiosity was piqued by the technical illustrations and fascinating explanations in *The Way Things Work* by David Macaulay or the illustrated anthology *Childcraft: The How and Why Library*. Perhaps you dreamed of space travel after reading the classic adventure *You Will Go to the Moon* by Mae and Ira Freeman. You may have seen a little of yourself in *Madeline* by Ludwig Bemelmans, *Where the Wild Things Are* by Maurice Sendak, *Ramona the Pest* by Beverly Cleary, or *The Snowy Day* by Ezra Jack Keats. Perhaps your imagination was stirred by *Cloudy With a Chance of Meatballs* by Judi and Ronald Barrett or *A Wrinkle in Time* by Madeleine L'Engle. You most likely remember the cozy feeling of having a treasured book such as Don Freeman's *Corduroy*, Margery Williams's *The Velveteen Rabbit* illustrated by William Nicholson, or Robert Munsch's *Love You Forever* illustrated by Sheila McGraw being read to you by a parent or grandparent. But chances are your favorite book as a child was not one of your elementary school science textbooks!

TEACHERS LOVE USING PICTURE BOOKS

There's no question that STEM plays a critical role in K–12 education today. But did you know that one of the most effective ways to get kids interested in STEM learning and expose them to STEM careers is through children's literature? The format of picture books in particular offers certain unique advantages over both textbooks and chapter books for engaging students in a STEM lesson. More often than other books, fiction and nonfiction picture books stimulate students on both an emotional and intellectual level. They are appealing and memorable because children readily connect with the engaging storylines, imaginative illustrations, vivid photographs, exciting adventures of characters, fascinating information that supports them in their quest for knowledge, and warm emotions that surround read-aloud time. The positive experiences and memories of listening to picture books being read aloud by a family member or beloved teacher can inspire a lifelong love of reading. With *Picture-Perfect STEM Lessons, Grade 2, Expanded Edition*, you will learn how to tap into the magic of a good picture book to inspire STEM learning in your classroom.

What characterizes a picture book? We like what *Beginning Reading and Writing* says: "Picture books are unique to children's literature as they are defined by format rather than content. That is, they are books in which the illustrations are of equal importance as or more important than the text in the creation of meaning" (Strickland and Morrow 2000, p. 137). Because picture books are more likely to hold children's attention, they lend themselves to reading-comprehension strategy instruction and to engaging students within an inquiry-based cycle of science instruction. "Picture books, both fiction and nonfiction, are more likely to hold our attention and engage us than reading dry, formulaic text … Engagement leads to remembering what is read, acquiring knowledge and enhancing understanding" (Harvey and Goudvis 2017, p. 50). We wrote the Picture-Perfect STEM series so teachers can take advantage of the positive features of children's picture books by supplementing the traditional textbook or kit program with a wide variety of high-quality fiction and nonfiction STEM-related picture books.

What Is STEM?

Turn on the television news, open a newspaper, or browse an internet news source, and you'll likely find a story about a new STEM initiative or program at a school, library, or museum—STEM is everywhere these days! Historically, these four disciplines (science, technology, engineering, and mathematics) have been taught independently (see the box on the next page for more details about each discipline), with engineering often overlooked. But over the past several years, STEM education has gained momentum as an interdisciplinary way of teaching that goes beyond what is being learned in these disciplines to include the *application* of what is being learned, with increased efforts to include engineering in elementary classrooms.

So what exactly is meant by "STEM education"? STEM education first gained prominence as a result of efforts to keep the United States competitive in the global economy, with the argument that most jobs (and some of the best paying jobs) in the 21st-century workforce would require the application of the STEM disciplines. U.S. policy makers have called for increasing the pool of highly skilled college graduates in STEM, including women and minorities who are often underrepresented in these fields. Nearly all of the emerging careers for 2025 identified by the World Economic Forum's The Future of Jobs Report 2020 are in STEM fields, ranging from data science to software development. But even students who do not pursue STEM jobs need to become STEM literate in order to understand the world around them, to make informed decisions, and to seek sustainable solutions to human problems. The National Science and Technology Council's Committee on STEM Education describes it this way:

STEM literacy depends on access to high-quality, lifelong STEM learning for all Americans. Even for those who may never be employed in a STEM-related job, a basic understanding and comfort

The Four STEM Disciplines

Science is the study of the natural world, including the laws of nature associated with physics, chemistry, and biology, and the treatment or application of facts, principles, concepts, or conventions associated with these disciplines. Science is both a body of knowledge that has been accumulated over time and a process—scientific inquiry—that generates new knowledge. Knowledge from science informs an engineering design process.

Technology includes the entire system of people and organizations, knowledge, processes, and devices that go into creating and operating technological artifacts, as well as the artifacts themselves. Throughout history, humans have created technology to satisfy their wants and needs. Much of modern technology is a product of science and engineering, and technological tools are used in both fields.

Engineering is both a body of knowledge—about the design and creation of human-made products—and a process for solving problems. This process is design under constraint. One constraint in engineering design is the laws of nature, or science. Other constraints include time, cost, available materials, ergonomics, environmental regulations, manufacturability, and repairability. Engineering uses concepts in science and mathematics as well as technological tools.

Mathematics is the study of patterns and relationships among quantities, numbers, and shapes. Specific branches of mathematics include arithmetic, geometry, algebra, trigonometry, and calculus. Mathematics is used in science and in engineering.

Source: National Academy of Engineering and National Research Council 2009.

with STEM and STEM-enabled technology has become a prerequisite for full participation in modern society. STEM education teaches thinking and problem-solving skills that are transferrable to many other endeavors. STEM literacy gives individuals a better capacity to make informed choices on personal health and nutrition, entertainment, transportation, cybersecurity, financial management, and parenting. A STEM-literate public will be better equipped to conduct thoughtful analysis and to sort through problems, propose innovative solutions, and handle rapid technological change, and will be better prepared to participate in civil society as jurors, voters, and consumers (Committee on STEM Education 2018, p. 5).

Our approach to teaching STEM is simple. It involves making natural connections among the STEM disciplines as you help your students investigate and problem solve within a meaningful context. In the Picture-Perfect STEM series, picture books provide this meaningful context. The books help engage and motivate students, introduce topics and establish themes, set up investigations and real-world problem-solving opportunities, spark creativity and innovation, explain science and engineering concepts, and develop the empathy needed to design solutions to human problems. Science and engineering standards provide the learning framework, while reading strategies, technology, and mathematics are used as tools within this framework to support and extend student learning. The lessons are written so the connections among the four disciplines are natural, not forced. For example, mathematics is applied where it fits within the overall goal of the lesson (not simply to meet a mathematics objective). So you will not see all four STEM disciplines given equal emphasis in every lesson.

Why STEM in Grades K–2?

Young children are natural STEM learners. Whether it is counting toy cars, building with blocks, testing buoyancy in the bathtub, observing pendulums on the playground, or marveling at the changing Moon, children tend to demonstrate an affinity for STEM learning early in life. And no doubt you've noticed how readily young students embrace digital technology, from video games to tablets to computers. High-quality STEM experiences in the primary grades help foster these early inclinations and set the stage for later success. If children do not have access to engaging and meaningful early STEM experiences, they may lose confidence in their STEM abilities or lose interest in STEM altogether. STEM literacy is necessary for all learners, not just those who will someday enter the STEM fields. The authors of *STEM Starts Early: Grounding Science, Technology, Engineering, and Math Education in Early Childhood* put it this way:

> *Just as the industrial revolution made it necessary for all children to learn to read, the technology revolution has made it critical for all children to understand STEM. To support the future of our nation, the seeds of STEM must be planted early, along with and in support of the seeds of literacy. Together, these mutually enhancing, interwoven strands of learning will grow well-informed, critical citizens prepared for a digital tomorrow (McClure et al. 2017, p. 4).*

Another reason to address STEM in the early grades is that children's attitudes about STEM and about themselves as STEM learners form early. A 2017 report from the Early Childhood STEM Working Group states,

> *"Children's earliest experiences with science, technology, engineering, and mathematics set the stage for their later engagement and success in those fields; if we fail to give all children access to high-quality early STEM experiences, instead providing either inferior quality STEM expe-*

> *riences or no STEM at all, they may very well lose interest in STEM topics or lose confidence that they can 'do' STEM." (Early Childhood STEM Working Group 2017, p. 7)*

We can't underestimate the value of these early STEM experiences where students feel empowered by "doing" STEM. In our lessons, students not only read about STEM but also actively participate in STEM activities, such as designing simple investigations, collecting data, and solving design problems.

Why Picture Books?

Context for Concepts

One reason for using picture books to teach STEM is that they can provide a context for the concepts students are exploring. Understanding a new idea depends on whether learners can connect it to concepts that they already know about. Picture books help build that background knowledge, creating a common experience that gives all students a shared frame of reference for their learning. The wide array of high-quality STEM-related children's literature currently available can help you explain concepts and model reading-comprehension strategies in a meaningful context. Children's picture books have interesting storylines that can help students understand and remember concepts better than they would by using only textbooks, which tend to present science as lists of facts to be memorized (Butzow and Butzow 2000). As more and more content is packed into the school day and higher expectations are placed on student performance, teachers must make more efficient use of their time. Zemelman, Daniels, and Hyde (2012) suggest that connecting various content areas can lead to deep engagement as students read, write, talk, view, watch, explore, create, and interact around a topic.

Our previous Picture-Perfect Science books are based on research that shows that integrating science with literacy makes science more meaningful to students and can lead to increases in achievement in both subjects. Although research is limited on the impact of picture books on STEM learning, we believe these benefits apply to STEM and

literacy integration because students are provided with a meaningful context in which to investigate, innovate, and communicate.

Simple Explanations

Nonfiction children's picture books can be excellent tools to help students make sense of their world. Nonfiction reading is reading to learn, and nonfiction picture books are very good at helping students transform information into knowledge. There are many picture book writers who are masterful at making abstract concepts more child-friendly and relatable using simple words, everyday examples, and a conversational tone. Headings, captions, bold-print words, and other features used in nonfiction picture books can signal importance and scaffold understanding as students read to learn. In addition, research has shown that the colorful pictures and graphics in picture books are superior to many texts for explaining abstract ideas (Kralina 1993).

More Depth

Science textbooks can be overwhelming for many children, especially those who have reading problems. Textbooks often contain unfamiliar vocabulary and tend to cover a broad range of topics (Casteel and Isom 1994; Short and Armstrong 1993; Tyson and Woodward 1989). However, fiction and nonfiction picture books tend to focus on fewer topics and give more in-depth coverage of the concepts. It can be useful to pair an engaging fiction book with a nonfiction book to round out the science content being presented.

For example, the Picture-Perfect STEM kindergarten lesson titled "The Handiest Things" features *The Handiest Things in the World* by Andrew Clements, an engaging book about some commonplace inventions that make our everyday lives easier. It is paired with *Engineering in Our Everyday Lives* by Reagan Miller, which explains how engineers design technologies to solve everyday problems. The engaging verse and illustrations in *The Handiest Things in the World* hook the reader, whereas the information in *Engineering in Our Everyday Lives* helps students understand how engineering design processes are used in the real world. Together, those books offer a balanced, in-depth look at what engineers do and how engineering affects our everyday lives.

Improvement in Science, Reading, and Mathematics

Research by Morrow and colleagues (1997) on using children's literature and literacy instruction in the science program indicated gains in science and literacy. Romance and Vitale (1992) found significant improvement in the science and reading scores of fourth graders when the regular basal reading program was replaced with reading in science that correlated with the science curriculum. They also found an improvement in students' attitudes toward the study of science. Many studies, including one by Van den Heuvel-Panhuizen, Elia, and Robitzsch (2014), show that reading picture books can have a positive influence on children's mathematical performance as well.

Opportunities to Correct Science Misconceptions

Students often have strongly held misconceptions about science that can interfere with their learning. "Misconceptions, in the field of science education, are preconceived ideas that differ from those currently accepted by the scientific community" (Colburn 2003, p. 59). Children's picture books, reinforced with hands-on inquiries, can help students correct their misconceptions. Repetition of the correct concept by reading several books, doing a number of experiments, and inviting scientists to the classroom can facilitate a conceptual change in children (Miller, Steiner, and Larson 1996).

But teachers must be aware that scientific misconceptions can be inherent in the picture books. Although many errors are explicit, some of the misinformation is more implicit or may be inferred from text and illustrations (Rice 2002). This problem is more likely to occur in fictionalized material. Mayer's (1995) study demonstrated that when both inaccuracies and science facts are presented in the same book, children do not necessarily remember the correct information. The nonfiction picture books in these lessons have been carefully reviewed

for accuracy. When reading fiction as a part of a STEM lesson, it is important to identify which parts of the book are make-believe.

Tools for Building Empathy

Picture books can help children gain awareness of people and situations outside their own experience and develop a sense of empathy. Neuroscientists generally define *empathy* as the ability to recognize, understand, and share the thoughts and feelings of another person, animal, or fictional character. It's like stepping into the shoes of someone else. Empathy is not only crucial for establishing relationships and behaving compassionately, it is also the first stage in what is known as "design thinking." When designing anything meant to be used by another person, the designers must set aside their own assumptions and perceptions about the world to understand what that person—or the end user—wants or needs. In the Picture-Perfect STEM series, we often use true stories to engage students' emotions and generate empathy before a design challenge in order to make the task more meaningful for the designer and the end product more beneficial to the user. For example, in the first-grade lesson "Let's Drum!", we read *Drum Dream Girl* by Margarita Engle, the true story of a girl who persevered after being told she was not allowed to play the drums. This motivates students to learn about the science of sound and then design and play their own drums just like the main character in the story.

Fiction can also be an effective tool for building empathy and giving purpose to a design challenge. Writer Neil Gaiman, in his 2013 lecture to the Reading Agency, said, "[When you read fiction], you get to feel things, visit places and worlds you would never otherwise know. You learn that everyone else out there is a 'me,' as well. You're being someone else, and when you return to your own world, you're going to be slightly changed." That change, born of the experience of being in someone else's shoes, can be a powerful motivator for the design process. For instance, a kindergarten lesson titled "Feel the Heat" features the book *Summer Sun Risin'* by W. Nikola-Lisa and Don Tate, a fictional story set on a Texas farm. Students make personal connections to the young boy in the story as they discover how the Sun affects his daily activities. Then they design a shade structure that could help someone like him keep cool on a hot day.

A truly engaging picture book, whether a fictional story or a narrative about a real person, can build empathy, ground an engineering challenge in a meaningful context, motivate students to work together for a common purpose, and ignite the imagination and creativity necessary to solve real-world problems.

STEM Role Models

In *Strategies That Work*, Harvey and Goudvis (2017) say, "What better way to combine science and literacy than to read all about scientists and how they think about, study, and investigate topics they are passionate about" (p. 250). Reading, writing, and talking about people we call STEM role models can help students understand how those people use science and engineering practices in their work and can even inspire students' future career choices. *A Framework for K–12 Science Education* (NRC 2012) states:

> *Discussions involving the history of scientific and engineering ideas, of individual practitioners' contributions, and of the applications of these endeavors are important components of a science and engineering curriculum. For many students, these aspects are the pathways that capture their interest in these fields and build their identities as engaged and capable learners of science and engineering (p. 249).*

In the Picture-Perfect STEM series, we feature a variety of narrative information texts featuring inspiring, real-life STEM role models. Female role models in particular need to be visible in picture books to help develop girls' early interest in STEM. Some examples of women STEM career role models in our books include Wangari Maathai, who started Kenya's Green Belt movement; Marie Tharp, who mapped the ocean floor; and Isatou Ceesay, who

initiated a grassroots recycling movement in The Gambia that solved an environmental problem and empowered women.

We also use a variety of fictional stories with diverse and relatable characters who use STEM to solve problems. *Rosie Revere, Engineer* by Andrea Beaty is a tale about a shy girl who puts her creativity to work as she builds a flying machine and learns the value of persistence along the way. Another book in the same series, *Ada Twist, Scientist*, also by Andrea Beaty, features a young Black girl whose curiosity, imagination, and STEM skills help her solve a mystery.

In the absence of STEM role models, children receive messages that STEM is only for certain types of people. The good thing is that over the last several years, a growing number of picture books have been published that feature diverse characters as well as real-life scientists and engineers from underrepresented groups. Representation matters! As Vashti Harrison writes in her introduction to *Little Leaders: Bold Women in Black History*, "To be able to see yourself in someone else's story can be life-changing. To know a goal is achievable can be empowering" (p. viii).

Selection of Books

Each lesson in *Picture-Perfect STEM Lessons, Grade 2, Expanded Edition* focuses on the *Next Generation Science Standards* (*NGSS*; NGSS Lead States 2013) and *A Framework for K–12 Science Education* (NRC 2012). We've selected fiction and nonfiction children's picture books that closely relate to these standards. An annotated "More Books to Read" section is provided at the end of each lesson. If you would like to find more high-quality children's literature to use in your STEM classroom, check out both the Outstanding Science Trade Books for Students K–12 list and the Best STEM Books K–12 list, which are published each year by the National Science Teaching Association (NSTA). The books are carefully vetted by book-review panels composed of both science education and children's literature experts. Each year, new lists are featured in *Science and Children*, NSTA's journal for elemen-

tary school teachers. See the "Websites" section for archived lists. And, of course, make friends with your local and school librarians! They possess a wealth of knowledge about children's literature and often find out about new and exciting titles well before the general public.

When you select children's picture books for science instruction, you might consult with a knowledgeable colleague who can help you check them for errors or misinformation. Young and Moss (2006) describe five essential things to consider when selecting nonfiction trade books for science:

1. The authority of the author (i.e., the author's credibility and qualifications for writing the book)
2. The accuracy of the text, illustrations, and graphics
3. The appropriateness of the book for its intended audience (e.g., the book makes complex concepts understandable for young readers)
4. The literary artistry and quality of writing
5. The appearance or visual impact of the book

Using a rubric may also be valuable to help you make informed decisions about the science trade books you use in your classroom. One such tool that provides a systematic framework to simplify the trade book evaluation process is the Science Trade Book Evaluation Rubric, found in the article "Making Science Trade Book Choices for Elementary Classrooms" (Atkison, Matusevich, and Huber 2009).

Finding the Picture-Perfect Books and Materials

Each lesson in this book includes a "Featured Picture Books" section with titles, author and illustrator names, publication details, and summaries of each book. All the picture books featured in the lessons were in print as of the publication date of this book and can be found at your local bookstore or from an online retailer or library. NSTA has also created ClassPacks that contain the materials needed to do each lesson. ClassPacks are available for purchase from NSTA's Picture-Perfect Science web page (see the "Websites" section).

Considering Genre

Taking genre into account when you determine how to use a particular picture book within a STEM lesson is important. Donovan and Smolkin (2002) identify four different genres frequently recommended for teachers to use in their science instruction: story, non-narrative information, narrative information, and dual purpose. The genre of each picture book we use in a lesson is identified in the "Featured Picture Books" section at the beginning of the lesson. Summaries of the four genres, a representative picture book for each genre, and suggestions for using each genre within the Biological Sciences Curriculum Study (BSCS) 5E learning cycle follow. (Chapter 4 describes in detail the science learning cycle, known as the BSCS 5E Instructional Model, which we employ.)

Storybooks

Storybooks center on specific characters who work to resolve a conflict or problem. The major purpose of stories is to entertain, not to present factual information. The vocabulary is typically commonsense, everyday language. An engaging storybook can spark interest in a science topic and move students toward informational texts to answer questions inspired by the story. For example, a second-grade lesson titled "Build It!" (Chapter 12) begins with a read-aloud of *Iggy Peck, Architect* by Andrea Beaty, an amusing book about a boy who is obsessed with building. The charming story hooks learners and engages them in explorations of architecture.

Non-Narrative Information Books

Non-narrative information books are nonfiction texts that introduce a topic, describe the attributes of the topic, or describe typical events that occur. The focus of these texts is on the subject matter, not specific characters. The vocabulary is typically technical. This type of book is generally not meant to be read out loud from cover to cover, so readers can enter the text at any point. When planning a read-aloud of a non-narrative information book, choose the parts of the book that help students make sense of the STEM concepts they are exploring.

Many non-narrative information books contain features found in nonfiction, such as a table of contents, bold-print vocabulary words, a glossary, and an index. Some research suggests that these types of books are "the best resources for fostering children's scientific concepts as well as their appropriation of science discourse" (Pappas 2006). Young children tend to be less familiar with this genre and need many opportunities to experience this type of text. Using non-narrative information books will help students become familiar with the structure of textbooks, as well as real-world reading, which is primarily nonfiction. Teachers may want to read only those sections that provide the concepts and facts needed to meet particular STEM objectives.

One example of non-narrative information writing is the book *What is Pollination?*, which contains nonfiction text features such as a table of contents, diagrams, insets, a glossary, and an index. This book is featured in a second-grade Picture-Perfect STEM lesson: "Flight of the Pollinators" (Chapter 14). The appropriate placement of non-narrative information text in a science learning cycle is typically after students have had the opportunity to explore concepts through hands-on activities. At that point, students are engaged in the topic and are motivated to read the non-narrative information text to learn more.

Narrative Information Books

Narrative information books, another subset of nonfiction text, are sometimes called hybrid books. They provide an engaging format for factual information. They communicate a sequence of factual events over time and sometimes recount the events of a specific case to generalize to all cases. When using these books within STEM instruction, it can be useful to establish a purpose for reading so students focus on the science content rather than the storyline. In some cases, teachers may want to read the book one time through for the aesthetic components of the book and a second time to help

explain or reinforce specific STEM content. *Flip! How the Frisbee took Flight* by Margaret Muirhead is an example of a narrative information text and is used in the second-grade lesson called "Imaginative Inventions" (Chapter 7). This narrative tells the true story of how Fred Morrison's persistence and ingenuity led to the invention of the Frisbee. The narrative information genre can be used at any point in a science learning cycle. This genre can be both engaging and informative

Dual-Purpose Books

Dual-purpose books are intended to serve two purposes: to entertain and to inform. Part of the book presents a story or poem and the other part includes informational text. Sometimes, information can be found in the running text, but more frequently information appears in insets, diagrams, or separate pages. You may want to read only the story or poem component of a dual-purpose book to engage readers at the beginning of the science learning cycle. In the first-grade lesson "Nature Did It First", we use the dual-purpose book *Nature Did It First: Engineering Through Biomimicry*, which is part playful poetry and part fascinating nonfiction. The reader is introduced to a plant or an animal in rhyme and then provided an explanation of how engineers were inspired by that organism to solve a problem.

Dual-purpose books typically have little science content within the story. If the insets and diagrams are read, discussed, explained, and related to the story, these books can be very useful in helping students refine concepts and acquire scientific vocabulary after they have had opportunities for hands-on exploration.

Using Fiction and Nonfiction Texts

It can be useful to pair fiction and nonfiction books in read-alouds to round out the science or engineering content being presented. Because fiction books tend to be very engaging for students, they can be used to hook students at the beginning of a science lesson. However, most of the reading people do in everyday life is nonfiction. We are immersed in informational text every day, and we must be able to comprehend it to be successful in school, at work, and in society. Nonfiction books and other informational text such as articles should be used frequently in the elementary classroom. They often include text structures that differ from stories, and the opportunity to experience these structures in read-alouds can strengthen students' abilities to read and understand informational text. Duke (2004) recommends four strategies to help teachers improve students' comprehension of informational text:

1. Increase students' access to informational text.
2. Increase the time students spend working with informational text.
3. Teach comprehension strategies through direct instruction.
4. Create opportunities for students to use informational text for authentic purposes.

The Picture-Perfect STEM series addresses these recommendations in several ways. The lessons expose students to a variety of nonfiction picture books, articles, and websites on science topics, thereby increasing access to informational text. Various tools (e.g., card sorts, anticipation guides, and "stop and try it" ideas; see Chapter 2 for a complete list of these tools) help enhance students' comprehension of the informational text by increasing the time they spend working with it. Each lesson includes instructions for explicitly teaching comprehension strategies within the learning cycle. The inquiry-based lessons provide an authentic purpose for reading informational text, as students are motivated to read or listen to find the answers to questions generated in the inquiry activities.

In summary, we feel that picture books have an important place in STEM education in the elementary grades. Engaging stories and interesting nonfiction can activate prior knowledge and build schema, explain science and engineering concepts, establish a meaningful context for sensemaking, motivate students to read to learn while they learn to read,

inspire their interest in STEM, and help foster the empathy they need to be effective designers. Used within a constructivist framework, picture books can assist readers in transforming information into knowledge and help prepare them to meet the challenges of a rapidly changing world.

Websites

 Best STEM Books K–12
www.nsta.org/best-stem-books-k-12

 Outstanding Science Trade Books for Students K–12
www.nsta.org/outstanding-science-trade-books-students-k-12

 Picture-Perfect Science Web Page
www.nsta.org/book-series/picture-perfect-science

References

Atkison, T., M. N. Matusevich, and L. Huber. 2009. Making science trade book choices for elementary classrooms. *The Reading Teacher* 62 (6): 484–497.

Butzow, J., and C. Butzow. 2000. *Science through children's literature: An integrated approach*. Portsmouth, NH: Teacher Ideas Press.

Casteel, C. P., and B. A. Isom. 1994. Reciprocal processes in science and literacy learning. *The Reading Teacher* 47 (7): 538–544.

Colburn, A. 2003. *The lingo of learning: 88 education terms every science teacher should know*. Arlington, VA: NSTA Press.

Committee on STEM Education. 2018. Charting a course for success: America's strategy for STEM education. Washington, DC: National Science & Technology Council.

Donovan, C., and L. Smolkin. 2002. Considering genre, content, and visual features in the selection of trade books for science instruction. *The Reading Teacher* 55 (6): 502–520.

Duke, N. K. 2004. The case for informational text. *Educational Leadership* 61 (6): 40–44.

Early Childhood STEM Working Group. 2017. Early STEM matters: Providing high-quality STEM experiences for all young learners. Chicago: UChicago STEM Education & Erickson Institute.

Gaiman, N. 2013. Why our future depends on libraries, reading and daydreaming. Lecture to the Reading Agency, London.

Harvey, S., and A. Goudvis. 2017. *Strategies that work: Teaching comprehension for understanding, engagement, and building knowledge, grades K–8*. 3rd ed. Portland, ME: Stenhouse Publishers.

Kralina, L. 1993. Tricks of the trades: Supplementing your science texts. *The Science Teacher* 60 (9): 33–37.

Mayer, D. A. 1995. How can we best use children's literature in teaching science concepts? *Science and Children* 32 (6): 16–19, 43.

McClure, E. R., L. Guernsey, D. H. Clements, S. N. Bales, J. Nichols, N. Kendall-Taylor, and M. H. Levine. 2017. STEM starts early: Grounding science, technology, engineering, and math education in early childhood. New York: The Joan Ganz Cooney Center at Sesame Workshop.

Miller, K. W., S. F. Steiner, and C. D. Larson. 1996. Strategies for science learning. *Science and Children* 33 (6): 24–27.

Morrow, L. M., M. Pressley, J. K. Smith, and M. Smith. 1997. The effect of a literature-based program integrated into literacy and science instruction with children from diverse backgrounds. *Reading Research Quarterly* 32 (1): 54–76.

National Academy of Engineering and National Research Council. 2009. *Engineering in K–12 education: Understanding the status and improving the prospects*. Washington, DC: National Academies Press.

National Research Council (NRC). 2012. *A framework for K–12 science education: Practices, crosscutting concepts, and core ideas*. Washington, DC: National Academies Press.

NGSS Lead States. 2013. *Next Generation Science Standards: For states, by states*. Washington, DC: National Academies Press. *www.nextgenscience.org/next-generation-science-standards*.

Pappas, C. 2006. The information book genre: Its role in integrated science literacy research and practice. *Reading Research Quarterly* 41 (2): 226–250.

Rice, D. C. 2002. Using trade books in teaching elementary science: Facts and fallacies. *The Reading Teacher* 55 (6): 552–565.

Romance, N. R., and M. R. Vitale. 1992. A curriculum strategy that expands time for in-depth elementary science instruction by using science-based reading strategies: Effects of a year-long study in grade four. *Journal of Research in Science Teaching* 29 (6): 545–554.

Short, K. G., and J. Armstrong. 1993. Moving toward inquiry: Integrating literature into the science curriculum. *New Advocate* 6 (3): 183–200.

Strickland, D. S., and L. M. Morrow, eds. 2000. B*eginning reading and writing*. New York: Teachers College Press.

Tyson, H., and A. Woodward. 1989. Why aren't students learning very much from textbooks? *Educational Leadership* 47 (3): 14–17.

Van den Heuvel-Panhuizen, M., I. Elia, and A. Robitzsch. 2014. Effects of reading picture books on kindergartners' mathematics performance. *Educational Psychology* 36 (2): 323–346.

World Economic Forum. 2020. The future of jobs report 2020. *www.weforum.org/reports/the-future-of-jobs-report-2020*.

Young, T. A., and B. Moss. 2006. Nonfiction in the classroom library: A literary necessity. *Childhood Education* 82 (4): 207–212.

Zemelman, S., H. Daniels, and A. Hyde. 2012. *Best practice: Bringing standards to life in America's classrooms*. 4th ed. Portsmouth, NH: Heinemann.

Children's Books Cited

Ansberry, K. 2020. *Nature did it first: Engineering through biomimicry*. Nevada City, CA: Dawn Publications.

Barrett, J., and R. Barrett. 1978. *Cloudy with a chance of meatballs*. New York: Atheneum Books for Young Readers.

Beaty, A. 2007. *Iggy Peck, architect*. New York: Abrams Books for Young Readers.

Beaty, A. 2013. *Rosie Revere, engineer*. New York: Abrams Books for Young Readers.

Beaty, A. 2016. *Ada Twist, scientist*. New York: Abrams Books for Young Readers.

Bemelmans, L. 1958. *Madeline*. New York: Penguin Young Readers Group.

Childcraft Editors. 1973. *Childcraft: The how and why library*. New York: World Book.

Cleary, B. 1968. *Ramona the pest*. New York: HarperCollins.

Clements, A. 2010. *The handiest things in the world*. New York: Atheneum Books for Young Readers.

Engel, M. 2015. *Drum dream girl: How one girl's courage changed music*. New York: HMH Books for Young Readers.

Freeman, D. 1968. *Corduroy*. New York: Viking Press.

Freeman, M., and I. Freeman. 1959. *You will go to the Moon*. New York: Random House Children's Books.

Harrison, V. 2017. *Little leaders: Bold women in Black history*. New York: Little, Brown Books for Young Readers.

Hughes, L. 1954. *The first book of rhythms*. New York: Franklin Watts.

Kalman, B. 2010. What is pollination? New York: Crabtree Publishing Company.

Keats, E. 1962. The snowy day. New York: Viking Press.

L'Engle, M. 1963. *A wrinkle in time*. New York: Farrar, Straus & Giroux.

Macaulay, D. 1988. *The way things work*. New York: Houghton Mifflin/Walter Lorraine Books.

Miller, R. 2014. *Engineering in our everyday lives*. New York: Crabtree.

Muirhead, M. 2021. *Flip! How the Frisbee Took Flight*. Watertown, MA: Charlesbridge.

Munsch, R. 1986. *Love you forever*. Scarborough, Ontario: Firefly Books.

Nikola-Lisa, W. 2005. *Summer Sun risin'*. New York: Lee & Low Books.

Sendak, M. 1988. *Where the wild things are*. New York: HarperCollins.

Seuss, Dr. 1960. *Green eggs and ham*. New York: Random House Books for Young Readers.

Silverstein, S. 1964. *The giving tree*. New York: Harper & Row.

Stone, J. 2003. *The monster at the end of this book*. New York: Golden Books.

Williams, M. 1922. *The velveteen rabbit*. New York: Doubleday & Company.

Reading Aloud

This chapter addresses some of the research supporting the benefits of reading aloud, lists 10 tips to make your read-aloud time more valuable, outlines seven key reading-comprehension strategies, and describes a variety of tools you can use to enhance students' comprehension during read-aloud time.

Why Read Aloud?

Reading aloud is a social activity that gives all the students in your classroom a shared frame of reference for making sense of their world. It activates their prior knowledge, builds vocabulary, promotes empathy, and provides a common experience to help foster a sense of community. The wealth of personal connections students make between their own lived experiences and the ideas and information they process during an interactive read-aloud helps them understand why things happen and how things work. Children of all ages enjoy the rich interactions that surround the read-aloud experience. We like what writer Neil Gaiman has to say about reading aloud: "We have an obligation to read aloud to our children. To read them things they enjoy. To read to them stories we are already tired of. To do the voices, to make it interesting, and not to stop reading to them just because they learn to read to themselves" (2013).

There are many research-based benefits to reading aloud. First and foremost, reading aloud to children appears to be the single most important activity for building understandings and skills essential for later success with independent reading (Neuman, Copple, and Bredekamp 2000). Being read to not only improves students' reading skills but also increases their interest in reading and literature, and it can even improve their overall academic achievement. A read-aloud performed by a good reader demonstrates fluent, expressive

reading and makes visible the thinking strategies of proficient readers. Experiencing books read aloud can fine-tune students' listening skills and enhance their learning of content. When a teacher does the reading, children's minds are free to anticipate, infer, connect, question, and comprehend (Calkins 2000). In addition, being read to is risk-free. In *Yellow Brick Roads: Shared and Guided Paths to Independent Reading, 4–12*, Allen (2000) says, "For students who struggle with word-by-word reading, experiencing the whole story can finally give them a sense of the wonder and magic of a book" (p. 45). Likewise, the *Common Core State Standards for English Language Arts* (*CCSS ELA*; NGAC and CCSSO 2010) advocate the use of reading aloud:

By reading a story or nonfiction selection aloud, teachers allow children to experience written language without the burden of decoding, granting them access to content that they may not be able to read and understand by themselves. Children are then free to focus their mental energy on the words and ideas presented in the text, and they will eventually be better prepared to tackle rich written content on their own. (Appendix A, p. 27)

The benefits of reading aloud apply to children in all grades. Appendix A of the *CCSS ELA* states that "children in the early grades—particularly kindergarten through grade 3—benefit from participating in rich, structured conversations with an adult in response to written texts that are read aloud, orally comparing and contrasting as well as analyzing and synthesizing" (NGAC and CCSSO 2010, p. 27). Reading aloud is important not only when children can't read well on their own but also after they have become proficient readers (Anderson et al. 1985). Allen (2000) supports this view: "Given

the body of research supporting the importance of read-aloud for modeling fluency, building background knowledge, and developing language acquisition, we should remind ourselves that those same benefits occur when we extend read-aloud beyond the early years" (p. 44).

Ten Tips for Reading Aloud

We have provided a list of tips to help you get the most from your read-aloud time. Using these suggestions can help set the stage for learning, improve comprehension of STEM concepts, and make the read-aloud experience richer and more meaningful for both you and your students.

1. Preview the Book

Select a book that is engaging, lends itself to being read aloud, and helps meet your STEM objectives by introducing a phenomenon, setting up a design challenge, or (after the explore phase of the lesson) explaining a concept. Preview it carefully before sharing it with your students. Are there any scientific errors, inaccurate or misleading diagrams, or misconceptions that could be inferred from the text or illustrations? If the book is not in story form, is there any nonessential information you could omit to make the read-aloud experience better? If you are not going to read the whole book, choose appropriate starting and stopping points before reading. If the book is written in a "stop and try it" format, prepare materials for explorations or demonstrations in advance. Consider generating questions, predictions, or inferences about the text and placing them on sticky notes inside the book to help you model your thought processes as you read. Practice reading the book aloud, especially when the book is written in verse!

2. Set the Stage

Because reading aloud is a performance, pay attention to the atmosphere and physical setting of the session. Gather the students in a special reading area, such as on a carpet or in a semicircle of chairs. Some teachers like to assign each child a designated spot on the floor or reading carpet. If you have a large class, consider adding a bench or comfy couch

for students in the back row. Seat yourself slightly above them. Do not sit in front of a bright window where the glare will keep students from seeing you well or in an area where students can be easily distracted. You may want to turn off the overhead lights and read by the light of a lamp or use soft music as a way to draw students into the mood of the text. Establish expectations for appropriate behavior during read-aloud time, and, before reading, give students an opportunity to settle in, perhaps by using a "countdown to listening" before they focus their attention on the book.

3. Celebrate the Author and Illustrator

Honor the hard work and dedication that goes into creating a picture book! Announce the title of the book and the names of the author and the illustrator before reading. Build connections to the book by asking students if they have read other works by the author or illustrator. Increase interest by sharing facts about the author or illustrator from their websites or from the book jacket. Share online "book trailers" before reading a book to help students understand the author's purpose, discover how the art is created, or just create excitement around the read-aloud experience. Consider inviting mentor authors or illustrators to virtually join your classroom to motivate readers and inspire writers and artists.

4. Introduce the Book

Have students look at the title and the cover and predict what the book is about. Point out the cover illustration and ask students how they think it was made. Flip through a few pages and ask students to identify whether the book is fiction or nonfiction and why they think so. Invite them to share their wonderings or talk about how the book might connect to their own experiences or to other books they've heard or read. You can also share your own connections to the book and give a brief explanation of why you selected it. In some cases, you may want to make clear the purpose for reading the book or ask students to listen for specific information or answers to questions as you read the book aloud.

5. Read With Expression

Reading aloud, like acting in a play or musical, is really a performance. Intentional practice makes perfect! Can you read with more expression to more fully engage your audience? Try matching your tone of voice to the mood of the text. Experiment with louder or softer speech, funny voices, facial expressions, or gestures. Make eye contact with your students every now and then as you read. This strengthens the bond between reader and listener, helps you gauge your audience's response, and cuts down on off-task behaviors. Read slowly enough that your students have time to build mental images of what you are reading but not so slowly that they lose interest. When reading a nonfiction book aloud, you may want to pause after reading about a key concept to let it sink in and then reread that part. At suspenseful parts in a storybook, use dramatic pauses for emphasis or read in a whisper. This can move the audience to the edges of their seats!

6. Share the Pictures

Don't forget the power of visual images to help students connect with and comprehend what you are reading. Make sure that you hold the book in such a way that students can see the pictures on each page. Allow time for students to study the pictures and make observations or connections. Ask students what they notice or what they are wondering about the illustrations or photographs. Read captions when appropriate. In some cases, you may want to hide certain pictures so students can visualize what is happening in the text before you reveal the illustrator's interpretation. After reading, you may want to discuss the illustrator's choices and analyze how the pictures enhance the story or content.

7. Encourage Interaction

Children learn the most from read-alouds when they are actively involved. Read-aloud time should be a social event—a shared experience filled with both verbal and nonverbal interactions between the reader and listener. So be sure to stop from time to time during the read-aloud to invite children to share their connections with you and one another,

ask and answer questions, close their eyes and visualize a scene from the book, or predict what might happen next. When students make predictions, honor all their ideas, not just the "correct" ones. Try using comments such as "Nice thinking, let's see what the author had in mind"; "That's one possibility, let's find out what happens on the next page"; or "What an interesting idea! How did you come up with that?" Build empathy and understanding by having students consider how they might react in a similar situation; how the events in a story might affect people, animals, or the environment; or maybe just how they think a character is feeling. A fun way to have students connect to the story is to have them mime emotions, for example, "On the count of three, show me how you think so-and-so is feeling," or "Make your best roller-coaster face!"

For some lessons, you may want to ask students to interact with the text by signaling when they hear a certain word or when they recognize an answer to a prereading question. Signals can be simple, such as thumbs-up/thumbs-down or touching their ear when they hear an answer. Signals can also be descriptive, such as wiggling fingers when they hear an example of humans giving animals "a helping hand" or doing the American Sign Language sign for "Sun" when they hear an example of how the Sun affects Earth.

You may want to provide students with "think pads" in the form of dry-erase boards or sticky notes to write on as you read aloud. Not only does this help extremely active children keep their hands busy while listening, but it also encourages sense-making as students jot down questions, comments, or even a "sketch to stretch." After the read-aloud, have students share their questions and comments. They can place their sticky notes on a class chart on the topic being studied. Another way to encourage interaction without taking the time for each student to ask questions or comment is to do an occasional "turn and talk" during the read-aloud. Stop reading, ask a question, allow thinking time, and then have each student share ideas with a partner. If a book is a bit longer than your students' attention spans, consider taking a "brain break" by incorporating movement into the read-aloud

session. For example, pose a discussion question related to the reading and then have students stand for a "stretch and share" or even a quick "walk and talk" around the room.

When planning for an interactive read-aloud, don't overdo it! Too much back and forth between the reader and listener can interrupt the flow of the reading or even reduce the need for students to think independently. Aim for a balance between allowing students to hear the language of the book uninterrupted and providing them with opportunities to share connections, make comments, and ask and answer questions. You may want to read the book all the way through one time so students can enjoy the aesthetic components of the story, and then go back and read the book for the purpose of encouraging interaction with the text and meeting your STEM objectives.

8. Model Reading Strategies

As you read aloud, it is important that you help children access what they already know and build bridges to new understandings. Think out loud; model your questions to the author; and make connections to yourself, other books, and the world. Show students how to determine the important parts of the text or story, and demonstrate how you synthesize meaning from the text. Modeling these reading comprehension strategies when appropriate before, during, and after reading helps students internalize the strategies and begin to use them in their own reading. Seven key strategies are described in detail in the next section (Reading-Comprehension Strategies).

9. Don't Put It Away ... Yet!

After the read-aloud, ask text-dependent questions that help you reach your STEM goals, but also leave time for open-ended questions that don't have right or wrong answers. For instance, ask students what they liked (or didn't like) about the book and why. Find out what connections they made to their own experiences, to other books, or to the world. If the read-aloud is a storybook or a narrative information text, ask about the theme, the characters, or how the problem was solved. If the read-aloud is a non-nar-

rative information book, ask how the information presented connects to their own lives or other areas of science. Keep the read-aloud book accessible to students after you read it. They will want to get a close-up look at the pictures and will enjoy reading the book independently. Don't be afraid of reading the same book more than once—younger children enjoy and benefit from the repetition.

10. Have Fun!

Let your passion for books show. It is contagious! Be a reading role model by sharing your preferred genres, talking about your favorite authors, and letting your students know what books you are reading for pleasure. Tap into the current trend of "unboxing" videos by recording and sharing your reaction to opening a new book at home. Tell them about your favorite reading spot, whether it's a soft chair, a cozy nook, or a porch swing. When reading a story out loud, let your feelings show—voice your own opinions and connections to the text, wonder aloud about the author's purpose, laugh at the funny parts, and cry at the sad parts. Seeing an authentic response from the reader is important for students. Share nonfiction books with emotion too. Make your sensemaking process visible to students by identifying your own misconceptions about a scientific concept ("I used to think ..."), celebrating new learning ("Now I know ...!"), and verbalizing your wonderings about the topic. Model how you use nonfiction books to search for answers to your own questions. No matter the book, sharing it with enthusiasm will make read-aloud time special and enjoyable for everyone involved. As Debbie Miller (2012) writes in *Reading With Meaning, 2nd Edition: Teaching Comprehension in the Primary Grades*, "Learning to read should be a joyful experience. Give children the luxury of listening to well-written stories with interesting plots, singing songs and playing with their words, and exploring a wide range of fiction, nonfiction, poetry and rhymes ... Be genuine. Laugh. Love. Be patient. You're creating a community of readers and thinkers" (p. 26).

Reading-Comprehension Strategies

Children's author Madeleine L'Engle (1995) says, "Readers usually grossly underestimate their own importance. If a reader cannot create a book along with the writer, the book will never come to life. The author and the reader … meet on the bridge of words" (p. 34). It is our responsibility as teachers, no matter what subjects we are assigned to teach, to help children realize the importance of their own thoughts and ideas as they read. Modeling our own thinking as we read aloud is the first step. Becoming a proficient reader is an ongoing, complex process, and children need to be explicitly taught the strategies that good readers use. In *Strategies That Work,* Harvey and Goudvis (2017) identify seven key reading strategies essential to achieving full understanding when we read. These strategies are used where appropriate in each lesson and are seamlessly embedded into the lessons. The strategies should be modeled as you read aloud to students from both fiction and nonfiction texts.

Research shows that explicit teaching of reading-comprehension strategies can foster comprehension development (Duke and Pearson 2002). Explicit teaching of the strategies is the initial step in the gradual-release-of-responsibility approach to delivering reading instruction (Fielding and Pearson 1994). During this first phase of the gradual-release method, the teacher *explains* the strategy, demonstrates *how* and *when* to use the strategy, explains *why* it is worth using, and *thinks aloud* to model the mental processes used by good readers. Duke (2004) describes the process in this way:

> *I often discuss the strategies in terms of good readers, as in "Good readers think about what might be coming next." I also model the uses of comprehension strategies by thinking aloud as I read. For example, to model the importance of monitoring understanding, I make comments such as, "That doesn't make sense to me because …" or "I didn't understand that last part—I'd better go back." (p. 42)*

Using the teacher-modeling phase within a science learning cycle will reinforce what students do during reading instruction, when the gradual-release-of-responsibility model can be continued. When students have truly mastered a strategy, they are able to apply it to a variety of texts and curricular areas and can explain how the strategy helps them construct meaning.

Descriptions of the seven key reading-comprehension strategies featured in *Strategies That Work* (Harvey and Goudvis 2017) follow. These strategies will be highlighted within the lessons by this icon: .

Monitoring Comprehension

According to Harvey and Goudvis (2017), monitoring comprehension is more of a thinking disposition than a specific strategy. You can model this anytime you read aloud by verbalizing your "inner conversation." For instance, you might pause to say, "I don't get this part, I'm going to reread it." Then, "Oh, now I understand." When you encounter new information in the text, you might say, "Wow, I never knew that before." Or you might verbalize how you use context clues to figure out the meaning of a difficult word. Harvey and Goudvis describe monitoring comprehension to students this way: "Nothing is more important than the reader's thinking. When readers pay attention and think about the words and ideas in the text, they carry on an inner conversation with the text. It is a quiet conversation that happens in the reader's head" (p. 89).

The following prompts can help your students monitor their comprehension as they read, write, listen, or explore in order to make sense of and apply STEM concepts:

? What are you thinking about this?

? What is confusing to you?

? How can you figure it out?

? Does this sound right to you?

? What is new information for you?

Making Connections

This strategy requires readers to activate their background knowledge and make meaningful connections to the reading. Background knowledge (often referred to as *schema*) is made up of a person's experiences with the world, along with their concepts of how text is structured. Research has established that readers' existing knowledge is critical in determining their ability to comprehend what they read—our brains learn by connecting the new to the known. Making meaningful connections during reading can improve learners' comprehension and engagement by helping them better relate to what they read. Comprehension breakdown that occurs when reading or listening to expository text can come from a lack of prior knowledge. These three techniques can help readers activate their schema and connect what they know to what they read:

- *Text-to-self connections* occur when readers and listeners link the text to their past experiences or background knowledge.
- *Text-to-text connections* occur when readers and listeners recognize connections from one book to another.
- *Text-to-world connections* occur when readers and listeners connect the text to events or issues in the real world.

The following prompts can help your students leverage these connections as they read, write, listen, or explore in order to make sense of and apply STEM concepts:

? What does this remind you of?

? Do you know anyone who does (*STEM career*) for a living?

? How does (*STEM concept in the book*) relate to (*STEM concept in another book*)?

? How might you use what you've learned in this book in your own life?

? How could you apply what you've learned to solve the problem of (*engineering design challenge*)?

Questioning

Proficient readers ask themselves questions before, during, and after reading. Questioning allows readers to construct meaning, find answers, solve problems, and eliminate confusion as they read. Harvey and Goudvis (2017) write, "Questioning is the strategy that propels readers on. If we didn't wonder about the text, why would we bother to continue reading? Human beings are driven to understand the world. Questions open the door to understanding" (p. 18). They suggest modeling your own questioning process by writing your questions on sticky notes as you read, placing them next to the passages that spurred them, and coding them with a question mark. Point out that some questions are answered in the text, some answers can be inferred from the text, some answers require further research, and some questions are not answered. Above all, students need to know that their questions matter!

Asking questions not only is a critical reading skill but also lies at the heart of scientific inquiry. Asking good questions can lead students into meaningful investigations. Questioning as a scientific practice is clearly articulated in *A Framework for K–12 Science Education,* which suggests that students ask questions based on observations to find more information or to design an investigation (NRC 2012).

The following prompts can help your students practice good questioning strategies as they read, write, listen, or explore in order to make sense of and apply STEM concepts:

? What are you wondering about …?

? What would happen if …?

? How do you know …? What is your evidence?

? How could you find out the answer?

? What do you predict will happen next? What clues support your prediction?

Visualizing

Visualizing is the creation of mental images while reading or listening to text. Mental images are created from the learner's emotions and senses, making the text more concrete and memorable.

Imagining the sensory qualities of things described in a text can help engage learners and stimulate their interest in the reading. During a read-aloud, stop and ask students to visualize the scene. What sights, sounds, smells, and colors are they imagining? When readers form pictures in their minds, they are more likely to stick with a challenging text. This ability can be an indication that a reader understands the text. Research by Pressley (1976) suggests that readers who visualize as they read are better able to recall what they have read than those who do not visualize.

Visualizing is valuable when used in the context of a story, but it can also be applied to informational texts. Having students visualize steps in a process or draw how something works as they listen to a text can be a powerful STEM sensemaking strategy. The practice of visualizing can help students form mental models, which serve as tools for making sense of phenomena.

The following prompts can help your students use visualizing strategies as they read, write, listen, or explore in order to make sense of and apply STEM concepts:

? What do you think this would feel like?
? What do you think this would look like?
? What do you think this would smell like?
? What do you think this would sound like?
? What are you picturing?
? How could you draw this?

Inferring

Reading between the lines, or inferring, involves a learner's merging clues from the text and illustrations with prior knowledge and experiences to draw conclusions and interpret the text. Good readers make inferences before, during, and after reading. In fact, research by Hansen and Pearson (1983) indicates that the ability to make inferences is crucial to successful reading.

Inferential thinking is also an important science skill and can be reinforced during reading instruction. To make an inference, scientists connect prior knowledge to new evidence collected through observation. Over time, as scientists gather more evidence, they can become more confident in the inferences they have made. Prior knowledge + new evidence = inference!

The following prompts can help your students make inferences as they read, write, listen, or explore in order to make sense of and apply STEM concepts:

? What do you predict?
? What could this mean?
? Based on your observation(s) of (*phenomenon*), what can you infer?
? What do the data show?
? What can you conclude?

Determining Importance

Reading to learn requires readers to identify essential information by distinguishing it from nonessential details. How readers decide what is important in the text depends on the purpose for reading and the genre of the book. In storybooks and narrative information texts, determining importance often requires students to infer the big ideas and themes of the story. Non-narrative information books typically provide features such as headings, bold-print words, captions, and other text structures that help students sift the essential information from less important details. In some Picture-Perfect STEM lessons, the lesson's objectives determine the importance of the information in the supporting text. Learners might read or listen to the text to find answers to specific questions, to gain understanding of certain concepts, or to identify misconceptions.

The following prompts can help your students use the strategy of determining importance as they read, write, listen, or explore in order to make sense of and apply STEM concepts:

? What important details did you learn about (*STEM concept*)?
? What is the most valuable point?
? What is the main idea?
? What is the most compelling evidence?
? What matters to you the most about this?

Synthesizing

In synthesizing, readers summarize information and combine it with prior knowledge and experience to form new ideas. To synthesize, readers must stop, think about what they have read, and contemplate its meaning before continuing on through the text. Using a variety of text types and reading strategies, pairing images or media clips with text, explaining their thinking to others, and leveraging hands-on learning experiences can help students synthesize new information. Sometimes when readers synthesize, they are adding to their store of knowledge to reinforce what they already know, or their thinking evolves slowly over time. But at other times—those "aha!" moments—readers have a flash of insight based on new information and, as a result, change their thinking. We suggest encouraging synthesis by asking students to think about what a word, a book title, an illustration, or a concept means to them before reading. Have them discuss, write, or sketch their ideas on a sticky note or in a notebook. Then, after reading, ask students to reflect on how their thinking has changed and discuss it, write about it, and/or add to their sketch.

The following prompts can help your students use synthesis as they read or listen in order to make sense of and apply STEM concepts:

? What does this mean?

? How have your ideas changed?

? You used to think _____ but now you know _____.

? What new ideas can you add to …?

? How can you apply (*new learning*) to (*engineering design challenge*)?

Tools to Enhance Comprehension

We have identified several activities and organizers that can enhance students' science understanding and reading-comprehension in the lessons. These tools, which support the reading-comprehension strategies from *Strategies That Work* (Harvey and Goudvis 2017) listed in the previous section, are

briefly described on the following pages and in more detail within the lessons.

Anticipation Guides

Anticipation guides (Herber 1978) are sets of questions that serve as a pre- and post-reading activity for a text. They can be used to activate and assess prior knowledge, determine misconceptions, focus thinking on the reading, and motivate reluctant readers by stimulating interest in the topic. An anticipation guide should revolve around four to six key concepts from the reading that learners make predictions about before reading. Students will be motivated to read or listen carefully to find the evidence that supports their predictions. After reading, learners revisit their anticipation teaching guide to check their responses. In a revised extended anticipation guide (Duffelmeyer and Baum 1992), learners are required to justify their responses and explain why their choices were correct or incorrect.

Card Sorts and Sequencing

Card sorts help learners understand the relationships among key concepts and help teach classification. They can also reveal misconceptions and increase motivation to read when used as a pre-reading activity. Learners are asked to sort words or phrases written on cards into different categories or sequence the events described on the cards. In an "open sort," learners sort the cards into categories of their own making or sequence events any way they wish. They can re-sort and re-sequence to help refine their understanding of concepts or events.

Card sequencing

In a "closed sort," the teacher gives them the categories for sorting or provides more information for correctly sequencing their cards.

Chunking

Chunking is dividing the text into manageable sections and reading only a section at any one time. This gives learners time to digest the information in a section before moving on. Chunking is also a useful technique for weeding out nonessential information when reading nonfiction books. Reading only those parts of the text that meet your learning objectives focuses the learning on what is important. Remember: Nowhere is it written that you must read nonfiction books cover to cover when doing a read-aloud. Feel free to omit parts that are inaccurate, out of date, or don't contribute in a meaningful way to the lesson.

Visual Representations

Organizers such as T-charts, Venn diagrams, semantic maps, word webs (Billmeyer and Barton 1998), and the Frayer Model (Frayer, Frederick, and Klausmeier 1969) can help learners activate prior knowledge, organize their thinking, understand the essential characteristics of concepts, or see relationships among concepts. They can be used for prereading, assessment, summarizing, or reviewing material. Visual representations are effective because they help learners perceive abstract ideas in a more concrete form. Examples of these visual representations, with instructions for using them within the lesson, can be found throughout this book.

New Vocabulary List

A new vocabulary list, sometimes called a personal vocabulary list (Beers and Howell 2004) is a "guess and check" type of visual representation. Students develop vocabulary as they draw and write predictions about the meanings of new words, read the words in context, and draw and write their definitions of the words.

Cloze Strategy

"Cloze" refers to an activity that helps readers infer the meanings of unfamiliar words. In the cloze strategy, key words are deleted in a passage. Students then fill in the blanks with words that make sense and sound right. Words can be printed on cards for students to place in the blanks before reading a passage so they can predict where they go. Then, after reading the passage, students can move them if necessary.

Picture Walk

A picture walk consists of showing students the cover of a book and browsing through the pages in order, without reading the text. The purpose of this tool is to establish interest in the story and expectations about what is to come. It also reinforces the importance of using visual cues while reading. Students look at the pictures and talk about what they see, what may be happening in each illustration, and how the pictures come together to make a story. Some useful questions to ask during a picture walk include the following:

? From looking at the cover, what do you think this book is about?

? What do you notice?

? What are you wondering?

? What does this remind you of?

? What do you think is happening?

? What do you think will happen next?

Stop and Try It

"Stop and try it" is a read-aloud format in which the teacher stops reading the text periodically to allow students to observe a demonstration or take part in a hands-on activity to better understand the content being presented. This way, students have an experience that connects to the information they are learning from the book.

STOP AND TRY IT

Turn and Talk

With "turn and talk," learners pair up to share their ideas, explain concepts in their own words, or talk about a connection they have to the book. This method allows each child to respond so everyone in the group is involved as either a talker or a listener. Saying, "Take a few minutes to share your thoughts with someone" gives students an opportunity to satisfy their needs to express their own ideas about the reading. "Walk and talk" and "stretch and share" are variations of this strategy that incorporate movement.

Using Features of Nonfiction

Many nonfiction books include a table of contents, index, glossary, bold-print words, picture captions, diagrams, and charts that provide valuable information. Because children are generally more used to narrative text, they often skip over these text structures. It is important to model how to interpret the information these features provide the reader. To begin, show the cover of a nonfiction book and read the title and table of contents. Ask students to predict what they'll find in the book. Show students how to use the index in the back of the book to find specific information. Point out other nonfiction text structures as you read, and note that these features are unique to nonfiction. Model how nonfiction books can be entered at any point in the text, because they generally don't follow a storyline.

Rereading

Nonfiction text is often full of unfamiliar ideas and challenging vocabulary. Rereading content for clarification and deeper understanding is an essential skill of proficient readers, and you should model this frequently. Rereading content for a different purpose can aid comprehension. For example, you might read aloud a text for enjoyment and then revisit the text to focus on specific science content. Younger students especially benefit from and enjoy listening to a book multiple times, and the more they hear it, the more they comprehend it.

USING THE TABLE OF CONTENTS

How Do Picture Books Enhance Comprehension?

Students should be encouraged to read a wide range of print materials, but picture books offer many advantages when teaching reading-comprehension strategies. Harvey and Goudvis (2017) not only believe that interest is essential to comprehension but also maintain that because picture books are extremely effective for building background knowledge and teaching content, instruction in reading-comprehension strategies during picture book read-alouds allows students to better access that content. In summary, picture books are invaluable for teaching reading-comprehension strategies because they are extraordinarily effective at keeping readers engaged and thinking.

This chapter has provided a variety of tips, tools, and strategies to enhance comprehension and maximize the many other benefits of reading aloud, but remember that first and foremost a read-aloud should be a joyful celebration for you and your students. In *The Ramped Up Read Aloud: What to Notice as You Turn the Page,* Maria Walther (2019) writes:

In my mind, a picture book is a piece of art created to be cherished and applauded. Right from the start, I give you permission to simply READ ALOUD—no questions, no stopping, no after-reading conversations. When your students are having a bad day—read aloud. If you need a break from a tough topic in math—read aloud. When you just want to have fun with your kids—read aloud. Enjoy the book and the experience! (p. 1)

References

Allen, J. 2000. *Yellow brick roads: Shared and guided paths to independent reading*, 4–12. Portland, ME: Stenhouse Publishers.

Anderson, R. C., E. H. Heibert, J. Scott, and I. A. G. Wilkinson. 1985. *Becoming a nation of readers: The report of the Commission on Reading*. Washington, DC: National Institute of Education, U.S. Department of Education.

Beers, S., and L. Howell. 2004. *Reading strategies for the content areas: An action toolkit*. Vol. 2. Alexandria, VA: ASCD.

Billmeyer, R., and M. L. Barton. 1998. *Teaching reading in the content areas: If not me, then who?* Aurora, CO: McREL.

Calkins, L. M. 2000. *The art of teaching reading*. Boston: Pearson Allyn & Bacon.

Duffelmeyer, F. A., and D. D. Baum. 1992. The extended anticipation guide revisited. *Journal of Reading* 35 (8): 654–656.

Duke, N. K. 2004. The case for informational text. *Educational Leadership* 61 (6): 40–44.

Duke, N. K., and P. D. Pearson. 2002. Effective practices for developing reading comprehension. In *What research has to say about reading instruction*, ed. A. E. Farstrup and S. J. Samuels, 205–242. Newark, DE: International Reading Association.

Fielding, L., and P. D. Pearson. 1994. Reading comprehension: What works? *Educational Leadership* 51 (5): 62–67.

Frayer, D. A., W. E. Frederick, and H. J. Klausmeier. 1969. *A schema for testing the level of concept mastery*. Madison, WI: University of Wisconsin Research and Development Center for Cognitive Learning.

Gaiman, N. 2013. Why our future depends on libraries, reading and daydreaming. Lecture to the Reading Agency, London.

Hansen, J., and P. D. Pearson. 1983. An instructional study: Improving the inferential comprehension of fourth grade good and poor readers. *Journal of Educational Psychology* 75: 821–829.

Harvey, S., and A. Goudvis. 2017. *Strategies that work: Teaching comprehension for understanding, engagement, and building knowledge, grades K–8*. 3rd ed. Portland, ME: Stenhouse Publishers.

Herber, H. 1978. *Teaching reading in the content areas*. Englewood Cliffs, NJ: Prentice Hall.

L'Engle, M. 1995. *Walking on water: Reflections on faith and art*. New York: North Point Press.

Miller, D. 2012. *Reading with meaning: Teaching comprehension in the primary grades*. 2nd ed. Portland, ME: Stenhouse Publishers.

National Governors Association Center for Best Practices and Council of Chief State School Officers (NGAC and CCSSO). 2010. *Common core state standards*. Washington, DC: NGAC and CCSSO.

National Research Council (NRC). 2012. *A framework for K–12 science education: Practices, crosscutting concepts, and core ideas*. Washington, DC: National Academies Press.

Neuman, S. B., C. Copple, and S. Bredekamp. 2000. *Learning to read and write: Developmentally appropriate practices for young children*. Washington, DC: National Association for the Education of Young Children.

Pressley, G. M. 1976. Mental imagery helps eight-year-olds remember what they read. *Journal of Educational Psychology* 68: 355–359.

Walther, M. 2019. *The ramped up read aloud: What to notice as you turn the page*. Thousand Oaks, CA: Corwin.

Three-Dimensional Learning

There have been some important changes in science education since the publication of our first Picture-Perfect Science book in 2005. The most significant change came with the release of the *Next Generation Science Standards* (*NGSS*; NGSS Lead States 2013). The *NGSS* are based on *A Framework for K–12 Science Education* (the *Framework*; NRC 2012), which presents three dimensions of learning science—science and engineering practices (SEPs), crosscutting concepts (CCCs), and disciplinary core ideas (DCIs). These three dimensions are meant to be used in an integrated manner to help students make sense of phenomena or design solutions to problems. In *Picture-Perfect STEM Lessons, Grade 2, Expanded Edition* (and the updated editions of the other grade-level books), we have made significant revisions to previously published lessons and written new ones in order to fully integrate the three dimensions.

In this chapter, we give some brief background on the *Framework*, discuss what three-dimensional learning looks like in the K–2 classroom, explore the role of picture books within this model, and offer opportunities for differentiation and more student-directed learning.

A Framework for K–12 Science Education

The *Framework* was developed by the National Research Council (NRC), whose overarching goal was "to ensure that by the end of 12th grade, all students have some appreciation of the beauty and wonder of science; possess sufficient knowledge of science and engineering to engage in public discussions on related issues; are careful consumers of scientific and technological information related to their everyday lives; are able to continue to learn about science outside school; and have the skills to enter careers of their choice, including (but not limited to) careers in science, engineering, and technology" (NRC 2012, p. 1).

As previously mentioned, the *Framework* was developed around three major dimensions: (1) science and engineering practices (SEPs), (2) crosscutting concepts (CCCs), and (3) disciplinary core ideas (DCIs). These three dimensions are the key components of the *NGSS* and many other state standards.

Dimension 1: Science and Engineering Practices

This dimension describes eight fundamental practices that scientists use as they investigate and build models and theories about the world, as well as the engineering practices that engineers use as they design and build systems (NRC 2012, p. 42). These practices are as follows:

1. Asking questions (for science) and defining problems (for engineering)
2. Developing and using models
3. Planning and carrying out investigations
4. Analyzing and interpreting data
5. Using mathematics and computational thinking
6. Constructing explanations (for science) and designing solutions (for engineering)
7. Engaging in argument from evidence
8. Obtaining, evaluating, and communicating information

Dimension 2: Crosscutting Concepts

The *Framework* identifies seven CCCs that apply to and connect all the disciplines of science. Making these CCCs explicit for students will help them see how all the fields of science are connected and provide a common vocabulary for them to explain these connections. The CCCs are as follows:

1. Patterns
2. Cause and effect
3. Scale, proportion, and quantity
4. Systems and system models
5. Energy and matter
6. Structure and function
7. Stability and change

Dimension 3: Disciplinary Core Ideas

DCIs are grouped into four domains: (1) physical science; (2) life science; (3) Earth and space science; and (4) engineering, technology, and applications of science. The *Framework* committee has identified these core ideas of science and engineering as meeting at least two of the following criteria (NRC 2012):

1. Have broad importance across multiple sciences or engineering disciplines or be a key organizing principle of a single discipline.

2. Provide a key tool for understanding or investigating more complex ideas and solving problems.

3. Relate to the interests and life experiences of students or be connected to societal or personal concerns that require scientific or technological knowledge.

4. Be teachable and learnable over multiple grades at increasing levels of depth and sophistication. That is, the idea can be made accessible to younger students but is broad enough to sustain continued investigation over years. (p. 31)

The DCIs are listed in a quick-reference chart in Table 3.1.

Three-dimensional learning involves students using all three dimensions—SEPs, CCCs, and DCIs—to make sense of the world and solve problems. Instead of just learning *about* science and engineering, students are *doing* science and engineering and recognizing themes that cross through all areas of science and engineering.

What Happened to Inquiry?

When we first started writing *Picture-Perfect Science Lessons* in 2005, inquiry-based instruction served as the foundation for our lessons. We even included an entire chapter about teaching science through inquiry in our original Picture-Perfect Science books. If you have been teaching science for a while, you might have been part of the inquiry-based science movement and may be wondering, "What happened to inquiry?" You will be glad to hear it is still around! Three-dimensional learning has not replaced inquiry; instead, it has provided more specifics about the practices of inquiry and how they can be used by students to both make sense of the content and make connections to the world.

The National Science Teaching Association (NSTA) published a position statement in 2018, *Transitioning From Scientific Inquiry to Three-Dimensional Teaching and Learning*, with some helpful history on inquiry-based instruction and the rationale for the transition to three-dimensional learning. The statement includes the following:

Scientific inquiry was first introduced as a method of thinking that was equally important to science content, but often interpreted as a set of steps and procedures, such as the "scientific method." Later, scientific inquiry became understood as a hands-on and minds-on approach requiring more than a set of steps, and was referred to as a "habit of the mind" (Minstrell 2000). The National Science

Table 3.1. The Framework's Disciplinary Core Ideas

Disciplinary Core Ideas in Physical Science	Disciplinary Core Ideas in Life Science	Disciplinary Core Ideas in Earth and Space Science	Disciplinary Core Ideas in Engineering, Technology, and Applications of Science
PS1: Matter and Its Interactions PS1.A: Structure and Properties of Matter PS1.B: Chemical Reactions PS1.C: Nuclear Processes **PS2: Motion and Stability: Forces and Interactions** PS2.A: Forces and Motion PS2.B: Types of Interactions PS2.C: Stability and Instability in Physical Systems **PS3: Energy** PS3.A: Definitions of Energy PS3.B: Conservation of Energy and Energy Transfer PS3.C: Relationship Between Energy and Forces PS3.D: Energy in Chemical Processes and Everyday Life **PS4: Waves and Their Applications in Technologies for Information Transfer** PS4.A: Wave Properties PS4.B: Electromagnetic Radiation PS4.C: Information Technologies and Instrumentation	**LS1: From Molecules to Organisms: Structures and Processes** LS1.A: Structure and Function LS1.B: Growth and Development of Organisms LS1.C: Organization for Matter and Energy Flow in Organisms LS1.D: Information Processing **LS2: Ecosystems: Interactions, Energy, and Dynamics** LS2.A: Interdependent Relationships in Ecosystems LS2.B: Cycles of Matter and Energy Transfer in Ecosystems LS2.C: Ecosystem Dynamics, Functioning, and Resilience LS2.D: Social Interactions and Group Behavior **LS3: Heredity: Inheritance and Variation of Traits** LS3.A: Inheritance of Traits LS3.B: Variation of Traits **LS4: Biological Evolution: Unity and Diversity** LS4.A: Evidence of Common Ancestry and Diversity LS4.B: Natural Selection LS4.C: Adaptation LS4.D: Biodiversity and Humans	**ESS1: Earth's Place in the Universe** ESS1.A: The Universe and Its Stars ESS1.B: Earth and the Solar System ESS1.C: The History of Planet Earth **ESS2: Earth's Systems** ESS2.A: Earth Materials and Systems ESS2.B: Plate Tectonics and Large-Scale System Interactions ESS2.C: The Roles of Water in Earth's Surface Processes ESS2.D: Weather and Climate ESS2.E: Biogeology **ESS3: Earth and Human Activity** ESS3.A: Natural Resources ESS3.B: Natural Hazards ESS3.C: Human Impacts on Earth Systems ESS3.D: Global Climate Change	**ETS1: Engineering Design** ETS1.A: Defining and Delimiting an Engineering Problem ETS1.B: Developing Possible Solutions ETS1.C: Optimizing the Design Solution **ETS2: Links Among Engineering, Technology, Science, and Society** ETS2.A: Interdependence of Science, Engineering, and Technology ETS2.B: Influence of Engineering, Technology, and Science on Society and the Natural World

Source: Willard 2015, p. 3.

Education Standards (NSES; NRC 1996) further developed our understanding of scientific inquiry, defining it as encompassing both knowledge and skill (NRC 2000, p. 23), and giving it prominent position as its own content area (AIR & WDPI 2016). Even so, scientific inquiry continued to have numerous meanings and be applied to a broad range of classroom activities (AIR & WDPI 2016). As a result, an uneven implementation of scientific inquiry has occurred in science classrooms.

The NSTA position statement goes on to say, "It's important to note that this transition is not a rejection of scientific inquiry, but represents further evolution of our understanding about what is essential to promote student learning."

With three-dimensional learning, the basic features of inquiry still apply. Learners are engaged in questions, give priority to evidence, formulate explanations, evaluate explanations, and communicate and justify their explanations. However, three-dimensional learning gives us specific SEPs for students to use as they inquire and provides a scaffold for the increase in sophistication of these practices as students advance through grades K–12. In other words, students in all grades are learning about science by doing science, which puts them at the center of their learning.

In revising previously published Picture-Perfect Science lessons and writing new ones for this project, we have not abandoned our commitment to inquiry-based science. We have just more explicitly integrated the SEPs and identified the CCCs as they apply throughout the lessons. We have added more open-ended questions as well as opportunities for students to ask their own questions, and we provide prompts to elicit connections to the CCCs. So, in the pages of this book, you will find our same Picture-Perfect Science inquiry-based philosophy enriched by integration of the three dimensions of the *Framework*. We believe this transition to three-dimensional learning will improve student understanding of STEM concepts in elementary school as well as prepare them for making sense of concepts as they advance beyond grades K–5.

Making Sense of Phenomena

A word you will often hear in discussions about three-dimensional learning is *phenomena*. Phenomena are simply observable events in the natural and designed world.

In three-dimensional lessons, students are presented with a phenomenon and use the three dimensions to make sense of it. Likewise, engineering requires students to understand a phenomenon well enough to define problems related to it and use that understanding to design a solution. Phenomena are central to the work of both scientists and engineers, but they can also be investigated by students in the early grades. The *Framework* states that "building progressively more sophisticated explanations of natural phenomena is central throughout grades K–5, as opposed to focusing only on description in the early grades and leaving explanation to the later grades" (NRC 2012, p. 25). Even in grades K–2, students can engage in making sense of phenomena. The *Framework* suggests that "in grades K–2, we choose ideas about phenomena that students can directly experience and investigate" (p. 33). For example, in the lesson "Wind and Water" (Chapter 16), learners explore the phenomenon that wind and water can change Earth's surface. In their efforts to make sense of this, students observe the effects of wind and water on a pile of sand and implement strategies to reduce the impact of erosion on Earth's surface. We have carefully chosen a phenomenon for these lessons that students in second grade can directly observe. These phenomena are clearly identified in the lesson description directly beneath the title of each lesson.

Three-Dimensional Learning in the K–2 Classroom

So what does three-dimensional learning look like in the K–2 classroom? We like how Paul Andersen from Bozeman Science simplifies the three dimensions in his video titled "Three-Dimensional Learning" (see the "Websites" section at the end of this chapter). He suggests thinking of the three dimensions this way:

- DCIs—What students learn
- SEPs—What students do
- CCCs—How students think

As previously mentioned, in three-dimensional lessons, students are typically presented with a phenomenon to figure out. The phenomenon is tied to the disciplinary core idea. For example, in the second-grade lesson "Wind and Water" (Chapter 16), students are presented with the phenomenon that wind and water can change the shape of the land and remove soil. This ties to the DCI "Wind and water can change the shape of the land." Students use SEPs as they observe both media and a model to describe patterns of weathering and erosion. They apply the CCC of stability and change as they discuss slow and rapid changes caused by wind and water. Finally, they use the SEP of designing solutions as they compare multiple solutions to an erosion problem. At the beginning of each lesson, the three dimensions are outlined in three separate columns (Figure 3.1). But, when you examine

Figure 3.1. Using the Three Dimensions: An Example

Alignment with the *Next Generation Science Standards*

> What students
> LEARN

> What students
> DO

> How students
> THINK

Performance Expectations

2-ESS1-1: Use information from several sources to provide evidence that Earth events can occur quickly or slowly.

2-ESS2-1: Compare multiple solutions designed to slow or prevent wind or water from changing the shape of the land.

K-2-ETS1-3: Analyze data from tests of two objects designed to solve the same problem to compare the strengths and weaknesses of how each performs.

Science and Engineering Practices	Disciplinary Core Ideas	Crosscutting Concept
Analyzing and Interpreting Data Use observations (firsthand or from media) to describe patterns and/or relationships in the natural and designed world in order to answer scientific questions and solve problems. **Constructing Explanations and Designing Solutions** Compare multiple solutions to a problem.	**ESS1.C: The History of Planet Earth** Some events happen very quickly; others occur very slowly over a time period much longer than one can observe. **ESS2.A: Earth Materials and Systems** Wind and water can change the shape of the land. **ETS1.C: Optimizing the Design Solution** Because there is always more than one possible solution to a problem, it is useful to compare and test designs.	**Stability and Change** Things may change slowly or rapidly.

the actual lesson plan, you can see how the three dimensions are closely knit together.

To make it clear where the SEPs and CCCs are being used, there are boxes throughout each lesson noting them. The SEPs and CCCs are the same through grades K–12, growing in sophistication as students progress through the grade levels. So, the *Framework* provides "elements" that are targets for students at each grade band—K–2, 3–5, 6–8, and 9–12. The elements for K–2 are listed within the box to help you emphasize that particular practice or concept as you teach the lesson. See Figures 3.2 and 3.3.

Table 3.2 (pp. 31–32) and Table 3.3 (p. 33) show the elements of the SEPs and CCCs specific to grades K–2.

Figure 3.2. Sample SEP Box

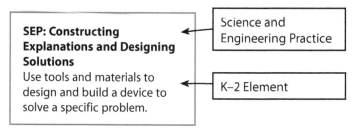

Figure 3.3. Sample CCC Box

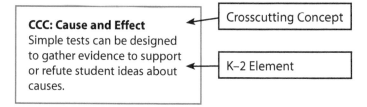

Table 3.2. Science and Engineering Practices for Grades K–2

Asking Questions and Defining Problems for Grades K–2

Asking questions and defining problems in K–2 builds on prior experiences and progresses to simple descriptive questions that can be tested.

- Ask questions based on observations to find more information about the natural and/or designed world(s).
- Ask and/or identify questions that can be answered by an investigation.
- Define a simple problem that can be solved through the development of a new or improved object or tool.

Developing and Using Models for Grades K–2

Modeling in K–2 builds on prior experiences and progresses to include using and developing models (i.e., diagram, drawing, physical replica, diorama, dramatization, or storyboard) that represent concrete events or design solutions.

- Distinguish between a model and the actual object, process, and/or events the model represents.
- Compare models to identify common features and differences.
- Develop and/or use a model to represent amounts, relationships, relative scales (bigger, smaller), and/or patterns in the natural and designed world(s).
- Develop a simple model based on evidence to represent a proposed object or tool.

Planning and Carrying Out Investigations for Grades K–2

Planning and carrying out investigations to answer questions or test solutions to problems in K–2 builds on prior experiences and progresses to simple investigations, based on fair tests, which provide data to support explanations or design solutions.

- With guidance, plan and conduct an investigation in collaboration with peers (for K).
- Plan and conduct an investigation collaboratively to produce data to serve as the basis for evidence to answer a question.
- Evaluate different ways of observing and/or measuring a phenomenon to determine which way can answer a question.
- Make observations (firsthand or from media) and/or measurements to collect data that can be used to make comparisons.
- Make observations (firsthand or from media) and/or measurements of a proposed object or tool or solution to determine if it solves a problem or meets a goal.
- Make predictions based on prior experiences.

Analyzing and Interpreting Data for Grades K–2

Analyzing data in K–2 builds on prior experiences and progresses to collecting, recording, and sharing observations.

- Record information (observations, thoughts, and ideas).
- Use and share pictures, drawings, and/or writings of observations.
- Use observations (firsthand or from media) to describe patterns and/or relationships in the natural and designed world(s) in order to answer scientific questions and solve problems.
- Compare predictions (based on prior experiences) to what occurred (observable events).
- Analyze data from tests of an object or tool to determine if it works as intended.

Continued

Table 3.2 (*continued*)

Using Mathematics and Computational Thinking for Grades K–2

Mathematical and computational thinking in K–2 builds on prior experience and progresses to recognizing that mathematics can be used to describe the natural and designed world(s).

- Use counting and numbers to identify and describe patterns in the natural and designed world(s).
- Describe, measure, and/or compare quantitative attributes of different objects and display the data using simple graphs.
- Use quantitative data to compare two alternative solutions to a problem.

Constructing Explanations and Designing Solutions for Grades K–2

Constructing explanations and designing solutions in K–2 builds on prior experiences and progresses to the use of evidence and ideas in constructing evidence-based accounts of natural phenomena and designing solutions.

- Use information from observations (firsthand or from media) to construct an evidence-based account for natural phenomena.
- Use tools and/or materials to design and/or build a device that solves a specific problem or a solution to a specific problem.
- Generate and/or compare multiple solutions to a problem.

Engaging in Argument From Evidence for Grades K–2

Engaging in argument from evidence in K–2 builds on prior experiences and progresses to comparing ideas and representations about the natural and designed world(s).

- Identify arguments that are supported by evidence.
- Distinguish between explanations that account for all gathered evidence and those that do not.
- Analyze why some evidence is relevant to a scientific question and some is not.
- Distinguish between opinions and evidence in one's own explanations.
- Listen actively to arguments to indicate agreement or disagreement based on evidence, and/or to retell the main points of the argument.
- Construct an argument with evidence to support a claim.
- Make a claim about the effectiveness of an object, tool, or solution that is supported by relevant evidence.

Obtaining, Evaluating, and Communicating Information for Grades K–2

Obtaining, evaluating, and communicating information in K–2 builds on prior experiences and uses observations and texts to communicate new information.

- Read grade-appropriate texts and/or use media to obtain scientific and/or technical information to determine patterns in and/or evidence about the natural and designed world(s).
- Describe how specific images (e.g., a diagram showing how a machine works) support a scientific or engineering idea.
- Obtain information using various texts, text features (e.g., headings, tables of contents, glossaries, electronic menus, icons), and other media that will be useful in answering a scientific question and/or supporting a scientific claim.
- Communicate information or design ideas and/or solutions with others in oral and/or written forms using models, drawings, writing, or numbers that provide detail about scientific ideas, practices, and/or design ideas.

Source: Willard 2015, pp. 88–89.

Table 3.3. The Framework's *Crosscutting Concepts for Grades K–2*

Crosscutting Concepts for Grades K–2	
Patterns	• Patterns in the natural and human-designed world can be observed, used to describe phenomena, and used as evidence.
Cause and Effect	• Events have causes that generate observable patterns. • Simple tests can be designed to gather evidence to support or refute student ideas about causes.
Scale, Proportion, and Quantity	• Relative scales allow objects and events to be compared and described (e.g., bigger and smaller, hotter and colder, faster and slower). • Standard units are used to measure length.
Systems and System Models	• Objects and organisms can be described in terms of their parts. • Systems in the natural and designed world have parts that work together.
Energy and Matter	• Objects may break into smaller pieces, be put together into larger pieces, or change shapes.
Structure and Function	• The shape and stability of structures of natural and designed objects are related to their function(s).
Stability and Change	• Some things stay the same while other things change. • Things may change slowly or rapidly.

Source: Willard 2015, p. 90.

See STEM Teaching Tools in the "Websites" section at the end of this chapter for a resource we have found helpful in understanding and implementing three-dimensional learning.

How Do the Picture Books Fit In?

How do the picture books tie in to three-dimensional learning? We think picture books support three-dimensional learning by providing a context for the learning and helping students build their understanding of science and engineering concepts.

Creating Context

We often use picture books to set up a relatable context for a phenomenon. For example, in the lesson "Wind and Water" (Chapter 16), we begin with a story titled *Kate, Who Tamed the Wind* in which a young girl solves a "windy" problem for her neighbor. This whimsical read-aloud leads into a simple investigation about how wind can change Earth's surface. The book not only helps students make connections to their own experiences with

weathering and erosion but also gives them a shared frame of reference for the phenomenon that wind and water can change Earth's surface.

Building Understanding

The informational text we select for our lessons helps students make sense of phenomena by providing simple explanations of the core ideas. These explanations are written specifically for children and are presented in a relatable context. For example, the book *How Do Wind and Water Change Earth?* in the "Wind and Water" lesson defines *weathering* and *erosion* using kid-friendly language and real-world examples.

Carefully selected picture books can make the DCIs, SEPs, and CCCs more meaningful for students by creating connections to themselves and the world.

Opportunities for Differentiated Instruction

In the lessons from the Picture-Perfect STEM series, students are engaged in three-dimensional learning in a guided manner. We encourage you to provide opportunities for students who need more guidance as well as opportunities for students who are ready for independent practice. One way to do so is to use the suggestions in the "Opportunities for Differentiated Instruction" box at the end of each lesson (Figure 3.4). This box lists questions and challenges related to the lesson that students may select to research, investigate, or innovate. Students may also use the questions as examples to help them generate their own questions.

For example, after the guided investigation in "Wind and Water," students can research what caused the Dust Bowl, investigate the soil in their own backyard, and apply what they have learned to design and model a solution to project a house on a riverbank from the effects of wind and water. Students can choose a question from the box or brainstorm some questions of their own. We believe that once students have participated in the guided format of Picture-Perfect STEM lessons, they are more likely to be able to apply SEPs on their own. The "Opportunities for Differentiated Instruction" box can help you provide those opportunities.

Figure 3.4. Sample "Opportunities for Differentiated Instruction" Box

Opportunities for Differentiated Instruction

This box lists questions and challenges related to the lesson that students may select to research, investigate, or innovate. Students may also use the questions as examples to help them generate their own questions. These questions can help you move your students from the teacher-directed investigation to engaging in the science and engineering practices in a more student-directed format.

Extra Support

For students who are struggling to meet the lesson objectives, provide a question and guide them in the process of collecting research or help them design procedures or solutions..

Extensions

For students with high interest or who have already met the lesson objectives, have them choose a question (or pose their own question), conduct their own research, and design their own procedures or solutions.

After selecting one of the questions in the box or formulating their own question, students can individually or collaboratively make predictions, design investigations or surveys to test their predictions, collect evidence, devise explanations, design solutions, or examine related resources. They can communicate their findings through a science notebook, at a poster session or gallery walk, or by producing a media project.

Continued

Figure 3.4. (*continued*)

Research

Have students brainstorm researchable questions:

? What is topsoil and what is it made of?

? What was the Dust Bowl?

? What can farmers do to protect their topsoil from erosion?

Investigate

Have students brainstorm testable questions to be solved through science or math:

? What observations can you make of soil in your area?

? Can you change the course of a river using pebbles? Make a model.

? Does the slope of a hill affect the shape a river makes when running down it? Make two models using soil or sand and compare.

Innovate

Have students brainstorm problems to be solved through engineering:

? Can you build a model of a house located on a riverbank?

? Can you design and model a solution to protect the house you built from a flood?

? Can you design and model a solution to protect the house you built from a dust storm?

In summary, the Picture-Perfect STEM series engages students in three-dimensional learning by capturing their interest, helping them make sense of phenomena and solve problems, and above all instilling in them a sense of wonder about the natural and designed worlds. The end result is that by actually doing science and engineering rather than merely learning about it, students will recognize that the work of scientists and engineers is creative and rewarding and deeply influences their world.

Websites

 STEM Teaching Tools
   http://stemteachingtools.org

 "Three-Dimensional Learning" with Paul Andersen (video)
   www.youtube.com/
   watch?v=1g9CUY1TBS8

References

Midwest Comprehensive Center at the American Institutes for Research (AIR) and the Wisconsin Department of Public Instruction (WDPI). 2016. *What ever happened to scientific inquiry? A look at evolving notions of inquiry within the science education community and national standards.* Chicago: AIR.

Minstrell, J. 2000. Implications for teaching and learning inquiry: A summary. As quoted in Barrow, L. H. 2006. A brief history of inquiry: From Dewey to standards. *Journal of Science Teacher Education* 17: 265–278.

National Research Council (NRC). 1996. *National science education standards.* Washington, DC: National Academies Press.

National Research Council (NRC). 2000. *Inquiry and the national science education standards: A guide for teaching and learning.* Washington, DC: National Academies Press.

National Research Council (NRC). 2012. A framework for K–12 science education: Practices, crosscutting concepts, and core ideas. Washington, DC: National Academies Press.

National Science Teaching Association (NSTA). 2018. Transitioning from scientific inquiry to three-dimensional teaching and learning. NSTA position statement. *www.nsta.org/nstas-official-positions/ transitioning-scientific-inquiry-three-dimensional-teaching-and-learning.*

NGSS Lead States. 2013. *Next Generation Science Standards: For states, by states.* Washington, DC: National Academies Press. *www.nextgenscience.org/next-generation-science-standards.*

Willard, T., ed. 2015. *The NSTA quick-reference guide to the NGSS: Elementary school.* Arlington, VA: NSTA Press.

Children's Books Cited

Hyde, N. 2015. *How Do Wind and Water Change Earth?* New York: Crabtree Publishing.

Scanlon, L. G. 2018. *Kate, Who Tamed the Wind.* New York: Schwartz and Wade Books.

BSCS 5E Instructional Model

Teaching in three dimensions can feel like trying to put together the pieces of a puzzle. The *Next Generation Science Standards* (*NGSS*; NGSS Lead States 2013) identify core ideas students should understand, practices they need to learn in order to "do" science, and crosscutting concepts that they can use to describe how the core ideas relate to one another and to other disciplines. This approach is much different than previous science standards that typically outlined content students needed to know, and, separately, skills students needed to master. But what does three-dimensional learning look like at the instructional level? Luckily, there is a model that can help you weave together the three dimensions so students are making sense of core ideas, using practices, and thinking about connections as they cycle through an instructional sequence.

The guided lessons in this book are designed using this model, commonly referred to as the 5Es. The Biological Sciences Curriculum Study (BSCS), led by Rodger Bybee, developed the 5E Model in 1987. It is a learning cycle based on a constructivist view of how students make sense of their world. Constructivism embraces the idea that learners bring with them preconceived ideas about how the world works. According to the constructivist view,

learners test new ideas against that which they already believe to be true. If the new ideas seem to fit in with their pictures of the world, they have little difficulty learning the ideas ... if the new ideas don't seem to fit the learners' picture of reality, then they won't seem to make sense. Learners may dismiss them ... or even-

tually accommodate the new ideas and change the way they understand the world (Colburn 2003, p. 59).

The objective of a constructivist model, therefore, is to provide students with experiences that make them reconsider their conceptions. Then, students "redefine, reorganize, elaborate, and change their initial concepts through self-reflection and interaction with their peers and their environment" (Bybee 1997, p. 176). The 5E Model (Figure 4.1) provides a planned sequence of instruction that places students at the center of their sensemaking

Figure 4.1. The BSCS 5Es as a Cycle of Learning

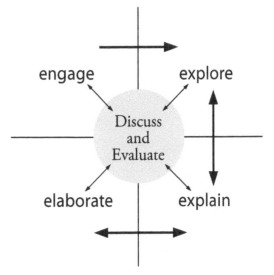

Source: Adapted from Barman, C. R. 1997. *The learning cycle revised: A modification of an effective teaching model.* Arlington, VA: Council for Elementary Science International.

experiences, encouraging them to use science and engineering practices to explore core ideas and to apply their learning to new situations. The phases of the 5E Model—*engage, explore, explain, elaborate,* and *evaluate*—are described here along with prompts that can guide students as they make sense of STEM concepts at each phase.

Phases of the 5E Model

engage

The purpose of this introductory phase, *engage,* is to capture students' interest and draw them into a STEM lesson. Here, you can uncover what students know and think about a topic as well as determine their misconceptions. The *engage* phase creates a common entry point for all students. We often use fiction or narrative nonfiction to set up a context for the core ideas featured in the lesson. These stories can introduce the phenomenon being investigated in a relatable way, raise questions about the subject, or help students connect with the topic. The *engage* phase sets up the opportunities for investigating that come next in the explore phase.

To promote sensemaking in the *engage* phase, you can use these prompts:

? What do you already know about this?

? Have you ever experienced this before?

? Where have you seen this in the real world?

? Why do you think this happens?

? What are you wondering about this?

ENGAGING WITH A READ-ALOUD

explore

In the *explore* phase, you provide students with exploration activities, giving them common, concrete experience with the phenomena being investigated. Students can ask questions, observe patterns, collect and organize data, test variables, and establish causal relationships. Your role is to observe and listen as students interact, ask probing questions, provide time for students to puzzle through problems, and act as a consultant for students as they explore the phenomenon.

To promote sensemaking in the *explore* phase, you can use these prompts:

? What do you notice?

? What do you think will happen?

? What do you think causes that?

? How could you find out?

? What other ideas could you try?

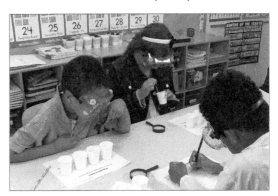

EXPLORING WITH MATTER OBSERVATIONS

explain

In the *explain* phase, it is important for learners to have the opportunity to explain what they have learned so far. They can share patterns they observed, hypothesize about relationships, and propose possible explanations for phenomena. After they share their own ideas, you can then begin to introduce the science and engineering vocabulary and explanations. In the Picture-Perfect STEM series, the explain phase is where we typically use informational text. As we read explanations and

EXPLAINING WITH A GRAPH

ELABORATING WITH A DESIGN CHALLENGE

introduce vocabulary, we refer back to the experiences students had in the *engage* and *explore* phases. We often use video, articles, and demonstrations to enhance explanations. In the *explain* phase, students can confront their own misconceptions and replace them with new learning.

To promote sensemaking in the *explain* phase, use these prompts:

? What could be the reason for this?

? How do your ideas compare with others or with what you have read?

? How did you figure this out? What science and engineering practices did you use?

? Can you give an example of (*vocabulary word*) from the activity?

? What evidence supports this?

elaborate

At the beginning of the *elaborate* phase, some students may understand the concepts only in the context of the previous exploration. Elaboration activities can help students generalize the concepts in a broader context. These activities challenge students to apply, extend, or elaborate on concepts and skills in a new situation, resulting in deeper understanding. The *elaborate* phase is often where we place design challenges that provide students with an opportunity to apply what they have learned and use the science and engineering practices in a meaningful context.

To promote sensemaking in the *elaborate* phase, you can use these prompts:

? How is this useful?

? How does this apply to your life or the lives of others?

? How can you use (*STEM concept*) to solve (*design challenge*)?

? How could you use what you've learned to improve an invention?

? How could you use something in nature to inspire your invention?

evaluate

In the *evaluate* phase, you evaluate students' understanding of concepts and their proficiency with various skills. You can use a variety of formal and informal procedures to assess conceptual understanding and progress toward learning outcomes. The *evaluate* phase also provides an opportunity for students to test their own understanding and skills.

Although the fifth phase is devoted to evaluation, a skillful teacher evaluates throughout the 5E Model, continually checking to see if students need more time or instruction to learn the key points in a lesson. Some ways to do this include informal questioning, formative assessment probes, teacher checkpoints, class discussions, and careful listening as students explain their thinking. Each Picture-Perfect STEM lesson also includes a formal evaluation such as a writing piece, poster, design challenge, or artwork. These formal evaluations take place at the end of the lesson.

Good resources for more information and practical suggestions for evaluating student understanding throughout the 5Es include *Seamless Assessment in Science: A Guide for Elementary and Middle School Teachers* by Abell and Volkmann (2006); *Uncovering Student Ideas in Primary Science, Volume 1: 25 New Formative Assessment Probes for Grades K–2* by Keeley (2013); and *The Power of Assessing: Guiding Powerful Practices* by Nyberg and McGough (2018).

To promote sensemaking in the *evaluate* phase, you can use these prompts:

? How have your ideas changed?

? Can you identify any new learnings or ways of thinking about (*STEM concept or practice*)?

? How would you explain (*STEM concept or practice*) to a friend?

? What are you still wondering about (*STEM concept or practice*)?

? How could you improve your design?

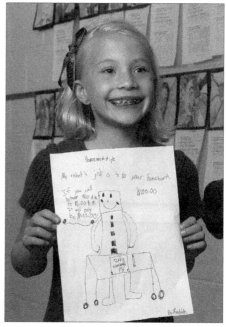

EVALUATING WITH A POSTER PROJECT

Roles of the Teacher and Student

The traditional roles of the teacher and student are virtually reversed in the 5E Model. Students take on much of the responsibility for learning as they construct knowledge through discovery, whereas in traditional models the teacher is responsible for dispensing information to be learned by the students. Table 4.1 shows actions of the teacher that are consistent with the 5E Model and actions that are inconsistent with the model.

In the 5E Model, the teacher acts as a guide: raising questions, providing opportunities for exploration or problem solving, asking for evidence to support student explanations, referring students to existing explanations, correcting misconceptions, and coaching students as they apply new concepts. This model differs greatly from the traditional format of lecturing, leading students step by step to a solution, providing definite answers, and testing isolated facts. Table 4.2 (p. 42) shows actions of the student that are consistent with the 5E Model and actions that are inconsistent with the model.

Three-Dimensional Learning and the 5Es

In his book *Translating the NGSS for Classroom Instruction*, Rodger Bybee (2013) suggests that when planning three-dimensional learning experiences with the *NGSS*, teachers use an integrated instructional sequence such as the 5E Model. We support this approach, because the 5E Model is a practical, research-based cycle of learning designed to facilitate sensemaking. Most notable is the placement of the *explore* phase BEFORE the *explain* phase. Students are provided with opportunities to explore phenomena, look for patterns, test relationships, and develop possible explanations before they are provided with scientific explanations and vocabulary. When they eventually receive the "formal" or known science explanations for the concepts they have explored, they are ready for them! Their experience in the *explore* phase gives them a mental hook on which to hang the explanations.

We have seen this simple modification of "explore before explain" work wonders with students. With many science topics, students may have not had much experience prior to coming into

Table 4.1. The BSCS 5E Instructional Model: What the Teacher Does

Stage of the Instructional Model	What the Teacher Does That Is …	
	Consistent With This Model	**Inconsistent With This Model**
Engage	• Creates interest • Generates curiosity • Raises questions • Elicits responses that uncover what students know or think about the concept or topic	• Explains concepts • Provides definitions and answers • States conclusions • Provides closure • Involves lectures
Explore	• Encourages the students to work together without direct instruction from the teacher • Observes and listens to students as they interact • Asks probing questions to redirect the students' investigations when necessary • Provides time for students to puzzle through problems • Acts as a consultant for students	• Provides answers • Tells or explains how to work through the problem • Provides closure • Tells students they are wrong • Gives information or facts that solve the problem • Leads students step by step to a solution
Explain	• Encourages students to explain concepts and definitions in their own words • Asks for justification (evidence) and clarification from students • Formally provides definitions, explanations, and new labels • Uses students' previous experiences as the basis for explaining concepts	• Accepts explanations that have no justification • Neglects to solicit students' explanations • Introduces unrelated concepts or skills
Elaborate	• Expects students to use formal labels, definitions, and explanations provided previously • Encourages students to apply or extend the concepts and skills in new situations • Reminds students of alternative explanations • Refers students to existing data and evidence and asks, "What do you already know?" "Why do you think x?" (Strategies from Explore also apply here.)	• Provides definitive answers • Tells students they are wrong • Involves lectures • Leads students step by step to a solution • Explains how to work through the problem
Evaluate	• Observes students as they apply new concepts and skills • Assesses students' knowledge and/or skills • Looks for evidence that students have changed their thinking or behaviors • Allows students to assess their own learning and group-process skills • Asks open-ended questions such as "Why do you think …?" "What evidence do you have?" "What do you know about x?" "How would you explain x?"	• Tests vocabulary words, terms, and isolated facts • Introduces new ideas or concepts • Creates ambiguity • Promotes open-ended discussion unrelated to the concept or skill

Table 4.2. The BSCS 5E Instructional Model: What the Student Does

Stage of the Instructional Model	What the Student Does That Is …	
	Consistent With This Model	**Inconsistent With This Model**
Engage	• Asks questions such as "Why did this happen?" "What do I already know about this?" "What can I find out about this?" • Shows interest in the topic	• Asks for the "right" answer • Offers the "right" answer • Insists on answers or explanations • Seeks one solution
Explore	• Thinks freely, within the limits of the activity • Tests predictions and hypotheses • Forms new predictions and hypotheses • Tries alternatives and discusses them with others • Records observations and ideas • Suspends judgment	• Lets others do the thinking and exploring (passive involvement) • Works quietly with little or no interaction with others (only appropriate when exploring ideas or feelings) • "Plays around" indiscriminately with no goal in mind • Stops with one solution
Explain	• Explains possible solutions or answers to others • Listens critically to others' explanations • Questions others' explanations • Listens to and tries to comprehend explanations that the teacher offers • Refers to previous activities • Uses recorded observations in explanations	• Proposes explanations from "thin air" with no relationship to previous experiences • Brings up irrelevant experiences and examples • Accepts explanations without justification • Does not attend to other plausible explanations
Elaborate	• Applies new labels, definitions, explanations, and skills in new but similar situations • Uses previous information to ask questions, propose solutions, make decisions, and design experiments • Draws reasonable conclusions from evidence • Records observations and explanations • Checks for understanding among peers	• "Plays around" with no goal in mind • Ignores previous information or evidence • Draws conclusions from "thin air" • Uses only those labels that the teacher provided in discussions
Evaluate	• Answers open-ended questions by using observations, evidence, and previously accepted explanations • Demonstrates an understanding or knowledge of the concept or skill • Evaluates his or her own progress and knowledge • Asks related questions that would encourage future investigations	• Draws conclusions without using evidence or previously accepted explanations • Offers only *yes* or *no* and memorized definitions or explanations as answers • Fails to express satisfactory explanations in his or her own words • Introduces new, irrelevant topics

the classroom. The *engage* and *explore* phases set up a common frame of reference so every student can be ready for the explanations and vocabulary, no matter their prior experiences or background. The sensemaking continues in the *explain* phase where students compare their thoughts and ideas to current scientific knowledge. They demonstrate (and continue to revise and expand on) what they have learned in the *elaborate* and *evaluate* phases by applying what they have learned to complete a task or solve a problem. In the *evaluate* phase, we have students reflect on their sensemaking by prompting them with questions about how their ideas have changed and what other questions they have about the topic.

All three dimensions of *A Framework for K–12 Science Education* (NRC 2012)—science and engineering practices (SEPs), crosscutting concepts (CCCs), and disciplinary core ideas (DCIs)—fit neatly into the 5E Model.

Science and Engineering Practices

As you will see with just a quick look through the lessons in this book, the SEPs are applied throughout the 5Es. For example, in the *engage* phase, students are often asking questions and defining problems. In the *explore* phase, they develop models, carry out investigations, analyze data, and use mathematics and computational thinking. The *explain* phase provides opportunities to construct their own explanations about core ideas, whereas the *elaborate* phase often involves designing solutions. One way we *evaluate* students is to have them engage in an argument from evidence. And throughout the 5Es, students obtain, evaluate, and communicate information by reading, writing, and speaking.

Crosscutting Concepts

The CCCs also appear throughout the 5Es. We have identified them at the beginning of each lesson but also throughout the text of the lesson. The way these themes connect the disciplines of science, technology, engineering, and mathematics may not be obvious to students at first, so we have been intentional about highlighting these connec-

tions by using the CCCs (or sometimes more age-appropriate words that express the same idea) in the questions we ask students. For example, we might ask the following:

? What patterns do you notice? (patterns)

? What do you think caused that to happen? (cause and effect)

? How does this compare to that? (scale, proportion, and quantity)

? What parts are working together here? (systems and system models)

? How could you take this apart and put it back together in a different way? (energy and matter)

? How do the parts of this object/animal/plant relate to what they are used for? (structure and function)

? What changed? What stayed the same? (stability and change)

For more questions to help your students make connections with the CCCs, see STEM Teaching Tool #41 in the "Websites" section at the end of the chapter.

Disciplinary Core Ideas

Of course, the DCIs are the focus of the lessons. We choose picture books that engage students in the core ideas; students explore phenomena related to the core ideas; nonfiction books, articles, and media are carefully selected to explain core ideas; design challenges require students to elaborate by applying the core ideas; and formal and informal assessments evaluate student understanding of the core ideas.

The 5E Model provides a framework for three-dimensional learning where all three dimensions can be integrated in a meaningful progression. Each phase—*engage, explore, explain, elaborate, and evaluate*—guides students through a sensemaking sequence where they use the practices of scientists and engineers to work toward a deeper understanding of STEM concepts and to design solutions to problems while beginning to see connections to the real world.

Using Picture Books in the 5Es

Both fiction and nonfiction picture books can be valuable components of the 5E Model when placed strategically within the cycle. We often begin lessons with a fiction book to pique students' curiosity or motivate them to want to learn more about a science concept. For example, the kindergarten lesson "Design a Habitat" begins with a read-aloud of *I Wanna Iguana* (Orloff 2004), a humorous story about a boy who is trying to convince his mom to let him have a pet iguana. This read-aloud during the *engage* phase inspires the question "What do you think you might need to take good care of an iguana?" and is followed by activities and a nonfiction read-aloud about animal habitats. A storybook, however, might not be appropriate to use during the *explore* phase of the 5Es, in which students are participating in concrete, hands-on experiences. Likewise, a storybook might not be appropriate to use during the *explain* phase to clarify scientific concepts and introduce vocabulary. Sometimes, a narrative nonfiction text can be used to engage students. For example, in the first-grade lesson titled "Let's Drum!" we use *Drum Dream Girl* (Engel 2015), the true story of a young girl from Cuba who wants to play the drums, to draw students into the STEM lesson. The inspirational message of one person's determination to pursue her dream serves as a powerful invitation to inquiry.

Too early in the learning cycle, you should avoid using books that contain a lot of scientific terminology or "give away" information students could discover on their own. It is important for students to have opportunities to construct meaning and articulate ideas in their own words before being introduced to scientific vocabulary. Nonfiction books, therefore, are most appropriate to use in the *explain* phase after students have had these opportunities. For example, in the *explain* phase of a second grade lesson titled "Flight of the Pollinators (Chapter 14)", students compare their observations of flowers with the information presented in the nonfiction book *What is Pollination?* (Kalman, 2010).

The 5Es provide an ideal format for a constructivist sequence of activities, allowing students to form their own ideas, collect evidence to confirm or discount their ideas, design solutions to real-world problems, apply what they have learned to new situations, and demonstrate what they have learned. Thoughtful placement of fiction and nonfiction picture books within the 5E Model can help you engage, motivate, and explain while immersing your students in meaningful, integrated STEM learning experiences.

Website

 STEM Teaching Tool #41: Prompts for Integrating Crosscutting Concepts Into Assessment and Instruction
http://stemteachingtools.org/assets/landscapes/STEM-Teaching-Tool-41-CrossCuttingConceptsRPC.pdf

Chapter 4

References

Abell, S. K., and M. J. Volkmann. 2006. *Seamless assessment in science: A guide for elementary and middle school teachers*. Portsmouth, NH: Heinemann; Arlington, VA: NSTA Press.

Barman, C. R. 1997. *The learning cycle revised: A modification of an effective teaching model*. Arlington, VA: Council for Elementary Science International.

Bybee, R. W. 1997. *Achieving scientific literacy: From purposes to practices*. Portsmouth, NH: Heinemann.

Bybee, R. W. 2013. *Translating the NGSS for classroom instruction*. Arlington, VA: NSTA Press.

Colburn, A. 2003. *The lingo of learning: 88 education terms every science teacher should know*. Arlington, VA: NSTA Press.

Keeley, P. 2013. *Uncovering student ideas in primary science, volume 1: 25 new formative assessment probes for grades K–2*. Arlington, VA: NSTA Press.

National Research Council (NRC). 2012. *A framework for K–12 science education: Practices, crosscutting concepts, and core ideas*. Washington, DC: National Academies Press.

NGSS Lead States. 2013. *Next Generation Science Standards: For states, by states*. Washington, DC: National Academies Press. *www.nextgenscience.org/next-generation-science-standards*.

Children's Books Cited

Engle, M. 2015. *Drum dream girl: How one girl's courage changed music*. New York: HMH Books for Young Readers.

Kalman, B. 2010. *What is Pollination?* New York: Crabtree Publishing.

Orloff, K. K. 2004. *I wanna iguana*. New York: Putnam.

Chapter
5

Connecting to the Standards

We realize that teaching in a primary classroom provides a unique challenge in that you are likely responsible for teaching all the state standards for your grade level. It often feels as if there are simply not enough hours in the school day to do so. As we travel around the country meeting teachers at our workshops, many K–2 teachers tell us how difficult it is to fit in the science standards in particular. Math and language arts often take priority over science and other subjects. We believe that integration with language arts and math is key in finding the time to teach science. In this chapter, we outline the standards that we have integrated in Picture-Perfect STEM lessons—the *Next Generation Science Standards* (*NGSS*; NGSS Lead States 2013) and the *Common Core State Standards* (*CCSS*; NGAC and CCSSO 2010) for English language arts and mathematics.

Even if your district has not adopted the *NGSS* and/or *CCSS*, we encourage you to read through these standards as they are noted throughout the lessons. Understanding how these lessons align to specific *NGSS* disciplinary core ideas (DCIs), crosscutting concepts (CCCs), and science and engineering practices (SEPs), as well as the *CCSS* will be helpful as you select and implement Picture-Perfect STEM lessons in your classroom. Throughout the lessons, you will find boxes titled "Connecting to the Common Core" noting the *Common Core State Standards for English Language Arts* (*CCSS ELA*) that are used during read-alouds and writing assignments and the *Common Core State Standards for Mathematics* (*CCSS Mathematics*) that are addressed in various activities. You will also see the CCCs and SEPs noted in boxes throughout the lessons. This chapter provides some background information about the *NGSS* and the *CCSS* and how our lessons connect to them..

Next Generation Science Standards

The *NGSS* are based on *A Framework for K–12 Science Education* (the *Framework*; NRC 2012). The three dimensions addressed in Chapter 3 come from the *Framework* and are the foundation of the *NGSS*. For K–5 science, the *Framework* places certain DCIs in grade bands (K–2 and 3–5), whereas the *NGSS* have the DCIs placed in specific grade levels. The CCCs and SEPs span all the grade levels, K–12. The *NGSS* also provide performance expectations that detail what students must do to show proficiency at each grade level. Performance expectations integrate all three dimensions of the *NGSS* into one task and are to be offered after students have had multiple experiences with the topic. The lessons in this book are intended to help students move toward specific performance expectations, which are identified at the beginning of each lesson. *However, a lesson will not by itself be sufficient to reach the performance expectations; rather, each lesson is meant to be one in a series of lessons that work toward the performance expectations.*

Table 5.1 (p. 48) shows the performance expectations and DCIs for grade 2 and the lessons in this book that address them.

Chapter
5

Table 5.1. *Performance Expectations and Disciplinary Core Ideas for Second Grade*

Performance Expectations	Disciplinary Core Ideas	Lesson Titles
2-LS1-1: Plan and conduct an investigation to determine if plants need sunlight and water to grow.	**LS2.A: Interdependent Relationships in Ecosystems** Plants depend on water and light to grow.	
2-LS2-2: Develop a simple model that mimics the function of an animal in dispersing seeds or pollinating plants.	**LS2.A: Interdependent Relationships in Ecosystems** Plants depend on animals for pollination or to move their seeds around.	Chapter 13: Seeds on the Move Chapter 14: Flight of the Pollinators
2-LS4-1: Make observations of plants and animals to compare the diversity of life in different habitats.	**LS4.D: Biodiversity and Humans** There are many different kinds of living things in any area, and they exist in different places on land and in water.	
2-ESS1-1: Use information from several sources to provide evidence that Earth events can occur quickly or slowly.	**ESS1.C: The History of Planet Earth** Some events happen very quickly; others occur very slowly over a time period much longer than one can observe.	Chapter 15: If You Find a Rock Chapter 16: Wind and Water
2-ESS2-1: Compare multiple solutions designed to slow or prevent wind or water from changing the shape of land.	**ESS2.A: Earth Materials and Systems** Wind and water can change the shape of the land.	Chapter 16: Wind and Water
2-ESS2-2: Develop a model to represent the shapes and kinds of land and bodies of water in an area.	**ESS2.B: Plate Tectonics and Large-Scale System Interactions** Maps show where things are located. One can map the shapes and kinds of land and water in any area.	Chapter 17: Our Blue Planet
2-ESS2-3: Obtain information to identify where water is found on Earth and that it can be solid or liquid.	**ESS2.C: The Roles of Water in Earth's Surface Processes** Water is found in the oceans, rivers, lakes, and ponds. Water exists as solid ice and in liquid form.	Chapter 17: Our Blue Planet

Continued

National Science Teaching Association

Table 5.1 (continued)

Performance Expectations	Disciplinary Core Ideas	Lesson Titles
2-PS1-1: Plan and conduct an investigation to describe and classify different kinds of materials by their observable properties.	**PS1.A: Structure and Properties of Matter** Different kinds of matter exist and many of them can be either solid or liquid, depending on temperature. Matter can be described and classified by its observable properties.	Chapter 8: Melting and Freezing Chapter 9: That Magnetic Dog Chapter 11: Science Mysteries Chapter 15: If You Find a Rock
2-PS1-2: Analyze data obtained from testing different materials to determine which materials have the properties that are best suited for an intended purpose.	**PS1.A: Structure and Properties of Matter** Different properties are suited for different purposes.	Chapter 7: Imaginative Inventions
2-PS1-3: Make observations to construct an evidence-based account of how an object made of a small set of pieces can be disassembled and made into a new object.	**PS1.A: Structure and Properties of Matter** A great variety of objects can be built up from a small set of pieces.	Chapter 12: Build It!
2-PS1-4: Construct an argument with evidence that some changes caused by heating or cooling can be reversed and some cannot.	**PS1.B: Chemical Reactions** Heating or cooling a substance may cause changes that can be observed. Sometimes these changes are reversible, and sometimes they are not.	Chapter 8: Melting and Freezing Chapter 10: Crayons
K-2-ETS1-1: Ask questions, make observations, and gather information about a situation people want to change to define a simple problem that can be solved through the development of a new or improved object or tool.	**ETS1.A: Defining and Delimiting Engineering Problems** A situation that people want to change or create can be approached as a problem to be solved through engineering. Such problems may have many acceptable solutions.	Chapter 6: How Big is a Foot? Chapter 7: Imaginative Inventions Chapter 10: Crayons
K-2-ETS1-2: Develop a simple sketch, drawing, or physical model to illustrate how the shape of an object helps it function as needed to solve a given problem.	**ETS1.B: Developing Possible Solutions** Designs can be conveyed through sketches, drawings, or physical models. These representations are useful in communicating ideas for a problem's solutions to other people.	Chapter 7: Imaginative Inventions Chapter 13: Seeds on the Move Chapter 14: Flight of the Pollinators

Continued

Table 5.1 (continued)

Performance Expectations	Disciplinary Core Ideas	Lesson Titles
K-2-ETS1-3: Analyze data from tests of two objects designed to solve the same problem to compare the strengths and weaknesses of how each performs.	**ETS1.C: Optimizing the Design Solution** Because there is always more than one possible solution to a problem, it is useful to compare and test designs.	Chapter 16: Wind and Water

Source: Willard 2015.

On the first page of each chapter, you will find a box that provides a detailed description of the three dimensions of the *NGSS* and the corresponding performance expectations (Figure 5.1).

Learning Progressions

We have also provided learning progressions at the beginning of each lesson that show how the DCIs students are learning in grades K–2 establish a foundation for what they will be learning in grades 3–5. Figure 5.2 (p. 52) shows the learning progression from Chapter 11: Crayons. These progressions come from *The NSTA Quick-Reference Guide to the NGSS: Elementary School* (Willard 2015). As you can see in the figure, the concepts learned in grades K–2 provide the foundation for the concepts students will learn in grades 3–5. Considering these progressions can help you see the importance of this foundational knowledge in grades K–2 and where this knowledge will eventually lead students. Awareness of the big picture can help you make decisions about how deep to go into a topic and how to set the stage for future learning.

Engineering Design Process

One notable shift with the *Framework* and *NGSS* is the elevation of engineering to the same level as science. In fact, engineering design is considered a "discipline" along with life science, physical science, and Earth and space science, and it has its own set of DCIs and performance expectations. Science and engineering are closely related and interdependent.

As stated in the *Framework*, "It is impossible to do engineering today without applying science in the process and, in many areas of science, designing and building new experiments requires scientists to engage in some engineering practices" (NRC 2012, p. 32).

There are many approaches to an engineering design process, but all of them follow the same basic pattern—a series of steps completed iteratively to solve a problem. In these lessons, we use the simple, three-component model described in the *NGSS* as our framework (see Figure 5.3, p. 52).

The *NGSS* make it clear that these component ideas do not always follow in order and that "at any stage a problem solver can redefine the problem or generate new solutions to replace an idea that is just not working out" (NGSS Lead States 2013, Appendix I).

The *NGSS* also provide the following explanation of engineering design in K–2:

Engineering design in the earliest grades introduces students to "problems" as situations that people want to change. They can use tools and materials to solve simple problems, use different representations to convey solutions, and compare different solutions to a problem and determine which is best. Students in all grade levels are not expected to come up with original solutions, although original solutions are always welcome.

Emphasis is on thinking through the needs or goals that need to be met and on which solutions best meet those needs and goals. (NGSS Lead States 2013, Appendix I)

Picture-Perfect STEM lessons integrate the three component ideas of engineering. Students are provided with opportunities to define problems, develop solutions, and optimize solutions. For example, in the first-grade lesson "Robots Everywhere," students learn how various types of robots are used every day to make our lives better. Next, they define a problem they have that a robot could solve, design a robot to solve that problem, and express their designs through words and pictures. Although students are not designing and building actual robots, they are learning about

how technologies are designed to solve problems. In a kindergarten lesson titled "Move It!" students learn about force and motion; design a way to get a toy dog and toy car into a plastic-cup "doghouse;" and then compare, test, and optimize their designs.

We do not think that every STEM lesson needs to include a specific design challenge. In some Picture-Perfect STEM lessons, students learn about engineering by using technologies that apply scientific concepts or developing an understanding of how the technologies related to the core idea of the lesson work. For example, the lesson titled "Our Blue Planet (Chapter 17)," students use Google Earth as a tool to explore Earth's water. Then they learn how satellite technology allows us to capture images of our planet. Students also begin to realize that maps are considered models

Figure 5.1. Sample "Alignment with the Next Generation Science Standards" Box

Performance Expectation

2-PS1-1: Plan and conduct an investigation to describe and classify different kinds of materials by their observable properties

Science and Engineering Practices	Disciplinary Core Idea	Crosscutting Concepts
Asking Questions and Defining Problems Ask and/or identify questions that can be answered by an investigation. **Planning and Carrying Out Investigations** Plan and conduct an investigation collaboratively to produce data to serve as the basis for evidence to answer a question. **Engaging in Argument From Evidence** Construct an argument with evidence to support a claim.	**PS1.A: Structure and Properties of Matter** Different kinds of matter exist and many of them can be either solid or liquid, depending on temperature. Matter can be described and classified by its observable properties.	**Energy and Matter** Objects may break into smalller pieces:, be put together into larger pieces, or change shape. **Patterns** Patterns in the natural and human-designed world can be observed, used to describe phenomena, and used as evidence.

Figure 5.2. Sample "Learning Progressions" Box

DCI	Grades K–2	Grades 3–5
PS1.A: Structure and Properties of Matter	• Different kinds of matter exist and many of them can be either solid or liquid, depending on temperature. Matter can be described and classified by its observable properties.	• Measurements of a variety of properties can be used to identify materials.

that can be used to learn more about our planet. Although students are not designing a solution to a problem, they are learning about a technology that has been developed to help us make models of our planet, and they are using that technology to learn more about Earth.

Common Core State Standards

The Common Core State Standards Initiative (*www.corestandards.org*) is a state-led effort to define the knowledge and skills students should acquire in their K–12 mathematics and ELA courses. It is part of an extended, broad-based effort by the states to craft the next generation of K–12 standards to ensure that all students are college and career ready by the end of high school. The standards are research and evidence based, aligned with college and work expectations, rigorous, and internationally benchmarked. The lessons in this book were not designed to teach the *CCSS ELA* and *CCSS Mathematics* standards but to provide opportunities for students to apply the standards appropriate to their grade level in an authentic way and in a meaningful context

Figure 5.3. Engineering Design in K–2

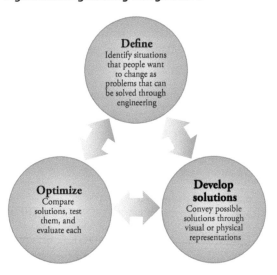

Source: NGSS Lead States 2013, Appendix I.

Common Core State Standards for English Language Arts

The *Common Core* suggests that the ELA standards be taught in the context of history/social studies, science, and technical subjects (NGAC and CCSO 2010). Grade-specific K–12 standards in reading, writing, speaking, listening, and language are included. Many of these grade-specific standards are used in the Picture-Perfect STEM series through the use of high-quality children's fiction and nonfiction picture books, research-based reading strategies, poster presentations, vocabulary development activities, and various writing assignments. In the boxes titled "Connecting to the *Common Core*" throughout each lesson, you will find the *CCSS ELA* strand(s) and topic the activity addresses, the grade level, and the standard number(s) (see Figure 5.4).

A DESIGN CHALLENGE

Figure 5.4. Sample CCSS ELA *Box*

Because the codes for the CCSS ELA standards are listed in the lessons instead of the actual standards statements, we have included the CCSS ELA grade-level statements in Table 5.2 (p. 54). This table is not a complete version of the CCSS ELA. Rather, it includes only the standards we address in our lessons for second grade: reading (literature and informational text), writing, speaking and listening, and language. You can access the complete CCSS ELA online (see the "Websites" section).

Table 5.2. Common Core State Standards for English Language Arts and Literacy in History/Social Studies, Science, and Technical Subjects for Grade 2

Reading Standards for Literature, Grade 2

Key Ideas and Details

1. Ask and answer such questions as who, what, where, when, why, and how to demonstrate understanding of key details in a text.

2. Recount stories, including fables and folktales from diverse cultures, and determine their central message, lesson, or moral.

3. Describe how characters in a story respond to major events and challenges.

Craft and Structure

4. Describe how words and phrases (e.g., regular beats, alliteration, rhymes, repeated lines) supply rhythm and meaning in a story, poem, or song.

5. Describe the overall structure of a story, including describing how the beginning introduces the story and the ending concludes the action.

6. Acknowledge differences in the points of view of characters, including by speaking in a different voice for each character when reading dialogue aloud.

Integration of Knowledge and Ideas

7. Use information gained from the illustrations and words in a print or digital text to demonstrate understanding of its characters, setting, or plot.

8. (Not applicable to literature)

9. Compare and contrast two or more versions of the same story (e.g., Cinderella stories) by different authors or from different cultures.

Range of Reading and Level of Text Complexity

10. By the end of the year, read and comprehend literature, including stories and poetry, in the grades 2–3 text complexity band proficiently, with scaffolding as needed at the high end of the range.

Reading Standards for Informational Text, Grade 2

Key Ideas and Details

1. Ask and answer such questions as *who, what, where, when, why,* and *how* to demonstrate understanding of key details in a text.

2. Identify the main topic of a multiparagraph text as well as the focus of specific paragraphs within the text.

3. Describe the connection between a series of historical events, scientific ideas or concepts, or steps in technical procedures in a text.

Craft and Structure

4. Determine the meaning of words and phrases in a text relevant to a grade 2 topic or subject area.

5. Know and use various text features (e.g., captions, bold print, subheadings, glossaries, indexes, electronic menus, icons) to locate key facts or information in a text efficiently.

6. Identify the main purpose of a text, including what the author wants to answer, explain, or describe.

Continued

Table 5.2 (continued)

Integration of Knowledge and Ideas

7. Explain how specific images (e.g., a diagram showing how a machine works) contribute to and clarify a text.

8. Describe how reasons support specific points the author makes in a text.

9. Compare and contrast the most important points presented by two texts on the same topic.

Range of Reading and Level of Text Complexity

10. By the end of year, read and comprehend informational texts, including history/social studies, science, and technical texts, in the grades 2–3 text complexity band proficiently, with scaffolding as needed at the high end of the range.

Writing Standards, Grade 2

Text Types and Purposes

1. Write opinion pieces in which they introduce the topic or book they are writing about, state an opinion, supply reasons that support the opinion, use linking words (e.g., *because, and, also*) to connect opinion and reasons, and provide a concluding statement or section.

2. Write informative/explanatory texts in which they introduce a topic, use facts and definitions to develop points, and provide a concluding statement or section.

3. Write narratives in which they recount a well-elaborated event or short sequence of events, include details to describe actions, thoughts, and feelings, use temporal words to signal event order, and provide a sense of closure.

Production and Distribution of Writing

4. (Begins in grade 3)

5. With guidance and support from adults and peers, focus on a topic and strengthen writing as needed by revising and editing.

6. With guidance and support from adults, use a variety of digital tools to produce and publish writing, including in collaboration with peers.

Research to Build and Present Knowledge

7. Participate in shared research and writing projects (e.g., read a number of books on a single topic to produce a report; record science observations).

8. Recall information from experiences or gather information from provided sources to answer a question.

9. (Begins in grade 4)

Range of Writing

10. (Begins in grade 3)

Continued

Table 5.2 (continued)

Speaking and Listening Standards, Grade 2

Comprehension and Collaboration

1. Participate in collaborative conversations with diverse partners about grade 2 topics and texts with peers and adults in small and larger groups.
   a. Follow agreed-upon rules for discussions (e.g., gaining the floor in respectful ways, listening to others with care, speaking one at a time about the topics and texts under discussion).
   b. Build on others' talk in conversations by linking their comments to the remarks of others.
   c. Ask for clarification and further explanation as needed about the topics and texts under discussion.

2. Recount or describe key ideas or details from a text read aloud or information presented orally or through other media.

3. Ask and answer questions about what a speaker says in order to clarify comprehension, gather additional information, or deepen understanding of a topic or issue.

Presentation of Knowledge and Ideas

4. Tell a story or recount an experience with appropriate facts and relevant, descriptive details, speaking audibly in coherent sentences.

5. Create audio recordings of stories or poems; add drawings or other visual displays to stories or recounts of experiences when appropriate to clarify ideas, thoughts, and feelings.

6. Produce complete sentences when appropriate to task and situation in order to provide requested detail or clarification. (See grade 2 Language standards 1 and 3 on pages 34–35 for specific expectations.)

Language Standards, Grade 2

Conventions of Standard English

1. Demonstrate command of the conventions of standard English grammar and usage when writing or speaking.
   a. Use collective nouns (e.g., group).
   b. Form and use frequently occurring irregular plural nouns (e.g., *feet, children, teeth, mice, fish*).
   c. Use reflexive pronouns (e.g., *myself, ourselves*).
   d. Form and use the past tense of frequently occurring irregular verbs (e.g., *sat, hid, told*).
   e. Use adjectives and adverbs, and choose between them depending on what is to be modified.
   f. Produce, expand, and rearrange complete simple and compound sentences (e.g., *The boy watched the movie; The little boy watched the movie; The action movie was watched by the little boy*).

2. Demonstrate command of the conventions of standard English capitalization, punctuation, and spelling when writing.
   a. Capitalize holidays, product names, and geographic names.
   b. Use commas in greetings and closings of letters.
   c. Use an apostrophe to form contractions and frequently occurring possessives.
   d. Generalize learned spelling patterns when writing words (e.g., *cage → badge; boy → boil*).
   e. Consult reference materials, including beginning dictionaries, as needed to check and correct spellings.

Knowledge of Language

3. Use knowledge of language and its conventions when writing, speaking, reading, or listening.
   a. Compare formal and informal uses of English.

Continued

Table 5.2 (continued)

Vocabulary Acquisition and Use

4. Determine or clarify the meaning of unknown and multiple-meaning words and phrases based on grade 2 reading and content, choosing flexibly from an array of strategies.

   a. Use sentence-level context as a clue to the meaning of a word or phrase.

   b. Determine the meaning of the new word formed when a known prefix is added to a known word (e.g., *happy/unhappy, tell/retell*).

   c. Use a known root word as a clue to the meaning of an unknown word with the same root (e.g., *addition, additional*).

   d. Use knowledge of the meaning of individual words to predict the meaning of compound words (e.g., *birdhouse, lighthouse, housefly; bookshelf, notebook, bookmark*).

   e. Use glossaries and beginning dictionaries, both print and digital, to determine or clarify the meaning of words and phrases.

5. Demonstrate understanding of word relationships and nuances in word meanings.

   a. Identify real-life connections between words and their use (e.g., describe foods that are *spicy* or *juicy*).

   b. Distinguish shades of meaning among closely related verbs (e.g., *toss, throw, hurl*) and closely related adjectives (e.g., *thin, slender, skinny, scrawny*).

6. Use words and phrases acquired through conversations, reading and being read to, and responding to texts, including using adjectives and adverbs to describe (e.g., *When other kids are happy, that makes me happy*).

Common Core State Standards for Mathematics

The *CCSS Mathematics* (NGAC and CCSO 2010) are divided into two parts: eight mathematical practices that apply to every grade level and grade-specific standards of mathematical content. Many of these grade-specific standards are used in Picture-Perfect STEM lessons as students measure, graph, compare, and design. In the boxes titled "Connecting to the *Common Core*," you will find the *CCSS Mathematics* domain the activity addresses, the grade level, and standard number(s) (see Figure 5.5).

Because the *CCSS Mathematics* codes are listed in the lessons instead of the actual standards statements, we have included the *CCSS Mathematics* grade-level standards in Table 5.3 (pp. 58–59). This table is not a complete version of the *CCSS Mathematics*. Rather, it includes only the domains we address in our lessons for grade 2. You can access the complete *CCSS Mathematics* online (see the "Websites" section).

Figure 5.5. Sample CCSS Mathematics Box

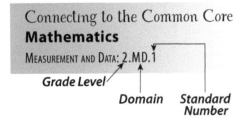

Picture-Perfect STEM Lessons, Grade 2, Expanded Edition

Table 5.3. Common Core State Standards *for Mathematics, Grade 2*

Operations and Algebraic Thinking	2.OA

Represent and solve problems involving addition and subtraction.

1. Use addition and subtraction within 100 to solve one- and two-step word problems involving situations of adding to, taking from, putting together, taking apart, and comparing, with unknowns in all positions, e.g., by using drawings and equations with a symbol for the unknown number to represent the problem.[1]

Add and subtract within 20.

2. Fluently add and subtract within 20 using mental strategies.[2] By end of Grade 2, know from memory all sums of two one-digit numbers.

Work with equal groups of objects to gain foundations for multiplication.

3. Determine whether a group of objects (up to 20) has an odd or even number of members, e.g., by pairing objects or counting them by 2s; write an equation to express an even number as a sum of two equal addends.

4. Use addition to find the total number of objects arranged in rectangular arrays with up to 5 rows and up to 5 columns; write an equation to express the total as a sum of equal addends.

Number and Operations in Base Ten	2.NBT

Understand place value.

1. Understand that the three digits of a three-digit number represent amounts of hundreds, tens, and ones; e.g., 706 equals 7 hundreds, 0 tens, and 6 ones. Understand the following as special cases:
   a. 100 can be thought of as a bundle of ten tens — called a "hundred."
   b. The numbers 100, 200, 300, 400, 500, 600, 700, 800, 900 refer to one, two, three, four, five, six, seven, eight, or nine hundreds (and 0 tens and 0 ones).

2. Count within 1000; skip-count by 5s, 10s, and 100s.

3. Read and write numbers to 1000 using base-ten numerals, number names, and expanded form.

4. Compare two three-digit numbers based on meanings of the hundreds, tens, and ones digits, using >, =, and < symbols to record the results of comparisons.

Use place value understanding and properties of operations to add and subtract.

5. Fluently add and subtract within 100 using strategies based on place value, properties of operations, and/or the relationship between addition and subtraction.

6. Add up to four two-digit numbers using strategies based on place value and properties of operations.

7. Add and subtract within 1000, using concrete models or drawings and strategies based on place value, properties of operations, and/or the relationship between addition and subtraction; relate the strategy to a written method. Understand that in adding or subtracting three- digit numbers, one adds or subtracts hundreds and hundreds, tens and tens, ones and ones; and sometimes it is necessary to compose or decompose tens or hundreds.

8. Mentally add 10 or 100 to a given number 100–900, and mentally subtract 10 or 100 from a given number 100–900.

9. Explain why addition and subtraction strategies work, using place value and the properties of operations.[3]

Continued

[1]See Glossary, Table 1.

[2]See standard 1.OA.6 for a list of mental strategies.

[3]Explanations may be supported by drawings or objects.

National Science Teaching Association

Table 5.3 (continued)

Measurement and Data	2.MD

Measure and estimate lengths in standard units.

1. Measure the length of an object by selecting and using appropriate tools such as rulers, yardsticks, meter sticks, and measuring tapes.

2. Measure the length of an object twice, using length units of different lengths for the two measurements; describe how the two measurements relate to the size of the unit chosen.

3. Estimate lengths using units of inches, feet, centimeters, and meters.

4. Measure to determine how much longer one object is than another, expressing the length difference in terms of a standard length unit.

Relate addition and subtraction to length.

5. Use addition and subtraction within 100 to solve word problems involving lengths that are given in the same units, e.g., by using drawings (such as drawings of rulers) and equations with a symbol for the unknown number to represent the problem.

6. Represent whole numbers as lengths from 0 on a number line diagram with equally spaced points corresponding to the numbers 0, 1, 2, ..., and represent whole-number sums and differences within 100 on a number line diagram.

Work with time and money.

7. Tell and write time from analog and digital clocks to the nearest five minutes, using a.m. and p.m.

8. Solve word problems involving dollar bills, quarters, dimes, nickels, and pennies, using $ and ¢ symbols appropriately. *Example: If you have 2 dimes and 3 pennies, how many cents do you have?*

Represent and interpret data.

9. Generate measurement data by measuring lengths of several objects to the nearest whole unit, or by making repeated measurements of the same object. Show the measurements by making a line plot, where the horizontal scale is marked off in whole-number units.

10. Draw a picture graph and a bar graph (with single-unit scale) to represent a data set with up to four categories. Solve simple put-together, take-apart, and compare problems[4] using information presented in a bar graph.

Geometry	2.G

Reason with shapes and their attributes.

1. Recognize and draw shapes having specified attributes, such as a given number of angles or a given number of equal faces.[5] Identify triangles, quadrilaterals, pentagons, hexagons, and cubes.

2. Partition a rectangle into rows and columns of same-size squares and count to find the total number of them.

3. Partition circles and rectangles into two, three, or four equal shares, describe the shares using the words *halves, thirds, half of, a third of,* etc., and describe the whole as two halves, three thirds, four fourths. Recognize that equal shares of identical wholes need not have the same shape.

[4]See Glossary, Table 1.

[5]Sizes are compared directly or visually, not compared by measuring.

Websites

CCSS ELA
https://learning.ccsso.org/ common-core-state-standards-initiative

CCSS Mathematics
https://learning.ccsso.org/ common-core-state-standards-initiative

References

National Governors Association Center for Best Practices and Council of Chief State School Officers (NGAC and CCSSO). 2010. *Common core state standards*. Washington, DC: NGAC and CCSSO.

National Research Council (NRC). 2012. *A framework for K–12 science education: Practices, crosscutting concepts, and core ideas*. Washington, DC: National Academies Press.

NGSS Lead States. 2013. *Next Generation Science Standards: For states, by states*. Washington, DC: National Academies Press. *www.nextgenscience.org/next-generation-science-standards*.

Willard, T., ed. 2015. *The NSTA quick-reference guide to the NGSS: Elementary school*. Arlington, VA: NSTA Press.

How Big Is a Foot?

Description

Learners explore the history of measurement from the ancient Egyptian use of nonstandard units to the modern-day metric system. They learn why standard measuring tools are useful and that their development was a problem-solving process that took centuries.

Alignment with the *Next Generation Science Standards*

Performance Expectation
K-2-ETS1-1: Ask questions, make observations, and gather information about a situation that people want to change to define a simple problem that can be solved through the development of a new or improved object or tool

Science and Engineering Practices	Disciplinary Core Ideas	Crosscutting Concept
Analyzing and Interpreting Data Analyze data from tests of an object or tool to determine if it works as intended. **Using Mathematics and Computational Thinking** Use quantitative data to compare two alternative solutions to a problem.	**ETS1.A: Defining and Delimiting Engineering Problems** A situation that people want to change or create can be approached as a problem to be solved through engineering. Such problems may have many acceptable solutions. Asking questions, making observations, and gathering information are helpful in thinking about problems. Before beginning to design a solution, it is important to clearly understand the problem.	**Scale, Proportion, and Quantity** Standard units are used to measure length.

Note: The activities in this lesson will help students move toward the performance expectations listed, which is the goal after multiple activities. However, the activities will not by themselves be sufficient to reach the performance expectations.

Contemporary research on how students learn science, reflected in the *Next Generation Science Standards* and other state standards based in *A Framework for K–12 Science Education,* requires that engineering lessons taught as part of the science curriculum provide students with opportunities to "acquire and use elements of disciplinary core ideas from physical, life, or Earth and space sciences together with elements of disciplinary core ideas from engineering design to solve design problems." (NGSS Lesson Screener, *www.nextgenscience.org/screener*)

Featured Picture Books

TITLE: ***How Big Is a Foot?***
AUTHOR: **Rolf Myller**
ILLUSTRATOR: **Rolf Myller**
PUBLISHER: **Young Yearling**
YEAR: **1991**
GENRE: **Story**
SUMMARY: *The King has a problem. He wants to give the Queen a bed for her birthday, but no one knows the answer to the question "How big is a bed?"*

TITLE: ***How Tall, How Short, How Faraway?***
AUTHOR: **David A. Adler**
ILLUSTRATOR: **Nancy Tobin**
PUBLISHER: **Holiday House**
YEAR: **1999**
GENRE: **Non-Narrative Information**
SUMMARY: *Colorful cartoons and easy-to-follow text introduce the history of measurement, from the ancient Egyptian system to the metric system.*

Time Needed

This lesson will take several class periods. Suggested scheduling is as follows:

Session 1: **Engage** with *How Big Is a Foot?* Read-Aloud and **Explore** with Measuring with Feet

Session 2: **Explain** with A Letter to the King

Session 3: **Explain** with *How Tall, How Short, How Faraway?* Read-Aloud and Measurement Activities

Session 4: **Elaborate** with Measuring the Playground

Session 5: **Evaluate** with A Better Way to Measure

Materials

For Measuring with Feet

• About 2 m of string or yarn (per pair of students)
• Roll of masking tape
• Yardstick

For Measurement Activities

• Meterstick
• Metric ruler (1 per student)

For Measuring the Playground

- Measuring wheel (1 per class)
- Metric ruler (per group of 4)
- Meterstick (per group of 4)
- Metric tape measure – soft, not metal (per group of 4)
- Clipboard (per group of 4)

Student Pages

- A Letter to the King
- Measuring the Playground
- A Better Way to Measure to Map a Buried Treasure
- STEM Everywhere

Background for Teachers

In this lesson, students learn how the development of standard measurements was a fascinating but lengthy problem-solving process.

Weights and measures were among the first tools invented by humans. Ancient people used their body parts and items in their surroundings as their first measuring tools. Early Egyptian and Babylonian records indicate that length was first measured with the forearm, hand, and fingers. As societies evolved, measurements became more complex. It became more and more important to be able to measure accurately time after time and to be able to reproduce the measurements in different places. By the 18th century, England had achieved a greater degree of standardization in measurement than other European countries. The English, or *customary system* of measurement, commonly used in the United States, is nearly the same as that brought by the colonists from England.

The need for a single, worldwide measurement system was recognized more than 300 years ago when a French priest named Gabriel Mouton proposed a comprehensive decimal measurement system. A century passed, however, and no action was taken. During the French Revolution, the National Assembly of France requested that the French Academy of Sciences "deduce an invariable standard for all the measures and all the weights." A system was proposed that was both simple and scientific: the *metric system*. The simplicity of the metric system is due to its being based on units of 10. The standardized structure and decimal features of the metric system made it well suited for scientific and engineering work, so it is not surprising that wide acceptance of the metric system coincided with an age of rapid technological development. By an Act of Congress in 1866, it became "lawful throughout the United States of America to employ the weights and measures of the metric system to all contracts, dealings, and court proceedings." By 1900, a total of 35 nations had accepted the metric system. Eventually, the name *Systeme Internationale d'Unites* (International System of Units) with the international abbreviation SI was given to the metric system. Although the customary system of measurement is commonly used in everyday situations in the United States, U.S. scientists primarily use the metric system (SI) in their daily work.

Adapted from: A Brief History of Measurement Systems
   www.dickeyphysics.com/Physics_Readings/History%20of%20Measurement%20Systems.pdf

In this lesson, students approach the topic of the development of standard measures as an engineering design process. They make sense of why we use standard units of measurement through reading a story that poses the problem with nonstandard units of measurement and by collecting and analyzing data from nonstandard measurements. They are engaged in the science and engineering practices (SEPs) of analyzing and interpreting data and using mathematics and computational thinking through these activities. The crosscutting concept (CCC) of scale, proportion, and quantity permeates the lesson as students compare standard and nonstandard units. The SEP of obtaining, evaluating, and communicating information comes into play as students read a nonfiction book about the history of measurement and as they communicate explanations and solutions in writing.

Learning Progressions

Below are the disciplinary core idea (DCI) grade band endpoints for grades K–2 and 3–5. These are provided to show how student understanding of the DCIs in this lesson will progress in future grade levels.

DCIs	Grades K–2	Grades 3–5
ETS1.A: Defining and Delimiting Engineering Problems	• A situation that people want to change or create can be approached as a problem to be solved through engineering. • Asking questions, making observations, and gathering information are helpful in thinking about problems. • Before beginning to design a solution, it is important to clearly understand the problem.	• Possible solutions to a problem are limited by available materials and resources (constraints). The success of a designed solution is determined by considering the desired features of a solution (criteria). Different proposals for solutions can be compared on the basis of how well each one meets the specified criteria for success or how well each takes the constraints into account.

Source: Willard, T., ed. 2015. *The NSTA quick-reference guide to the* NGSS: *Elementary school.* Arlington, VA: NSTA Press.

 engage

How Big Is a Foot? Read-Aloud

Connecting to the Common Core
Reading: Literature
Key Ideas and Details: 2.3

 **Inferring**

Show students the cover of the book *How Big Is a Foot?* Ask

❓ What can you infer from the title and illustration on the cover of this book?

Begin reading the book aloud but stop after reading, "Why was the bed too small for the Queen?" *Ask*

❓ Do you think it is fair that the King put the apprentice in jail? Why or why not?

Have students share their ideas with a partner, and then call on students to share with the class. *Ask*

? How big IS a foot?

Students will likely conclude that it depends on what you mean by "foot." Students might know that a foot is a unit of measure that is 12 inches long. But if you are talking about a person's foot, we'll have to find out!

explore

Measuring with Feet

Remind students that "the King took off his shoes and with his big feet walked carefully around the Queen. He counted that the bed must be three feet wide." Tell students that they are going to determine the length of three feet by using their own feet. Give each pair of students about 2 m of yarn or string. Then demonstrate the steps for measuring three "feet":

1. Have your partner hold the end of the string where the back of your heel touches the floor.

2. Place one foot right in front of the other for three steps, and then freeze.

3. Have your partner stretch the string to the big toe of your third step.

4. Cut the string. It will now represent the length of your three "feet."

5. Attach a piece of masking tape with your name on it to one end of the string.

6. Hang your string from the board.

7. Help your partner measure his or her three "feet."

When all students have hung their strings on the board, compare the various lengths. *Ask*

? Are all of the strings the same length? Why or why not?

MEASURING THREE "FEET"

> **SEP: Analyzing and Interpreting Data**
> Analyze data from tests of an object or tool to determine if it works as intended.

Hold up a yardstick and *ask*

? How many feet are in a yard? (Students may know there are three feet in a yard.)

? How does your string compare to three feet as measured by a yardstick?

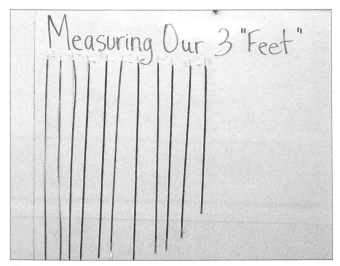

COMPARING THE STRINGS

explain

A Letter to the King

Connecting to the Common Core
Writing
TEXT TYPES AND PURPOSES: 2.1

 Writing

Refer back to the book *How Big Is a Foot?* and revisit the question:

? Do you think it is fair that the King put the apprentice in jail? Why or why not?

? What advice would you give the King about how he might be able to get a bed the right size for the Queen?

On the A Letter to the King student page, have students write a persuasive letter to the King about why he should let the apprentice out of jail. Ask them to explain why the bed is too small for the Queen and what he could do to get a bed that is the right size. Have students share their letters with a partner. Read the student letters to assess whether students understand that the bed is too

short because of the difference in foot size between the King and the apprentice. Students should also provide reasonable advice for getting a bed the right size.

Next, read the rest of the book to students. *Ask*

? How does the apprentice's solution in the book compare to the advice you gave in your letter?

? What measuring tool was created to solve the problem? (a model of the King's foot sculpted out of marble)

? Is there more than one correct solution? (yes)

? What are some other ways that the King could have had the bed built the right size? (by using a standard measurement tool with more precise markings)

? What tool would you use today to measure a bed? (tape measure, meterstick, ruler)

explain

How Tall, How Short, How Faraway? Read-Aloud

Connecting to the Common Core
Reading: Informational Text
INTEGRATION OF KNOWLEDGE AND IDEASS: 2.9

 Making Connections: Text to Text

Show students the cover of *How Tall, How Short, How Faraway? Ask*

? What do you think this book is about?

Hold up *How Tall, How Short, How Faraway?* and *How Big Is a Foot? Ask*

? What do you think these two books might have in common? (Examples of answers include that both are about measurement and about people's height.)

Ask students to signal when they hear or see any connections between the two books. Then read aloud pages 1–19 of *How Tall, How Short, How Faraway?* (ending after "5,280 feet are 1 mile"), stopping to discuss any text-to-text connections. Students may point out some of the following connections:

How Tall, How Short, How Faraway?	*How Big Is a Foot?*
Ancient Egyptians measured with their hands and arms (digits, cubits, palms, spans).	The King measured with his feet.
Measuring with hands and arms caused problems with getting accurate measurements.	Measuring with different-sized feet caused problems in getting a bed the right size for the Queen.
In the past, people often used their leader's or king's cubit or steps as a standard.	The apprentice decided to use the King's foot as a standard to remake the bed.
People made measuring sticks the size of their king's cubit or steps.	The apprentice made an exact marble copy of the King's foot and measured with it.

Measurement Activities

Connecting to the Common Core
Mathematics
2.MD.A.2

> **SEP: Using Mathematics and Computational Thinking**
> Use quantitative data to compare two alternative solutions to a problem.

Challenge students by *asking*

? Can you measure the length of my desk without a ruler?

As a class, brainstorm a list of ways that you could measure the desk without using any traditional measuring tools. Then *ask*

? How did the ancient Egyptians measure out a span? (A span is the distance from the tip of your thumb to the end of your little finger with your hand stretched wide.)

Make the following data table on the board:

Length of Desk

Names	Spans	

MEASURING THE DESK IN SPANS

> **SEP: Analyzing and Interpreting Data**
> Analyze data from tests of an object or tool to determine if it works as intended.

Call on a student to measure your desk with his or her hand span. Write that student's name and his or her number of spans on the data table. Call on another student who is noticeably taller or shorter than the first student to measure the desk in his or her spans. Write that number of spans on the data table. Then measure the desk using your own hand span, and write that number of spans on the data table. *Ask*

? Which is the correct answer for the length of my desk? (Students should begin to understand that there is no "correct" answer in spans.)

? Why did we get different answers for the length of the desk in spans? (Each person's span is a different size.)

? Why do you think the span is no longer used for measuring length? (It is not an accurate measurement because the length of the span varies from person to person.)

> Connecting to the Common Core
> **Reading: Informational Text**
> KEY IDEAS AND DETAILS: 2.1

Go back to *How Tall, How Short, How Faraway?* and read from page 20 ("The metric system was first proposed over 300 years ago …") to page 31 ("People have been measuring things for thousands of years."). After reading, state that in different times and parts of the world, there have been many systems of measurement. *Ask*

? What are the two systems of measurement most widely used today? (the customary, also known as the English system, and the metric system)

FINDING SOMETHING ONE METER LONG

COMPARING SPANS AND CENTIMETERS

> **CCC: Scale, Proportion, and Quantity**
> Standard units are used to measure length.

Explain that the units used in these systems are called standard units. *Standard units* are units of measurement that are accepted and used by most people. Some examples of standard units are feet, inches, pounds, centimeters, meters, grams, and liters. The other type of units is *nonstandard units*, which are everyday objects that can be used to obtain a measurement. Examples include spans, cubits, paces, and digits.

Explain that most people around the world, as well as scientists everywhere, use the metric system because it is simpler and less confusing than the customary system. Explain that, although the metric system was invented over 200 years ago, the United States has not entirely switched over to it. Some metric units are grams, kilograms, liters, centimeters, and meters. *Ask*

? What things do you know of that are measured in metric units? (Examples include 2 l bottles of soda, 100 m dash, grams of fat in food, distances in kilometers, and kilometers per hour on a speedometer.)

Connecting to the Common Core
Mathematics
2.MD.A.1

Give each pair of students a meterstick and a metric ruler. Have students use these tools to find something in the room that is about a centimeter long and something that is about a meter long. Next, label the third column on the data table "centimeters" and call on a student to measure your desk in centimeters with a meterstick. Write that student's name and the measurement on the data table. Call on another student to measure the desk with the meterstick. Write that measurement on the

data table. Then measure the desk yourself with a meterstick and write that measurement on the data table. *Ask*

? Why were the answers so different for the length of the desk in spans yet all the same for the length of the desk in centimeters? (Each person's span is a different size, but a centimeter is always the same size.

elaborate

Measuring the Playground

Connecting to the Common Core
Mathematics
2.MD.A.1

Tell students that an important part of using standard measurements is having the proper tools and using them correctly. *Ask*

? What are some of the tools we have used so far to make standard measurements? (rulers and metersticks)

? Would a ruler or meterstick be a good tool for measuring the circumference of (or distance around) the trunk of a tree or someone's head? (No, because they are flat and can't bend.)

Show students a metric tape measure and demonstrate how it can be used to measure things that are not flat because the tape is flexible. Model how to measure the circumference of something in the classroom that is round – like a student's head – or go outdoors and measure the circumference of a tree. *Ask*

? Would a tape measure be a good tool for measuring the distance from our classroom to the playground? (It is likely not long enough. Students might suggest marking the length of the tape measure at different points and measuring from there over and over again, but with that method, it is difficult to be exact.)

Next, show students a measuring wheel and model how it is used to measure long distances. Explain that all these tools are used to measure length. They were designed by engineers to be easy to use, precise, and suitable for different situations. There are many other types of measuring tools to measure things like weight, volume, temperature, time, and so on, but this lesson just focuses

on length. Explain that one of the most important things you can do to make sure you are taking precise measurements is to begin measuring at zero on the tool. Some rulers, metersticks, and tape measures begin with zero at the tip and others have some space before zero. Model where to find zero on all the measuring tools you are using for this activity. For the measuring wheel, model how to check that the device starts at zero before measuring.

> **SEP: Analyzing and Interpreting Data**
> Analyze data from tests of an object or tool to determine if it works as intended.

Give each group of four students a metric ruler, meterstick, metric tape measure, the Measuring the Playground student page, and a clipboard. Tell them that they are going to go to the playground (or the gym) to measure things using these tools. On the way to the playground, use the measuring wheel to measure the distance to the playground from your room or from the exit. Groups can take turns using the measuring wheel.

Optional: For fun, you may even want to try some high-tech measurement apps such as the Tape Measure App, Measure by Google, Measure by Apple, Ruler App, or Smart Measure.

After students practice measuring, have groups share some of the measurements they took and how they decided which tool to use to take those length measurements.

MEASURING ON THE PLAYGROUND

National Science Teaching Association

evaluate

A Better Way to Measure

Connecting to the Common Core
Writing
TEXT TYPES AND PURPOSES: 2.1

 *Writing*

Review what students have learned about the history of measurement and the need for standard measuring tools. Then distribute the assessment student page, A Better Way to Measure. Correct responses may include the following:

1. The pirates disagree because, when they measured the distance to the treasure, they each used their own paces. One is tall and one is short, so their paces are different lengths.

2. The pirates could measure in feet, yards, or meters.

3. We wouldn't know the exact distance to anything or anyplace.

> **SEP: Using Mathematics and Computational Thinking**
> Use quantitative data to compare two alternative solutions to a problem.

STEM Everywhere

Give students the STEM Everywhere student page as a way to involve their families and extend their learning. They can do the activity with an adult helper and share their results with the class. If students do not have access to internet at home, you may choose to have them complete this activity at school.

Opportunities for Differentiated Instruction

This box lists questions and challenges related to the lesson that students may select to research, investigate, or innovate. Students may also use the questions as examples to help them generate their own questions. These questions can help you move your students from the teacher-directed investigation to engaging in the science and engineering practices in a more student-directed format.

Extra Support

For students who are struggling to meet the lesson objectives, provide a question and guide them in the process of collecting research or help them design procedures or solutions.

Extensions

For students with high interest or who have already met the lesson objectives, have them choose a question (or pose their own question), conduct their own research, and design their own procedures or solutions.

Continued

Opportunities for Differentiated Instruction (continued)

After selecting one of the questions in the box or formulating their own question, students can individually or collaboratively make predictions, design investigations or surveys to test their predictions, collect evidence, devise explanations, design solutions, or examine related resources. They can communicate their findings through a science notebook, at a poster session or gallery walk, or by producing a media project.

Research

Have students brainstorm researchable questions:

? Which countries have not adopted the metric system as their official system of measurement? Why?

? How long is a marathon and what is the story behind it?

? What are some of the abbreviations for length measurements (centimeters, kilometers, inches, feet, miles)?

Investigate

Have students brainstorm testable questions to be solved through science or math:

? How tall is everyone in your family? Order them from shortest to tallest.

? Connect 10 small paper clips and use them to measure things around your room. Do paper clips make a good measuring tool? Why or why not?

? Design a way to compare the size of your "pace" (every two steps) to the "pace" of your friends. How do they compare?

Innovate

Have students brainstorm problems to be solved through engineering:

? What objects (that are always the same size) could be used to create a new way to measure? How would you use them?

? Can you create a scale model of your room?

? Can you make a scale drawing of the playground?

Website

 Ozomatli: "Measure It!" from PBS Kids Rock
*www.pbslearningmedia.org/
resource/4c3ca5c0-0e33-4504-8a16-
f6c29c9730f7/ozomatli-measure-it-pbs-
kids-rocks-video*

More Books to Read

Cleary, B. P. 2009. *How long or how wide? A measuring guide*. Minneapolis: Millbrook Press.
Summary: Part of the Math is CATegorical series, this book is a fun introduction to all the ways we measure length.

Jenkins, S. 2011. *Actual size*. New York: Houghton Mifflin.
Summary: With his colorful collage illustrations, Jenkins shows the actual sizes of many interesting animals. Some pages show the entire animal, whereas others show only a part of the animal.

Leedy, L. 2000. *Measuring penny*. New York: Square Fish.
Summary: Lisa learns about the mathematics of measuring by measuring her dog Penny with all sorts of units, including pounds, inches, dog biscuits, and cotton swabs.

Nagda, A. W. and Bickel, C. 2000. *Tiger math: Learning to graph from a baby tiger*. New York: Henry Holt.
Summary: At the Denver Zoo, a Siberian tiger cub named T. J. is orphaned when he is only a few weeks old. The zoo staff raises him, feeding him by hand until he is able to eat on his own and return to the tiger exhibit. The story is accompanied by graphs that chart T. J.'s growth, showing a wonderful example of real-world mathematics.

Pluckrose, H. 2018. *Length*. Chicago: Children's Press.
Summary: Photographs and simple text introduce the concept of length and ways to measure it.

Sweeny, J. 2019. *Me and the measure of things*. Decorah, IA: Dragonfly Books.
Summary: Simple text and playful illustrations explain the differences between wet and dry measurements, weight, length, and size in a fun and relatable context.

Weakland, M. A. 2013. *How tall? Wacky ways to compare height*. Minneapolis: Picture Window Books.
Summary: From the Wacky Comparisons series, this book compares the height of different objects in weird and wacky ways. Also in this series are *How Heavy? Wacky Ways to Compare Weight* and *How Long? Wacky Ways to Compare Length*.

Name: _____

A Letter to the King

Write a letter to the King to convince him to let the apprentice out of jail. In your letter, be sure to

- explain why the bed was made too small for the Queen, and
- tell what the King could do to have a bed made the right size for the Queen.

Your Royal Highness,

_____

_____

_____

_____

_____

_____

_____

_____

_____

Your Loyal Subject,

_____

National Science Teaching Association

Name: _____

Measuring the Playground

Can you find something that is…

About 1 centimeter long _____

About 10 centimeters long _____

About 1 meter long _____

Choose some things to measure on the playground. List the object, length, and tool that you used in the table below.

Object	Length	Tool

Name: _____

A Better Way to Measure
to Map a Buried Treasure!

1. Why do you think the pirates disagree about the distance to the treasure?

_____

_____

2. What would be a better way to measure the distance to the treasure?

_____

_____

3. What would happen if everyone used his or her own paces to measure distance or length?

_____

_____

Name: _____

STEM Everywhere

Dear Families,

At school, we have been learning about **the history of measurement**. We measured things in nonstandard units (like spans and paces) and standard units (like meters and feet). We identified tools that can be used to take exact measurements (like rulers and metersticks). To find out more, ask your learner questions such as:

- What did you learn?
- What was your favorite part of the lesson?
- What are you still wondering?

At home, you can watch a music video from PBS Kids about different tools we use to measure.

 Ozomatli: "Measure It!"
www.pbslearningmedia.org/resource/4c3ca5c0-0e33-4504-8a16-f6c29c9730f7/ozomatli-measure-it-pbs-kids-rocks-video

After watching the video, look around at home for tools you use to measure things like size, weight, temperature, and time. Draw and label the measuring tools below. Hint: the kitchen is a good place to start!

Imaginative Inventions

Description

Learners explore the properties of matter and the engineering design process as they learn about the invention of the Frisbee, test flying discs to compare the materials they are made of and the strengths and weaknesses of how each performs, analyze data from simple tests of other toys to compare their "fun" and "safe" ratings, and design a toy of their own.

Alignment with the *Next Generation Science Standards*

Performance Expectations

2-PS1-2: Analyze data obtained from testing different materials to determine which materials have the properties that are best suited for an intended purpose.

K-2-ETS1-1: Ask questions, make observations, and gather information about a situation that people want to change to define a simple problem that can be solved through the development of a new or improved object or tool.

K-2-ETS1-2: Develop a simple sketch, drawing, or physical model to illustrate how the shape of an object helps it function as needed to solve a given problem.

Science and Engineering Practices	Disciplinary Core Ideas	Crosscutting Concepts
Planning and Carrying Out Investigations Make observations (firsthand or from media) and/or measurements to collect data that can be used to make comparisons. **Engaging in Argument from Evidence** Distinguish between opinions and evidence in one's own explanation. **Analyzing and Interpreting Data** Analyze data from tests of an object or tool to determine if it works as intended.	**PS1.A: Structure and Properties of Matter** Different properties are suited to different purposes. **ETS1.A: Defining and Delimiting Engineering Problems** A situation that people want to change or create can be approached as a problem to be solved through engineering. Before beginning to design a solution, it is important to clearly understand the problem.	**Cause and Effect** Simple tests can be designed to gather evidence to support or refute student ideas about causes. **Structure and Function** The shape and stability of structures of natural and designed objects are related to their function(s)

Continued

Alignment with the Next Generation Science Standards *(continued)*

Science and Engineering Practices	Disciplinary Core Ideas	Crosscutting Concepts
Using Mathematics and Computational Thinking Describe, measure, and/or compare qualitative attributes of different objects and display the data using simple graphs.	**ETS1.B: Developing Possible Solutions** Designs can be conveyed through sketches, drawings, or physical models. These representations are useful in communicating ideas for a problem's solution to other people.	

Note: The activities in this lesson will help students move toward the performance expectations listed, which is the goal after multiple activities. However, the activities will not by themselves be sufficient to reach the performance expectations.

Featured Picture Books

TITLE: ***Imaginative Inventions***
AUTHOR: **Charise Mericle Harper**
ILLUSTRATOR: **Charise Mericle Harper**
PUBLISHER: **Little, Brown Books for Young Readers**
YEAR: **2001**
GENRE: **Dual Purpose**
SUMMARY: *The who, what, where, when, and why of roller skates, marbles, Frisbees, and more told in rhyming verse.*

TITLE: ***Flip! How the Frisbee Took Flight***
AUTHOR: **Margaret Muirhead**
ILLUSTRATOR: **Adam Gustavson**
PUBLISHER: **Charlesbridge**
YEAR: **2021**
GENRE: **Narrative Information**
SUMMARY: *This fascinating true story of how the Frisbee became a worldwide phenomenon begins on the East Coast in the 1920s, when college students were flinging "Frisbie's Pies" tins. Later, entrepreneur Fred Morrison and his wife Lu tried and failed to perfect the flying disc. Over the years, their perseverance paid off. In the 1950s, the Wham-O Corporation began manufacturing Frisbees, giving Fred and Lu lifetime royalties to the toy that would sweep the nation. For more than 20 years, Fred and Lu tried and failed to perfect a flying-disc concept. Eventually, they created what we know today as the Frisbee. Their story is full of good old-fashioned perseverance, success, and fun!*

Time Needed

NOTE: In advance, locate a suitable place outside for students to test Frisbees and other flying discs. A large field such as a soccer field is best, but a playground or even a gymnasium will work.

This lesson will take several class periods. Suggested scheduling is as follows:

Session 1: **Engage** with *Imaginative Inventions* Read-Aloud

Session 2: **Explore** with Frisbee Testing and Frisbee Testing Video (this session may take extra time depending on how long students take to test the flying discs)

Session 3: **Explain** with *Flip! How the Frisbee Took Flight* Read-Aloud and The Frisbee Design Process

Session 4: **Elaborate** with Toy Testing, Toy Testing Video, and Overall Class Testing

Session 5 and beyond: **Evaluate** with The Next Big Thing (journal, advertising posters, and optional toy fair)

Materials

For Frisbee Testing (per group of 4)

- One classic Frisbee flying disc
- One aluminum pie tin
- One foam flying disc

For Toy Testing

- 2 different inexpensive novelty toys (per student or pair of students) such as blow ball pipes, spin tops, or jumping frogs
- 1 or more child choke testers
- Fun Ratings page
- Safety Ratings page

For The Next Big Thing

- White poster paper (any size, 1 per student)
- Markers, crayons, and/or colored pencils
- Optional: Cardboard, fabric, Play-Doh, clay, recycled materials, etc. for making toy models

Spin tops, jumping frogs, and other novelty toys are available from

Oriental Trading
www.orientaltrading.com

Child Choke Testers and Floating Blow Pipe and Balls are available from

Amazon
Amazon.com

Student Pages

- Fun Ratings
- Safety Ratings
- Toy Testing
- The Next Big Thing: A Toy Design Journal
- STEM Everywhere

Background for Teachers

Inventors are problemsolvers. They think about people's problems and come up with solutions using the engineering design process. There are many variations of the design process, but in general it involves identifying and researching a problem or unmet need, brainstorming possible solutions, and then designing the solution. These steps are followed by an iterative cycle of building, testing and evaluating, and redesigning until the solution is ready to be shared (see Figure 7.1).

Exploring how toys are designed, and what they are made of, can be a relatable way for children to learn about the design process as well as the properties of materials. Toys have likely been around as long as humans have lived on Earth. Among the earliest toys were small balls or marbles made of natural materials such as stone or clay. Medieval toys were made of wood and included simple tops and cup-and-ball toys. Later, toymakers used materials such as tin and cast iron to fashion simple toys. As the Second Industrial Revolution transformed manufacturing in the 1800s, mass-produced toys became popular. In the early 1900s, walking and talking toys, toy pianos, and classics such as Lionel trains, Erector sets, the Flexible Flyer sled, Tinker Toys, Lincoln Logs, Crayola crayons, and teddy bears were introduced.

The choice of materials is a crucial part of the toy design process. By the late 1940s, Fisher-Price was the first toy company to make its entire product range in plastic. Today, 90% of toys on the market are made of plastic (source: *https://plastics-themag.com/Plastic-shakes-up-the-toy-industry*). *A Framework for K–12 Science Education* suggests that by the end of grade 2, students should understand that different materials (e.g., plastic) can be described and classified by their observable properties and that different properties (e.g., flexibility) are suited to different purposes. Toy design is an engaging way for students to explore these core science ideas.

Most students are familiar with this classic toy made entirely of plastic: the Frisbee flying disc. The evolution of the Frisbee began around the beginning of the 20th century when New England college students played with spinning "Frisbie's Pies" tins. In the 1930s, a high school student in California named Walter Frederick Morrison began spinning tin popcorn lids through the air. He and his girlfriend, Lu, tried pie plates too, then tin cake pans. He began selling the pans and thinking about ways to improve the design. He and Lu married in 1939. In 1947, when the UFO craze swept the United States, Fred came up with the idea to connect this fad with his spinning cake pan. He experimented with different materials and discovered that plastic worked much better than tin. In 1948, after several design modifications, he launched a plastic disc called the Flyin-Saucer with help from an investor named Warren Franscioni. However, the Flyin-Saucer's plastic became brittle and broke in cool temperatures. Fred didn't give up. In 1955, he and Lu used a more flexible plastic to invent the Pluto Platter.

This invention came to the attention of a California toy company called Wham-O, the makers of the famous Hula Hoop. Wham-O bought Morrison's design in 1957 and gave Fred and Lu

Figure 7.1 The Design Process

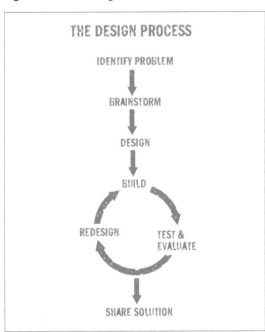

THE DESIGN PROCESS

IDENTIFY PROBLEM

BRAINSTORM

DESIGN

BUILD

REDESIGN — TEST & EVALUATE

SHARE SOLUTION

Chapter 7

National Science Teaching Association

lifetime royalties. The name of their invention was soon changed to Frisbee as a nod to the Frisbie tins still in use in New England. Wham-O added a band of raised edges on the disc's surface to stabilize flight and patented the modern Frisbee in 1967. By marketing Frisbee as a new sport, the company sold more than 100 million Frisbees by 1977. The Frisbee was inducted into the National Toy Hall of Fame in 1998. Today, more Frisbees are sold every year than footballs, baseballs, and basketballs combined! Other companies have put their own spin on the original Frisbee by adding lights or using materials such as nylon, foam, and even glow-in-the-dark plastic. A more drastic design change came with the Aerobie, a flexible flying ring made of a polycarbonate core surrounded by soft rubber bumpers. Manufacturers of flying discs and other toys seek to improve their market share by improving their designs and materials.

A Framework for K–12 Science Education suggests that by the end of grade 2, students should learn how science is utilized, particularly through the engineering design process. This process begins with identifying a problem to solve and specifying the *criteria* (desired features or goals that the final product must meet). Designers of toys such as Frisbees use the same engineering design process used by many other types of inventors. They begin by exploring possible criteria for the toy such as the needs and age range of the end-user and how the toy will function (what job it will perform and how). They use methods such as watching kids at play, talking with kids to see what they want for a new or improved toy, and interviewing parents to find out the types of toys they want to purchase for their children. They do market research to find out if their idea is unique or if similar toys are already being sold. They also research availability of materials and the costs associated with mass production. Toy trends come and go, so toy designers are always thinking about unique, cost-effective, and marketable ideas for "the next big thing."

The second step is to brainstorm ideas and create multiple concepts using methods such as sketches, sculptures, and 3D computer-aided designs (CADs). Once designers settle on a concept for a toy, the next step in the process is *prototype* development. A prototype is a first full-scale and usually functional physical model of a new design. Prototyping is an essential process that takes an invention from idea to reality. In this stage, designers fine tune the toys by creating a series of physical models, using technologies such as silicone molds or 3D printing. Prototyping gives designers a real, physical model of a toy to demonstrate the actual size and shape of the product, to test materials, to try out the model with focus groups, and to help sell their idea to toy manufacturers. Each prototype is refined through the iterative steps of the design process: building, testing and evaluating, and redesigning until the toy meets the criteria and is ready to market. As this iterative cycle progresses, designers get a better idea of constraints (limitations) such as the size and weight of the toy and the availability and cost of materials.

Toy designers often observe children in controlled settings to see how they play with a new toy and to assess the toy's durability and age-appropriateness. Toys must also be tested in labs to ensure that they are safe, they work as designed, and their materials don't break, bend, or fade. The U.S. Consumer Product Safety Commission publishes rigorous standards that toys must meet in order to be sold. Toys are tested for hazards such as flammability, sharp edges, and harmful chemicals. Toys must also pass a choke test using a tool called a choke gauge, a small cylinder with an angled bottom. If a toy part can fit inside the cylinder, the toy fails and must be labeled as not for children under 3 years old.

In this lesson, students learn about disciplinary core idea (DCI) ETS1.C: Optimizing the Design Solution as they compare and test toy designs. They are engaged in the crosscutting concept (CCC) of structure and function as they explore the properties and materials of a variety of flying discs and how they function in schoolyard play. They utilize the science and engineering practice (SEP) of planning and carrying out investigations as they make firsthand observations of the flying discs and other small,

simple novelty toys to collect data that can be used to make comparisons. They use the SEPs of both analyzing and interpreting data and using mathematics and computational thinking as they analyze tests of the novelty toys to determine if the toys are both fun and safe. They then compare the toys based on their individual fun ratings and safety ratings.

Finally, in the evaluate phase of this lesson, students use the SEP of obtaining, evaluating, and communicating information as they apply their knowledge of the design process to design their own new or improved toy: The Next Big Thing. They communicate their toy designs with one another in oral and/or written forms using models, drawings, and writing, detailing each step of the process, identifying which materials might be best suited for their toy, describing ways their toy might be tested, and creating a poster to advertise their toy. You may want to have students build simple, nonworking prototypes of their toys and invite others to view the toys and advertisements at a classroom toy fair. In this way, students are mirroring the design process used by real toy designers.

Special thanks to Karl Vanderbeek, VP of Design and Human Factors at Kaleidoscope Innovation.

Learning Progressions

Below are the DCI grade band endpoints for grades K–2 and 3–5. These are provided to show how student understanding of the DCIs in this lesson will progress in future grade levels.

DCIs	Grades K–2	Grades 3–5
PS1.A: Structure and Properties of Matter	• Different properties are suited to different purposes.	• Measurements of a variety of properties can be used to identify materials.
ETS1.A: Defining and Delimiting Engineering Problems	• A situation that people want to change or create can be approached as a problem to be solved through engineering. Such problems may have many acceptable solutions. • Asking questions, making observations, and gathering information are helpful in thinking about problems. • Before beginning to design a solution, it is important to clearly understand the problem.	• Possible solutions to a problem are limited by available materials and resources (constraints). The success of a designed solution is determined by considering the desired features of a solution (criteria). Different proposals for solutions can be compared on the basis of how each one meets the specified criteria for success or how well each takes the constraints into account.

Continued

Learning Progressions (continued)

DCIs	Grades K–2	Grades 3–5
ETS1.B: Developing Possible Solutions	• Designs can be conveyed through sketches, drawings, or physical models. These representations are useful in communicating ideas for a problem's solution to other people.	• Research on a problem should be carried out before beginning to design a solution. Testing a solution involves investigating how well it performs under a range of likely conditions.

Source: Willard, T., ed. 2015. *The NSTA quick-reference guide to the* NGSS: *Elementary school.* Arlington, VA: NSTA Press.

engage

Imaginative Inventions Read-Aloud

 ### Making Connections: Text to World

Show the cover of the book *Imaginative Inventions*, and introduce the author and illustrator. *Ask*

? What is an invention? (something that is made to meet a need or solve a problem)

? What is the difference between an invention and a discovery? (An invention is something that is created; a discovery is something that is found for the first time. For example, Ben Franklin discovered that lightning is electrical current, but he invented the lightning rod.)

? How are new things invented?

? Who invents new things?

? What is the first step when inventing something new?

? What is the final step when inventing something new?

 ### Turn and Talk

Next, build connections to the author by reading the inside flap of the book about author Charise Mericle Harper's favorite invention ("… muffins, which taste a lot like cake, but you get to eat them for breakfast!") Ask students to first discuss the following question with a partner, then share with the whole class.

? What do you think is the greatest invention ever and why? (Answers will vary.)

Connecting to the Common Core
Reading: Informational Text
KEY IDEAS AND DETAILS: 2.1

 ### Inferring

Tell students that the book *Imaginative Inventions* may not contain the invention they chose as the greatest, but it contains a lot of great inventions! Skipping pages 6–7 about the Frisbee, select several of the toys and other inventions in the book to read about. As you read each poem aloud, hide the illustrations and leave out the name of the invention. Instead, say "this invention." Ask students to make inferences about the identity of each invention using clues from the text. They can turn to a partner and whisper their guesses as you read. After reading each two-page spread, reveal the illustrations and name of the invention and read the facts in the sidebar on the right-hand side of each spread.

> **SEP: Obtaining, Evaluating, and Communicating Information**
> Communicate information or design ideas and/or solutions with others in oral and/or written forms using models, drawings, writing, or numbers that provide details about scientific ideas, practices, and/ or design ideas.

Then tell students that inventors think about people's unmet "needs" and "wants"(desires) and come up with ways to meet them. Ask students to identify the need or desire that each invention met. For example, a piggy bank met a need for a fun way to save loose change. A flat-bottomed paper bag met a need for a bag that could be filled while it was standing up. Potato chips met a customer's desire for a thinner fry.

Next, read pages 6–7 about the invention of the Frisbee and ask students to infer which toy the poem is describing. Reveal the toy and read the facts in the sidebar. Then ask students to identify the need or desire that the Frisbee met.

> **CCC: Structure and Function**
> The shape and stability of structures of natural and designed objects are related to their function(s).

Finally, hold up a classic Frisbee disc and *ask*

? Has anyone ever played with a Frisbee? (Answers will vary.)

? What is the function of a Frisbee? In other words, what is it designed to do? (to soar

COMPARING FLYING TOYS

through the air, to be used for fun, to be used for sports, etc.)

? What about its structure, or the way it is shaped, helps it do its job? (It is round, flat, smooth, lightweight, aerodynamic, etc.)

? What is a Frisbee made of? (plastic)

? Why is a Frisbee made of plastic? Why not rock, or glass, or cloth? (Students may laugh at this idea, but it will help them realize that a Frisbee is made of plastic because plastic has the right properties for the job. Plastic is not too hard, or sharp, or soft, etc. It is the best material to use for making Frisbees.)

? What is fun about playing with a Frisbee? (Answers will vary.)

? What is not so fun, or not so safe, about playing with a Frisbee? (Some Frisbees are hard for kids to throw or catch, a person could get hurt if hit by a Frisbee, a Frisbee could get stuck on a roof or sink in water, a Frisbee could be lost in the dark, and so on.)

? What are some ways that the shape or materials of the Frisbee could be changed to make it more fun, safer, or meet another need or desire? (Answers will vary.)

explore

Frisbee Testing

Tell students that instead of coming up with completely new inventions, inventors often think of ways to make an old one better. They might give the invention different features or make it out of different materials. A good example of this involves the improvements made to the classic Frisbee disc. Have students explore the improvements to the Frisbee's design. Provide each group of four a classic Frisbee, an aluminum pie tin, and a foam flying disc. Caution students not to throw them in the classroom!

As students are making observations of the flying discs, *ask*

? What do you notice about these designs? (They have the same basic shape but different colors, sizes, and profiles.)

? What do you wonder about these designs? (Answers will vary.)

Have groups put the flying discs in order of least fun to most fun. Have students hold up the flying disc they ranked as most fun. *Ask*

? What observations support your claims? In other words, how did you decide which would be the most fun? (Answers will vary.)

Then have each group hold up the disc they think would be the most fun and compare to other groups.

Next, have groups hold up the flying disc they ranked as least fun. *Ask*

? What observations support your claims? In other words, how did you decide which would be the least fun? (Answers will vary.)

Then have each group hold up the disc they think would be the least fun and compare to other groups.

Next, have groups put the flying discs in order of least safe to most safe. Have students hold up the flying disc they ranked as most safe. *Ask*

? What observations support your claims? In other words, how did you decide which would be the most safe? (Answers will vary.)

TESTING THE FLYING DISCS

Then have each group hold up the disc they think would be the most safe and compare to other groups.

Next, have groups hold up the flying disc they ranked as least safe. *Ask*

? What observations support your claims? In other words, how did you decide which would be the least safe? (Answers will vary.)

Then have each group hold up the disc they think would be the least safe and compare to other groups.

> **SEP: Engaging in Argument from Evidence**
> Distinguish between opinions and evidence in one's own explanation.

Next, tell students that the best way to make these claims is to actually play with the toys. *Ask*

? What observations could you make as you play with the flying discs to support your claims about the fun rankings? In other words, what could you observe in order to compare them? (Answers might include observing how well they fly, how far they fly, or how easy they are to throw or catch in comparison to one another.)

? What observations could you make as you play with the flying discs to support your claims about the safety rankings of the flying discs? (Answers might include observing how hard it hits your hand, how much control you have over where it goes, etc.)

> **CCC: Cause and Effect**
> Simple tests can be designed to gather evidence to support or refute ideas about causes.

Frisbee Testing Video

Tell students that testing is always done on toys, both by toy companies before the toy is sold and by end-users (people who buy or play with the toy) after the toy is on the market. Many students have likely seen toy testing videos on YouTube. Show the first 2:37 of the video "What is the Best Frisbee for Backyard Throwing?" (see "Websites") and ask students to listen and watch for what the man in the video wants to test. Then *ask*

? What kinds of things will he be testing for each flying disc? (how fast and far it flies, how straight and level it flies, how easy it is to throw, how comfortable it is to hold, etc.)

? How many of you would like to be flying disc testers? (It is likely that all students will want to be testers!)

Next, announce to the class that they will be going outside to test the flying discs! Caution them not to leave the playground, not to throw the discs onto a roof, and to use care when throwing so a flying disc doesn't hit someone. Remind them to be encouraging to one another, as some children may not have had much experience playing with Frisbees.

> **SEP: Planning and Carrying Out Investigations**
> Make observations (firsthand or from media) and/or measurements to collect data that can be used to make comparisons.

Students can choose what criteria they will use to determine what constitutes "fun" and "safe." Students will be collecting qualitative data using relative scales (easier to throw than, farther than, straighter than, faster than, etc.). They won't be measuring and recording distance or time in the air because of the difficulty involved. Some students may not have much experience throwing flying discs, so reassure them that it's OK if they aren't perfect with their throwing or catching. The goal is to explore ways to test toys and to have fun!

Then go outside to the playground or, even better, a large grassy field. Students should spread out and work in groups of four. Make sure all students in each group have at least one turn throwing and one turn trying to catch a flying disc. Continue until every group has had a chance to test each variation of flying disc (or until you run out of time).

 Turn and Talk

Return to the classroom and have each student turn and talk with a student from another group to compare their observations. Then *ask*

? Do you want to revise your initial claims about fun and safety based on new evidence? In other words, how would your rankings change?

? Which disc was the most comfortable to hold?

? Which one was the easiest to throw or catch?

? Which one had the longest, straightest, or most level flight?

? What material is each disc made of? (The pie tin is metal, the Frisbee is made of rigid plastic, and the other is made of soft foam.)

? How do those materials make them more or less fun?

? How do those materials make them more or less safe?

? Which one was the most fun? The least fun?

? Which one was the most safe? The least safe?

? Which one would you be most likely to buy? Why?

? How do you think the Frisbee was invented?

Tell students that they might be surprised to learn that the pie tin had something to do with how the Frisbee was invented!

explain

Flip! How the Frisbee Took Flight Read-Aloud

In advance, make a poster-sized version of The Design Process (Figure 7.1), which features the model used on the PBS show *Design Squad Global*. Two different color versions are available to print at *www.pictureperfectscience.com* (see Resources and click on the Extras tab).

Connecting to the Common Core
Reading: Informational Text
KEY IDEAS AND DETAILS: 2.1

Then *ask*

? Who did we learn designed the original Frisbee? (In the book *Imaginative Inventions*, students learned that the Frisbee was designed by a man named Walter, identified in the sidebar as Walter Frederick Morrison.)

? What did he first use as a flying disc? (a pie tin)

Tell students that you have another book that gives more background on how this inventor used the design process to go from a pie tin to a Frisbee. Introduce the author and illustrator of the book *Flip! How the Frisbee Took Flight*. Tell students that the inventor is referred to by his middle name (Fred) in this book. As you read the book aloud, ask students to listen for examples of how Fred Morrison used the design process.

The Frisbee Design Process

After reading, ask students to cite examples from the book for each step of the design process. They may need prompting to connect each step to an example from the text. Use Table 7.1 to help you facilitate this discussion.

Table 7.1 The Frisbee Design Process

Step	What it Means	Examples from the book *Flip!*
Identify Problem	Figure out something people need or want.	(page 7) Fred wanted something fun to do in the backyard after dinner.
Brainstorm	Come up with lots of ideas that might work.	(page 7) Fred tried using a tin popcorn lid. (page 8) Fred tried pie plates. (page 9) Fred tried cake pans.
Design	Imagine what the solution might look like and draw it.	(page 15) Fred imagined a flying tin with rounded edges or raised ridges. (*Note:* We don't know from reading if he just imagined it or also drew pictures of the solution.)
Build, Test, and Evaluate; Redesign	Build the solution, see if it works, make changes, test it again, and repeat until you are satisfied with the solution.	(page 19) Fred and Warren created the first Flyin-Saucer out of lightweight, pliable (bendable) plastic. (page 21) In cool temperatures, the Flyin-Saucer broke. (page 22) Fred and Lu tried a new design with a more flexible plastic and renamed it the Pluto Platter. It didn't break!
Share Solution	Tell others about the solution and try to use or sell it.	(page 22) Fred sold the Pluto Platter at fairs. (pages 24-26) A toy company called Wham-O took interest and bought the design from Fred and Lu. (page 29) Wham-O renamed it Frisbee and sales shot up. Millions of Frisbees have been sold.

Discuss the materials that Fred used while designing and improving the Frisbee. *Ask*

? What materials did he try? (metal, plastic, flexible plastic)

? How did those materials work? (The metal was not safe. The first plastic he tried broke when it got cold. The more flexible plastic was safe and did not break.)

Tell students that since Wham-O started making Frisbees, many improvements have been made using other materials such as foam, glow-in-the-dark plastic, and nylon. You may want to show them photos or real examples of improved Frisbees and

discuss the benefits of each type of material. For example, foam makes the toy soft and safe, glow-in-the-dark plastic makes it easy to see at night, and nylon makes it foldable and portable.

elaborate

Toy Testing

After discussing the Frisbee design process from the book *Flip!, ask*

? How do you think Fred Morrison tested his flying discs? (He played with them to see how well they flew, how durable they were, and how safe they were.)

? Why do toy designers and toy companies need to test toys? (to see if the toys work and if they are fun and safe)

Toy Testing Video

Tell students that real kids are the best toy testers! Many toy companies give children toys to test and observe their reactions to them. Kids can tell toy designers if a toy is truly fun, but safety is important, too. Toy companies are required by law to do safety tests on their toys. Explain that a magazine called *Good Housekeeping* runs a toy-testing lab where engineers test toys for safety and kids test toys for fun. Have them watch the 2:40 minute video called "Toy Testing at *Good Housekeeping*" (see "Websites") to observe a toy testing lab in action.

After watching the toy testing video, *ask*

? What did you notice?

? What do you wonder?

? Would you like to be a toy tester?

> **SEP: Planning and Carrying Out Investigations**
> Make observations to collect data that can be used to make comparisons

Tell students that they are going to have a chance to be toy testers! On the board, write the name of one of the toys they will be testing (see Materials) and label it "Toy A." Write the name of the other toy on the board and label it "Toy B." Then pass out a Toy Testing student page to each student. Point out that the student page has four different parts. Explain that first, they will play with both toys. In Part 1, they will draw and label the toys. In Part 2, they will rate the toys for how fun they are. In Part 3, they will rate the toys for how safe they are. In Part 4, they will decide which toy they would prefer to buy.

Next, give each student or pair of students both toys to test. Allow them several minutes to play with the toys. Then have them put the toys on their desks so they can complete the student page. For Part 1, ask them to determine what material(s) the toys are made of (they may need help with this) and to draw and label the materials and parts of each toy.

For Part 2, ask them to decide how fun the toys are (they may need more time to play with them!). *Ask*

? How did you decide what counted as fun when you tested the flying discs? (Answers will vary.)

? Can we use these same criteria for fun as we test and compare the toys? (Answers will vary.)

The "fun" rating will be relative. For example, a blow ball pipe might be considered "very fun" as compared to a "sort of fun" jumping frog or spinning top. However, to compare a blow ball pipe to a video game might not be fair!

For Part 3, ask students to consider the safety of each toy's materials and parts. Explain that most toys come with warning labels and/or directions for using the toy safely. These labels (if they are included on the toys or their packaging) can help them compare the safety of the toys. Return to students' initial criteria for "safe" and make connections between students' ideas and safety labels on toys.

Then discuss the possible risks of toys. Explain that toy testers look for sharp parts that could hurt a child. For this activity, students can gently run their fingers around the toy to assess if there are any pieces of plastic or other materials that could poke a child. Remind them to use caution! Toy testers also check for choking hazards. Babies and young children often put things in their mouths. If a toy is too small, or contains small parts, it could be a choking hazard for children under 3 years old. Show students a choke tester, a tool that can be used to determine whether toys have parts that young children can swallow. To use the choke tester, students can drop the toy or toy part into the clear cylinder. If it falls in, it is not safe because it could get caught in a child's throat. The diameter

of the tube is 1 ¼ inch, about the same size as a 3-year-old's throat. Students can use the warning labels, assessment of sharp parts, choke testing results, and anything else that might indicate the toy is unsafe to come up with their ratings. (Keep the choke tester accessible during the toy testing so students can use it to test the toys.) *Ask*

? How did you decide what counted as safe when you tested the flying discs?

? Can we use these same criteria for safety as we test and compare the toys? (Answers will vary, but students will likely want to add "sharp edges" and the choking test to their criteria.)

Then have students give a safety rating for each toy. Finally, students can compare the fun and safety ratings of the two toys to determine which toy they personally would prefer to buy.

Have them fill out the Toy Testing student page as shown:

1. Play with the toys! Then draw each toy below and label its parts and materials.

Toy A Drawing	Toy B Drawing

2. Give each toy a fun rating:

	Toy A	Toy B
Fun	☹ not fun 😐 sort of fun ☺ very fun	☹ not fun 😐 sort of fun ☺ very fun

3. Use the choke tester to test each toy and check for sharp parts. Then give each toy a safety rating:

	Toy A	Toy B
Safety	☹ not safe 😐 sort of safe ☺ very safe	☹ not safe 😐 sort of safe ☺ very safe

4. Which toy would you prefer to buy? Why?

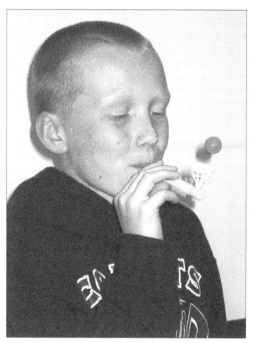

TESTING A BLOW BALL PIPE

WARNING LABEL FOR A BLOW BALL PIPE

Have students briefly share some of their ratings and discuss the criteria they used to come up with them. Point out that not everyone gave the toys the same ratings. Then *ask*

? Do you think companies use only one toy tester? (No. It is good to have more than one opinion about a toy.)

Overall Class Ratings

Discuss the idea that toy companies don't take just one person's opinion about a toy. They collect many people's opinions before making changes to the toy or before deciding to sell it in stores. Project the Fun Ratings page onto a screen. Point out the parts of the graph: the title, the x-axis label, the y-axis label, and the box with lines for summarizing the class ratings for Toy A and Toy B. Tell students that the graph will help them make a conclusion about the toy by showing everyone's ratings. Use a colored marker to color in the box for Toy A on the key. By a show of hands, count the number of "not fun" ratings and draw a bar using the color for Toy A. Then count the "sort of fun" and "very fun" ratings. Next, use a different-colored marker

to color in the box for Toy B on the key. By a show of hands, count the number of "not fun" ratings and draw a bar using the color for Toy B. Repeat for the other two ratings.

Have students look carefully at all of the ratings on the graph. Have them come up with an overall class fun rating for Toy A by *asking*

? Which fun rating did Toy A get most often?

Record that rating in the class rating box at the top of the graph. Then have students come up with an overall class fun rating for Toy B by *asking*

? Which fun rating did Toy B get most often?

Record that rating in the class rating box at the top of the graph.

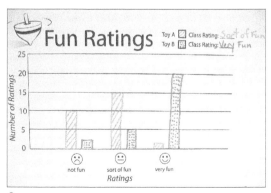

SAMPLE FUN RATINGS WHOLE-CLASS GRAPH

SEP: Using Mathematics and Computational Thinking
Describe, measure and/or compare qualitative attributes of different objects and display the date using simple graphs.

Project the Safety Rating page onto a screen. Follow the same process to come up with an overall class safety rating for both toys. Finally, ask students to compare the scores of both toys by comparing the class ratings. *Ask*

? Which toy scored higher for fun?

? Which toy scored higher for safety?

? What material is each toy made of? (Answers will vary depending on the toys used.)

? How do those materials make the toys more or less fun?

? How do those materials make the toys more or less safe?

? Which toy would you prefer to buy? Why?

? Which toy do you think a toy company would want to sell? Why?

? How could you improve on either of the toys?

evaluate

The Next Big Thing

Reread pages 24–25 in the book *Flip!*, where the California toy company Wham-O took interest in Fred's invention. Tell students that toy trends come and go, and toy companies like Wham-O are always looking for "the next big thing" to sell to their customers. *Ask*

? What other famous toy did Wham-O sell? (The book mentioned the Hula Hoop. Students may know of other Wham-O toys such as the Slip 'N Slide.)

? Has anyone ever played with a Hula Hoop? (Answers will vary.)

Tell students that, like the Frisbee, there have been many improvements to toys such as the Hula Hoop and the Slip 'N Slide. Often, toy manufacturers improve on existing toys rather than invent brand-new ones. Show the vintage Wham-O Frisbee & Hula Hoop commercial from the 1960s (see the "Websites") and *ask*

? What improvement was made to the Hula Hoop? (They gave it a "shoop shoop" sound.)

? How many different Frisbees were sold at the time this commercial was made? (seven)

? Is the Frisbee still a "big thing"? (Yes. Remind students that, according to the book *Imaginative Inventions*, more Frisbees have been sold than footballs, baseballs, and basketballs combined!)

? What are some of today's "big" (popular or bestselling) toys? (Answers will vary.)

? Would you like to design the next big thing in toys? (Students will likely say yes!)

Connecting to the Common Core
Writing
RESEARCH TO BUILD KNOWLEDGE: 2.7

Tell students that they are going to have the opportunity to be toy designers. Pass out The Next Big Thing student pages to each student. Tell them that they will be using the journal to guide them through the design process of creating "The Next Big Thing" – a new and improved toy! (Optional: You may want to have students build models of their toy designs.)

The journal takes students through each step of the design process:

1. **Identify Problem:** Figure out what kids need or want in a toy. Ask other students about a toy they like to play with. What do they think could be improved to make it more fun, more safe, or work better?

2. **Brainstorm:** Draw and/or write your ideas for improving some of the popular toys you discussed earlier (or other toys you have played with).

3. **Design:** Choose one of your ideas for a new and improved toy. Draw and label the toy in the box. Give the new and improved toy a name. Think about the materials it would be made of. What materials would make it fun? What materials would make it safe?

4. **Build, Test and Evaluate, Redesign:** How would you test the new and improved toy to decide if it were fun and safe?

5. **Share the Solution:** Tell others about the new and improved toy. Make an advertisement to sell it!

   - **3 points:** Make a drawing of the new and improved toy, label its parts, and give it a new name.

   - **2 Points:** Describe the material that would be used to make the toy and why you chose that material.

   - **1 Point:** Explain why the new and improved toy is more fun and/or safe than the original.

For fun, the students can include a catchy slogan on their advertisement to help sell the toy to consumers.

You may want to share and discuss a vintage Frisbee ad to give the students some ideas for their advertising poster (see "Websites"). Project the ad onto a screen and *ask*

? What does the ad say is new and improved about this Frisbee? (It has a new design.)

? What are some of the features of this Frisbee? (It flies like a plane, spins like a gyroscope, curves, boomerangs, flies straight, and comes in three colors.)

? Does the ad tell what the Frisbee is made of? (No.)

? What does the ad say about safety? (The Frisbee is soft, safe, and unbreakable.)

THE NEXT BIG THING

? How does the ad help sell the Frisbee? (It makes it seem new and exciting, it has pictures, it tells what it does, and it describes all of its unique features.)

? Does the ad have a catchy slogan – a short and memorable phrase used in advertising? ("If it's not Wham-O, it's not a Frisbee!")

> **SEP: Obtaining, Evaluating, and Communicating Information**
> Communicate information or design ideas and/or solutions with others in oral and/or written forms using models, drawings, writing, or numbers that provide detail about scientific ideas, practices, and/or design ideas.

Next, students can create three-dimensional, nonworking scale models of their toys out of cardboard, fabric, Play-Doh, clay, recycled materials, and so on. Consider holding a toy fair and inviting parents or other students to your classroom. In the design world, toy fairs are exciting conventions where toy industry professionals showcase their toy lines and reveal new products. Your students will enjoy displaying their journals, toy advertisements, and models for the toy fair "attendees." Have guests do a gallery walk through the classroom, using sticky notes to post questions and positive critiques on the students' posters. Writing on sticky notes encourages interaction, and the comments provide immediate feedback for the "exhibitors."

STEM Everywhere

Give students the STEM Everywhere student page as a way to involve their families and extend their learning. They can do the activity with an adult helper and share their results with the class. If students do not have access to these materials or the internet at home, you may choose to have them complete this activity at school.

Opportunities for Differentiated Instruction

This box lists questions and challenges related to the lesson that students may select to research, investigate, or innovate. Students may also use the questions as examples to help them generate their own questions. These questions can help you move your students from the teacher-directed investigation to engaging in the science and engineering practices in a more student-directed format.

Extra Support

For students who are struggling to meet the lesson objectives, provide a question and guide them in the process of collecting research or helping them design procedures or solutions.

Extensions

For students with high interest or who have already met the lesson objectives, have them choose a question (or pose their own question), conduct their own research, and design their own procedures or solutions.

After selecting one of the questions in this box or formulating their own questions, students can individually or collaboratively make predictions, design investigations or surveys to test their predictions, collect evidence, devise explanations, design solutions, or examine related resources. They can communicate their findings through a science notebook, at a poster session or gallery walk, or by producing a media project.

Research

Have students brainstorm researchable questions:

? What are the world records for Frisbee flight?

? Who invented the Aerobie and how is it different or better than the Frisbee?

? Who invented one of your favorite toys and how did they do it?

Investigate

Have students brainstorm testable questions to be solved through science or math:

? Test two different flying discs. Which flies the greatest distance?

? Does the size of a flying disc affect how far it goes?

? Which material is best for a flying disc that floats on water?

Innovate

Have students brainstorm problems to be solved through engineering:

? Can you make a flying disc out of cardboard or another safe material?

? Can you design a carrying case for a flying disc?

? Can you make a flying disc light up or make sound?

Websites

 What is the Best Frisbee for Backyard Throwing?
www.youtube.com/ watch?v=3lRNsXOT9TM

 Toy Testing at *Good Housekeeping*
www.youtube.com/ watch?v=Cd94h9wumbA

 Wham-O Frisbee & Hula Hoop Commercial (1960s)
www.youtube.com/ watch?v=tsJ9fwhFzE8

 Vintage Frisbee Ad
https://2.bp.blogspot.com/- _W-EASPFvFU/UKaBSwLzPul/ AAAAAAAAF0o/bCJBt7mhhdl/s640/ Frisbee_Adwhamo.png

More Books to Read

Barton, C. 2016. *Whoosh! Lonnie Johnson's super-soaking stream of inventions*. New York: Charlesbridge.
Summary: This picture book biography tells the story of Lonnie Johnson, an African American NASA scientist turned entrepreneur who invented the super-soaker water gun.

Ford, G 2016. *The marvelous thing that came from a spring: The accidental invention of the toy that swept the nation*. New York: Atheneum Books for Young Readers.
Summary: Using whimsical dioramic illustrations and simple, informative text, this book tells the story of how engineer Richard James accidently invented the iconic Slinky.

Kirkfield, V. 2021. *From here to there: Inventions that changed the way the world moves*. New York: Clarion Books.
Summary: This collective biography tells the stories of the visionaries who revolutionized the way people travel.

Rustad, M. 2015. *What is it made of? Noticing types of materials*. Minneapolis: Millbrook Press.
Summary: Colorful, cartoonish characters; lively narrative text; and fact-filled insets tell the story of a "treasure hunt" in Ms. Sampson's class. But the students aren't searching for real treasure – they are on the hunt for cloth, rock, glass, metal, and all of the different materials that make up objects in their school.

St. George, J. 2002. *So you want to be an inventor?* New York: Puffin Books.
Summary: This witty look at some of the world's best-known (and lesser-known) inventors features short, entertaining profiles and trivia accompanied by humorous illustrations.

Taylor, B. 2003. *I wonder why zippers have teeth: And other questions about inventions*. New York: Kingfisher.
Summary: "What did people use before they had refrigerators?" and "Where do inventors get their ideas?" are some of the questions answered in this intriguing question-and-answer book about common household inventions.

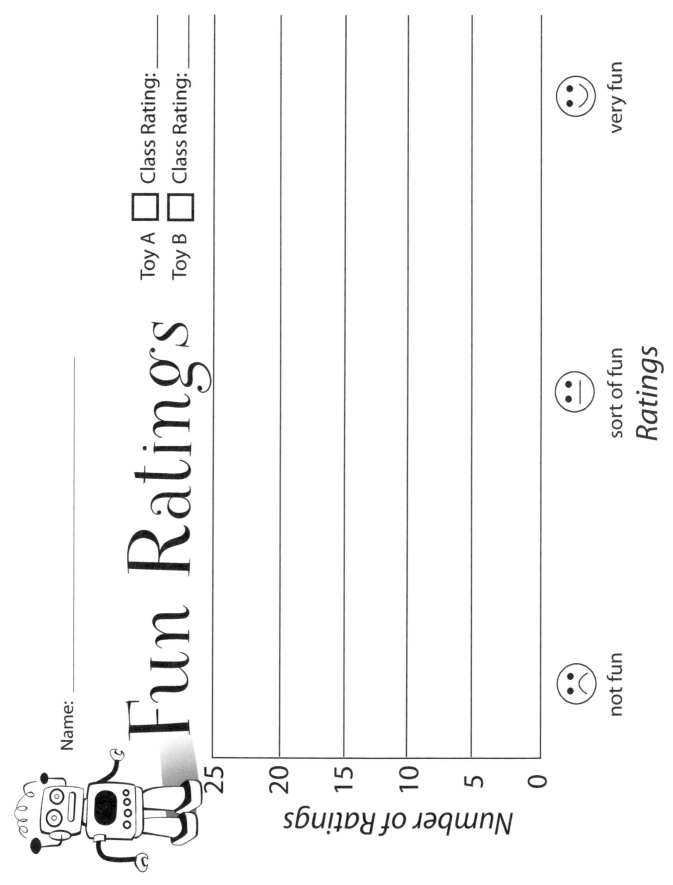

Name: _____

Fun Ratings

Toy A ☐ Class Rating: _____

Toy B ☐ Class Rating: _____

Number of Ratings

25

20

15

10

5

0

😞 not fun   😐 sort of fun   😊 very fun

Ratings

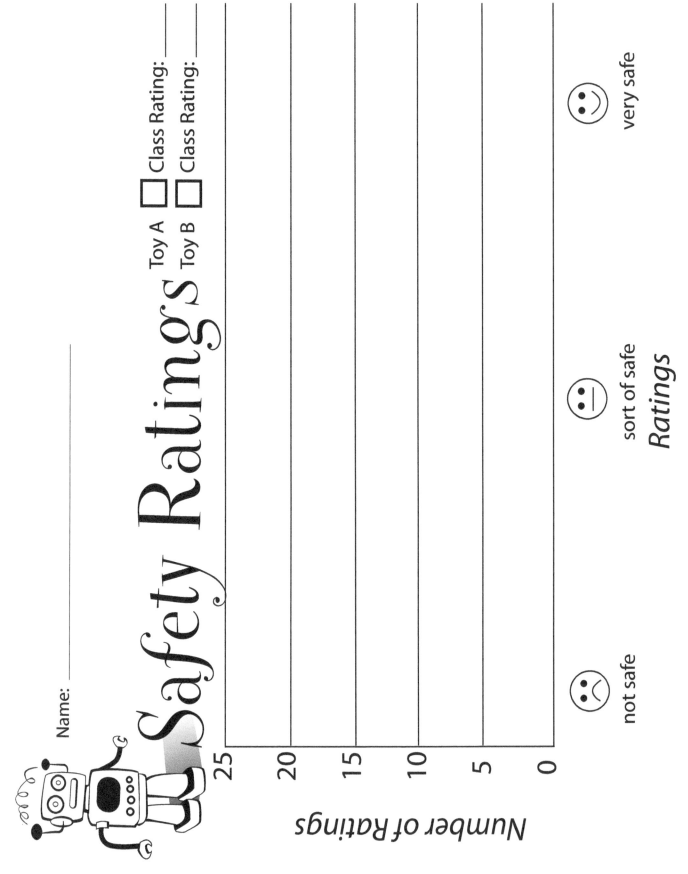

Name: _____

Safety Ratings

Toy A ☐ Class Rating: _____
Toy B ☐ Class Rating: _____

25

20

15

10

5

0

Number of Ratings

☹ not safe

😐 sort of safe

😊 very safe

Ratings

Name: _____

Toy Testing

1. Play with the toys!
   Then draw each toy below and label its parts and materials.

Toy A Drawing	Toy B Drawing

2. Give each toy a fun rating:

Toy A	Toy B
😟 not fun 😐 sort of fun 🙂 very fun	😟 not fun 😐 sort of fun 🙂 very fun

3. Use the choke tester to test each toy and check for sharp parts.
   Then give each toy a safety rating:

Toy A	Toy B
😟 not safe 😐 sort of safe 🙂 very safe	😟 not safe 😐 sort of safe 🙂 very safe

4. Which toy would you prefer to buy? Why? _____

   _____

The Next Big Thing
A Toy Design Journal

Name: _____

National Science Teaching Association

1. **Identify Problem:** Figure out what kids need or want in a toy. Ask other students about a toy they like to play with. What do they think could be improved to make it more fun, more safe, or work better?

Student's Name	Toy	Improvement

2. **Brainstorm:** Draw and/or write your ideas for improving some of the toys above (or other toys you have played with).

3. **Design:** Choose one of your ideas for a new and improved toy. Draw and label the toy in the box below. Give the new and improved toy a name. Think about the materials it would be made of.

Name of original toy: _____

Name of new and improved toy: _____

What materials would the new and improved toy be made of? Why?

_____

_____

_____

_____

4. **Build, Test and Evaluate, Redesign:** How would you test the new and improved toy to decide if it is fun and safe?

_____

_____

_____

_____

5. **Share the Solution:** Tell others about the new and improved toy. Make an advertisement to sell it!

3 Points: Make a drawing of the new and improved toy, label its parts, and give it a new name.

        3   2   1   0

2 Points: Describe the material that would be used to make the toy and why you chose that material.

        2   1   0

1 Point: Explain why the new and improved toy is more fun and/or safe than the original.

        1   0

For fun, include a catchy slogan!

Total Points_____/6

Comments: _____

_____

_____

Name: _____

STEM Everywhere

At school, we have been learning about **the design process**. This is a process used by inventors and other creative people to solve problems. To find out more, ask your learner questions such as:

- What did you learn?
- What was your favorite part of the lesson?
- What are you still wondering?

 At home, you can watch a video called "100 Years of Toys" and then talk about how toys have changed over the years: *www.youtube.com/watch?v=EDAPaEVr1Hk*

After Watching

Adult Helper: List some toys you liked to play with as a child.

_____   _____

_____   _____

_____   _____

Together: Brainstorm ideas for improving the toys above by making them safer or more fun. Then choose one toy and improve it.

Name of toy: _____

Learner: Draw and label the new and improved toy in the box below.

National Science Teaching Association

Melting and Freezing

Description

Frozen treats provide a fun, familiar phenomenon for learning about changes in matter. Through engaging read-alouds and some cool activities (pun intended) with Popsicles, students learn about liquids, solids, melting, and freezing.

Alignment with the *Next Generation Science Standards*

Performance Expectation

2-PS1-4: Construct an argument with evidence that some changes caused by heating or cooling can be reversed and some cannot.

Science and Engineering Practices	Disciplinary Core Ideas	Crosscutting Concepts
Obtaining, Evaluating, and Communicating Information Read grade-appropriate texts and/or use media to obtain scientific and/or technical information to determine patterns in and/or evidence about the natural and designed world(s). Communicate information or design ideas and/or solutions with others in oral and/or written forms using models, drawings, writing, or numbers that provide detail about scientific ideas, practices, and/or design ideas.	**PS1.A: Structure and Properties of Matter** Different kinds of matter exist and many of them can be either solid or liquid, depending on temperature. Matter can be described and classified by its observable properties. **PS1.B: Chemical Reactions** Heating or cooling a substance may cause changes that can be observed. Sometimes these changes are reversible, and sometimes they are not.	**Cause and Effect** Events have causes that generate observable patterns. **Scale, Proportion, and Quantity** Relative scales allow objects and events to be compared and described (e.g., bigger and smaller, hotter and colder, faster and slower).

Note: The activities in this lesson will help students move toward the performance expectations listed, which is the goal after multiple activities. However, the activities will not by themselves be sufficient to reach the performance expectations.

Featured Picture Books

TITLE: **The Boy Who Invented the Popsicle: The Cool Science Behind Frank Epperson's Famous Frozen Treat**
AUTHOR: **Anne Renaud**
ILLUSTRATOR: **Milan Pavlovic**
PUBLISHER: **Kids Can Press**
YEAR: **2019**
GENRE: **Narrative Information**
SUMMARY: *A fun biography of the inventor of the Popsicle. This book highlights his scientific process, determination, and the help he received along the way.*

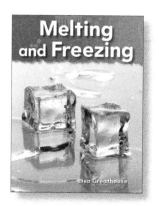

TITLE: **Melting and Freezing**
AUTHOR: **Lisa Greathouse**
PUBLISHER: **Teacher Created Materials**
YEAR: **2010**
GENRE: **Non-Narrative Information**
SUMMARY: *Simple text and photographs introduce the states of matter and the processes of melting and freezing.*

Time Needed

This lesson will take several class periods and will need to be taught on sunny days during the warmer months of the school year. Suggested scheduling is as follows:

Session 1: **Engage** with *The Boy Who Invented the Popsicle* Read-Aloud, and **Explore** with Popsicle Soup, Part 1

Session 2: **Explain** with *Melting and Freezing* Read-Aloud and Popsicle Soup, Part 2

Session 3: **Explain** with Changes in Matter Article Read-Aloud or Pairs Read and Reversible Change Frayer Model

Session 4: **Elaborate** with Making Frozen Treats

Session 5: **Evaluate** with Make a Frozen Treat in a Flash Booklet

Materials

For The Boy Who Invented the Popsicle *Read-Aloud and Popsicle Soup (per student)*

- Store-bought or homemade ice pop on a stick
- Bowl
- Spoon

For Making Frozen Treats (per student)

- ½ cup (125 ml) fruit juice
- 10 large ice cubes
- 1 cup (250 ml) salt
- 1 cup (250 ml) water
- Small plastic resealable bag (heavy duty)
- Large plastic resealable bag (heavy duty)
- Spoons
- 1 pair of winter gloves or oven mitts (*Note:* If you ask students to bring these from home, be sure to have a few extras for anyone who forgets to bring them.)

Note: The supplies for making treats are from the book *The Boy Who Invented the Popsicle.* Feel free to adapt to fit your learning situation. To cut down on single-use plastics, you could have students bring in reusable water bottles to hold the ice, salt, and water, instead of using the gallon-size plastic bags. You can also cut down on the amount of salt needed by using rock salt (the kind used in ice-cream makers).

For STEM Everywhere (per student)

- 2 individual-size vanilla coffee creamers

SAFETY
- Check with the school nurse regarding allergies and how to deal with them.
- Have students wash their hands with soap and water upon completing the activity (before and after when consuming food).
- When making food to be eaten (e.g., frozen treats), make sure that all surfaces and equipment for making the food have been sanitized.
- When working with cool or cold liquids/solids, have students use appropriate personal protective equipment (PPE), including thermal gloves, eye protection, and aprons.

Student Pages

- Popsicle Soup
- Changes in Matter
- Reversible Change Frayer Model
- How to Make a Frozen Treat in a Flash
- STEM Everywhere

Background for Teachers

Matter is all around us. Matter is defined as anything that has mass and takes up space. All matter is made of tiny *atoms*. They are so small that you cannot see them with your eyes or even with a standard microscope. Atoms combine to form *molecules,* and these molecules make up a variety of substances. Most matter on Earth is found in one of three states: solid, liquid, or gas. Each state of matter can be identified by its distinctive properties of shape and volume. A *solid* has a definite shape and a definite volume. Its molecules are the most tightly bound together of the three main states of matter. A *liquid* has a definite volume, but its shape changes more readily because its molecules are more loosely bound

together than those of a solid. A liquid, whether it is thick or thin, is a wet substance that can be poured and always takes the shape of its container. A *gas* has no particular shape or volume. It will expand to fill the space it is in. It can also be compressed to fit a smaller container. Gas has this property because the distances between the molecules of a gas are much greater than the distances between the molecules of a solid or a liquid. Much of the universe is composed of a fourth state of matter known as *plasma*. Plasma has properties different from the other three fundamental states of matter. Scientists can generate plasma in a lab, and it naturally exists inside stars.

The *Framework* suggests that in grades K–2, students focus on matter's solid and liquid states and the transitions between these two states of matter—melting and freezing. *Melting* describes the change from solid to liquid and is caused by heating a solid. Solids have different temperatures at which they turn to liquid. For example, ice melts at 0°C (32°F) and chocolate melts at around 36°C (97°F). This is why ice melts at room temperature, but a chocolate bar stays solid. However, when you put a piece of chocolate in your mouth, which is about 37°C (98.6°F), it begins to melt. (Note: Chocolate is not a pure substance, so the temperature at which it melts can vary due to its recipe, but in most cases, it is solid at room temperature.) Likewise, different kinds of matter have different temperatures at which liquid turns to solid. For many substances, like water, the freezing point and melting point are the same temperature. However, for some mixtures and organic compounds, the freezing point can be lower than the melting point.

Making frozen treats with fruit juice in the classroom is a fun way to explore freezing and melting. The key is getting the juice cold enough to become solid. In the lesson, we suggest you place juice in a quart-size zippered bag and then place that bag into a gallon-size zippered bag containing ice salt. The salt lowers the freezing point of water from its usual freezing point of 0°C (32°F) to –2°C (28°F), making the ice-salt-water mixture in the outside bag much colder than ice alone. This very cold outer mixture causes the juice to freeze and become solid. Shaking the bag distributes the cold outer mixture so it makes better contact with the inner bag. The frozen treats will not come out completely solid in this process but will be more like a slushie.

The *Framework* suggests that K–2 students observe that some of the changes caused by heating and cooling are reversible (e.g., freezing and melting) and some are not (e.g., baking a cake, burning fuel). In this lesson, students read an article about reversible changes that presents examples and nonexamples. They use the vocabulary-building strategy of a Frayer model to make sense of the term *reversible change* and then apply it to the changes they observed in the classroom. During this activity, students are engaged in the science and engineering practice (SEP) of obtaining, evaluating, and communicating information as they read grade-appropriate texts to make sense of the concept of reversible changes. The crosscutting concept (CCC) of cause and effect is addressed as students realize that warming and cooling are the cause of the changes in matter they observe in this lesson.

Later, in grades 3–5, students learn about matter's *gas* state, as well as the core idea that all matter is made up of particles that are too small to see. The concept of reversible change in grades K–2 falls under the disciplinary core idea (DCI) of chemical reactions and sets a foundation for students to later learn about chemical reactions and the conservation of matter. Providing students with experiences with freezing and melting also lays the groundwork for what they will learn about the structure and changes in matter in the upper elementary grades.

Learning Progressions

Below are the DCI grade band endpoints for grades K–2 and 3–5. These are provided to show how student understanding of the DCIs in this lesson will progress in future grade levels.

DCIs	Grades K–2	Grades 3–5
PS1.A: Structure and Properties of Matter	• Different kinds of matter exist and many of them can be either solid or liquid, depending on temperature. Matter can be described and classified by its observable properties.	• Matter of any type can be subdivided into particles that are too small to see, but even then, the matter still exists and can be detected by other means. A model that shows that gases are made from matter particles that are too small to see and are moving freely around in space can explain many observations, including the inflation and shape of a balloon and the effects of air on larger particles or objects. • The amount of matter is conserved when it changes form, even in transitions in which it seems to vanish.
PS1.B: Chemical Reactions	• Heating or cooling a substance may cause changes that can be observed. Sometimes these changes are reversible, and sometimes they are not.	• When two or more different substances are mixed, a new substance with different properties may be formed. • No matter what reaction or change in properties occurs, the total weight of the substances does not change.

Source: Willard, T., ed. 2015. *The NSTA quick-reference guide to the* NGSS: *Elementary school.* Arlington, VA: NSTA Press.

engage

The Boy Who Invented the Popsicle Read-Aloud

Making Connections

Show students the cover of *The Boy Who Invented the Popsicle* and share the title and subtitle. *Ask*

? What do you think this story is going to be about? (Answers will vary.)

? How many of you like Popsicles? (Answers will vary.)

? What are Popsicles made of? (Answers will vary.)

? How do you think Popsicles are made? (Answers will vary.)

? How do you think Popsicles got their name? (Answers will vary.)

Tell students that you are going to give each one of them a Popsicle. When they get it, you would like them to taste it (just one small bite) and then place it in a bowl while you read the book aloud. Call students away from their Popsicles (to the reading corner) and *ask*

? How did your Popsicle taste? (Answers will vary.)

? What flavor was it? (Answers will vary.)

? How did it feel on your tongue? (cold, hard)

? What do you think will happen to your Popsicle if we leave it in the bowl while we are reading this book? (Students may suggest that it will melt.)

> **CCC: Cause and Effect**
> Events have causes that generate observable patterns.

> Connecting to the Common Core
> **Reading: Literature**
> KEY IDEAS AND DETAILS: 2.1

Read the book aloud, skipping the four experiment pages. After reading, *ask*

? What was the original name of the Popsicle? (*Ep-sicle*, because the inventor's last name was Epperson.)

? Why did the name change to Popsicle? (His children called him "Pop" and would say, "Pop, can we have a 'sicle?")

? What characteristics did Frank Epperson have that made him a good inventor? (He was curious, hard-working, creative, and didn't give up.)

explore

Popsicle Soup, Part 1

After reading, have students check on their Popsicles. *Ask*

? What does your Popsicle look like now? (It will likely be at least partly melted.)

Tell students that they have made Popsicle soup! Give each student a copy of the Popsicle Soup student page. Have them draw the Popsicle before and after it became Popsicle soup. Ask them to raise

MAKING POPSICLE SOUP

their hand when they finish their drawings, and you will bring them a spoon so they can eat their Popsicle soup. Tell them they will be doing part 2 of the student page later.

? Did the soup have the same flavor as the Popsicle? (yes)

? Did it feel the same in your mouth? (no)

? What was the difference? (It was liquid, it was runny, it was not as cold)

? Would it be possible to turn the Popsicle soup back into a Popsicle? (Answers will vary.)

? What would we have to do? (Answers will vary, but some students may suggest putting it in the freezer or making it cold again.)

CCC: Scale, Proportion, and Quantity
Relative scales allow objects to be compared and described (e.g., hotter and colder).

---

explain

Melting and Freezing Read-Aloud

 **Features of Nonfiction**

Connecting to the Common Core
Reading: Informational Text
CRAFT AND STRUCTURE: 2.5

SEP: Obtaining, Evaluating, and Communicating Information
Read grade-appropriate texts to obtain scientific information to determine patterns about the natural world.

Show students the cover of *Melting and Freezing.* *Ask*

? Do you think this book is fiction or nonfiction? Why? (Students might guess that that book is nonfiction because the illustration is a photograph and the title is about a science topic.)

Invite students to look for more clues that the book is nonfiction. Point out the table of contents, bold-print words, charts, diagrams, captions, insets, glossary, and index and explain that these are all features that indicate the book is nonfiction. Discuss the purpose of each of these features, such as:

Feature	Purpose
Table of Contents	A quick overview of what is inside, or an easy way to locate specific information
Bold-print word	Tells you that it is an important word (that usually appears in the glossary)
Chart	An organized way to share a lot of information
Diagram	Explains a concept through a picture
Caption	Tells you what is in the picture
Inset	Shares a fun fact or related piece of information
Glossary	Provides definitions of important words
Index	Shows the page number where you can find a word or topic

Making Connections: Text to World

Read the book aloud. Below are some questions and comments to help students make connections to the content being presented.

Page 4

Let students know that "ice pop" is the generic name for a Popsicle. (In fact, Popsicle is a registered trademark.)

Page 6

Remind students that their ice pop turned into a liquid just sitting the room. *Ask*

? Would a chocolate bar melt just sitting in the room? (No) Why not? (Answers will vary.)

Page 8

After reading this page about matter, *ask*

? What are some examples of solid matter in our classroom? (pencils, chairs, etc.)

? What are some examples of liquid matter in our classroom? (water, juice, etc.)

? What is an example of a gas in our classroom? (air)

Page 10

Ask

? What causes a puddle to turn from liquid to solid? (The water in the puddle gets very cold.)

? What is that process called? (freezing)

Page 16

Ask

? Most of our ice pop was made of ice (with some flavor and sugar). At what temperature does ice melt? (Find ice on the chart: 32°F.)

? What is the temperature of this room? (It will likely be around 70°F.)

? What do you think would happen if we took our ice pops outside in the summer when it

is 85°F? (Answers will vary, but students may figure out that the ice pop would melt faster.)

? Have you ever had an ice pop or ice cream cone melt all over your hand on a hot summer day? (Answers will vary. Explain that ice pops melt faster at higher temperatures.)

? At what temperature does chocolate melt? (Find chocolate on the chart: 97°F. Explain that different types of chocolate have different recipes, so this number might not be exact for all types of chocolate.)

? What happens when you put chocolate in your mouth? (It melts.)

? What is your body temperature? (Students may know that normal body temperature is 98.6°F.)

? Why does chocolate melt in your mouth? (Because chocolate turns to liquid at 97°F and the inside of our mouths is warmer than 97°F.)

Optional: Give each student a small chocolate such as a chocolate kiss. This is a good time to let students experience chocolate melting in their mouths.

Page 19

? What do ice pops and chocolate bunnies have in common? (Students may say that they are both delicious, but they are also made in the same way. They are melted into liquid, poured into molds, and cooled until they freeze in a solid shape.)

Page 27

? Have you ever made ice pops in your freezer at home? (Answers will vary.)

? What did you use to make them? (Answers will vary but may include juice, sports drinks, etc.)

? How and where do you think the ice pops we buy at the store are made? (Answers will vary.)

After reading, you may want to show students a video of ice pops being made in a factory (see "Websites"). Have students look for solids and liquids as the ice pops are being made and note the different technologies (robots, conveyor belts, molds, etc.) being used.

Popsicle Soup, Part 2

Connecting to the Common Core
Language
VOCABULARY ACQUISITION AND USE: 2.6

Next, have students complete part 2 of the Popsicle Soup student page by filling in the blanks with the vocabulary they learned from the book. The sentences read:

My Popsicle started out as a solid.

My Popsicle got warmer and turned into a liquid.

Changing from a solid to a liquid is called melting.

Encourage the students to take their papers home and explain to someone how they made Popsicle soup and read their completed sentences aloud to that person.

explain

Changes in Matter Article

 *Pairs Read*

Pass out the Changes in Matter student page. Tell students this article will help them learn more about the changes they observed with their ice pops and other changes that matter can go through. You might choose to read the article aloud while students follow along, or have students do a pairs read. In a pairs read, students take turns reading aloud to each other. While one person reads a paragraph, the other listens and makes comments ("I think …"), asks questions ("I wonder …"), or shares new learnings ("I didn't know …").

Revisit *Melting and Freezing* to look for examples of reversible changes in the photos, such as:

- An ice pop melting (can be frozen into an ice pop again)
- Chocolate melting (can be cooled into solid chocolate again)
- A pond freezing (will melt into a liquid pond when the temperature rises)
- Chocolate cooling into a bunny shape (can be melted into liquid chocolate and made into a different shape)
- Icicles freezing on a fountain (will melt when the temperature rises)

Ask

? What are some examples of changes that are not reversible? (Frying an egg, because it can't be turned back into a liquid egg. Burning paper, because it turns into something else—ash and smoke. It can't be turned back into paper.)

Reversible Change Frayer Model

 *Frayer Model*

Connecting to the Common Core
Language
VOCABULARY ACQUISITION AND USE: 2.6

Next, give each student a copy of the Reversible Change Frayer Model student page. Students can use the information they learn from the article to complete the Frayer Model. The Frayer Model is a tool to help students develop their vocabularies by studying concepts in a relational manner. Students write a particular word in the middle of a box and proceed to include drawings, examples, nonexamples, and a definition in other quadrants of the box. They can proceed by using the examples and characteristics to help them formulate a definition or, conversely, by using the definition to

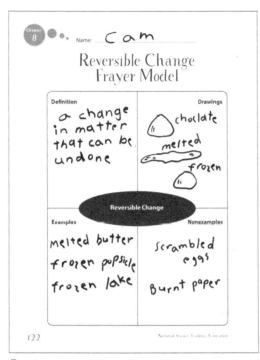

FRAYER MODEL

determine examples and nonexamples. In this case, have students use the preceding article to formulate a definition for *reversible change* in their own words in the top left box of the Reversible Change Frayer Model student page. Then have students write some characteristics of reversible changes in the top right box. Have students work in pairs to come up with examples and nonexamples from their own lives. As you observe students working, encourage them to use their previous experiences as a basis for their reversible change examples. Students can then present and explain their Frayer Models to other groups. As they present to one another, informally assess their understanding of the concept and clarify as necessary.

elaborate

Making Frozen Treats

In advance of this activity, ask each student to bring in a pair of winter gloves or oven mitts.

Ask

? How did Frank Epperson get his Popsicles to freeze quickly? (He added salt to lower the freezing point of the water so the Popsicles would get colder faster.)

? Do you think we could use that process to make a frozen treat right here in our classroom? (Answers will vary depending on if you have a freezer.)

? What materials do you think we would need? (Answers will vary.)

Have students explain their reasoning for each material or ingredient they suggest. Then show students page 21 of *The Boy Who Invented the Popsicle*, titled "A Frozen Treat in a Flash." Tell them that they can follow these instructions to make a frozen treat in only five minutes!

Note: You may want to have parent volunteers help out, or invite some older student "buddies" to help. If you are not able to get assistance, you can adapt this activity to be a demonstration.

MAKING A FROZEN TREAT IN A FLASH

Gather the materials listed on page 31 (also in the materials section of this lesson) and instruct students to follow these instructions (modified from page 31):

1. Pour ½ cup (125 ml) of juice into the small plastic bag. Seal the bag, trying to remove as much air as possible.

2. Pour the ice cubes, water, and salt into the large plastic bag.

3. Put the small bag into the large bag. Seal the large bag, and make sure it is tightly sealed.

4. Put on gloves and shake the bag back and forth for about five minutes to mix the ice, water, and salt around the small bag. (You may want play a song during this time.)

5. After five minutes, open the large bag and take out the small bag. Wipe off the salt water from the small bag and dispose of the large bag. (Students may need assistance.)

Give each student a spoon and allow them to eat their frozen treat!

Read the explanation titled "What happened?" on page 31 of *The Boy Who Invented the Popsicle* and *ask*

? Why did we add salt to the ice and water mixture? (The salt lowers the freezing point of water, making the water much colder than 32°F. This made the treat freeze faster.)

If you have access to a freezer, you could place ½ cup of juice in a plastic bag for five minutes to show how it does not freeze as fast as when the salt was added to the mixture of ice and water. *Ask*

? Was this a reversible change? (yes)

? Why? (Because you can turn it back into liquid juice by letting it warm up.)

While students enjoy their frozen treats, show some videos of Popsicles being made in factories (see "Websites"). They can compare the processes in the videos to the process they used to make their frozen treats.

evaluate

Make a Frozen Treat in a Flash Booklet

Writing

Connecting to the Common Core
Writing
RESEARCH TO BUILD AND PRESENT KNOWLEDGE: 2.7
Language
VOCABULARY ACQUISITION AND USE: 2.6

SEP: Obtaining, Evaluating, and Communicating Information
Communicate information with others in written forms using drawings and writing that provide detail about scientific ideas.

Give each student a copy of the How to Make a Frozen Treat in a Flash student pages. Have each student write the correct word to complete each sentence and then illustrate each sentence in the box. Encourage students to go back to each page and add more details. For example, the sentences should read:

First, place liquid juice in the small plastic bag.

Next, add solid ice and salt to the large plastic bag.

The salt lowers the temperature of the ice so the treat can freeze faster.

Then place the small bag into the large bag. Shake the large bag to turn the liquid in the small bag into a solid.

Last, take the solid treat out of the bag and eat it before it melts. Remember, this is a reversible change. If it melts, you can freeze it again!

STEM Everywhere

Give students the STEM Everywhere student page as a way to involve their families and extend their learning. They can do the activity with an adult helper and share their results with the class. You will need to send home two individual coffee creamers with each student for this activity.

Opportunities for Differentiated Instruction

This box lists questions and challenges related to the lesson that students may select to research, investigate, or innovate. Students may also use the questions as examples to help them generate their own questions. These questions can help you move your students from the teacher-directed investigation to engaging in the science and engineering practices in a more student-directed format.

Extra Support

For students who are struggling to meet the lesson objectives, provide a question and guide them in the process of collecting research or help them design procedures or solutions.

Extensions

For students with high interest or who have already met the lesson objectives, have them choose a question (or pose their own question), conduct their own research, and design their own procedures or solutions.

After selecting one of the questions in the box or formulating their own question, students can individually or collaboratively make predictions, design investigations or surveys to test their predictions, collect evidence, devise explanations, design solutions, or examine related resources. They can communicate their findings through a science notebook, at a poster session or gallery walk, or by producing a media project.

Research

Have students brainstorm researchable questions:

? How do the melting points of various substances compare? Make a chart!

? How is ice cream made?

? How do companies keep ice pops and ice-cream bars from melting when they ship them to stores?

Continued

National Science Teaching Association

Opportunities for Differentiated Instruction (continued)

Investigate

Have students brainstorm testable questions to be solved through science or math:

? How does the volume of liquid water change when you freeze it?

? What is your class's favorite flavor of ice pop? Take a survey!

? Does the amount of a liquid affect how fast it freezes?

Innovate

Have students brainstorm problems to be solved through engineering:

? Can you design something to keep an ice cube from melting?

? Can you design something to make an ice cube melt quickly?

? Can you come up with a recipe for a new frozen treat?

Websites

How Twin Pops are Made: The Ziegenfelder Company
www.youtube.com/watch?v=y02TBgkBUhg

How Red White and Blue Pops are Made
www.youtube.com/watch?v=P2hCDq2qUrk

Ice Pop Manufacturing at the Ice Pop Factory
www.youtube.com/watch?v=GLFQRmWJadY

More Books to Read

Boothroyd, J. 2011. *Many kinds of matter: A look at solids, liquids, and gases.* New York: Lerner
Summary: Full-color photographs and simple text provide everyday examples of solids, liquids, and gases.

Diehn, A. 2018. *Matter: Physical science for kids.* White River Junction, VT: Nomad Press.
Summary: From the Picture Book Science series, this book provides a simple definition of *matter*, information on the states of matter, and examples of things that are not matter.

Hansen, A. 2011. *Matter comes in all shapes.* Vero Beach, FL: Rourke Educational Media.
Summary: Simple text and photographs explain the differences between solids, liquids, and gases.

Hansen, A. 2011. *Solid or liquid?* Vero Beach, FL: Rourke Educational Media.
Summary: Simple text and photographs explain the differences between solids and liquids.

Mason, A. 2006. *Change it!: Solids, liquids, gases and you.* Toronto: Kids Can Press.
Summary: Filled with information and activities, this book provides a simple introduction to the states of matter.

Willems, M. 2011. *Should I share my ice cream?* New York: Hyperion Books for Children.
Summary: From the Elephant and Piggie series, this book follows Gerald the elephant as he makes a big decision: Should he share his ice cream? He waits too long and it melts, but Piggie brings more and saves the day.

Zoehfeld, K. W. 2015. *What is the world made of?: All about solids, liquids, and gases.* New York: HarperCollins.
Summary: From the Let's-Read-and-Find-Out Science series, this book gives examples of each state of matter and some simple activities that demonstrate the attributes of each.

Name: _____

Popsicle Soup

Part 1

Draw a picture of your Popsicle before and after it became Popsicle soup in the boxes below:

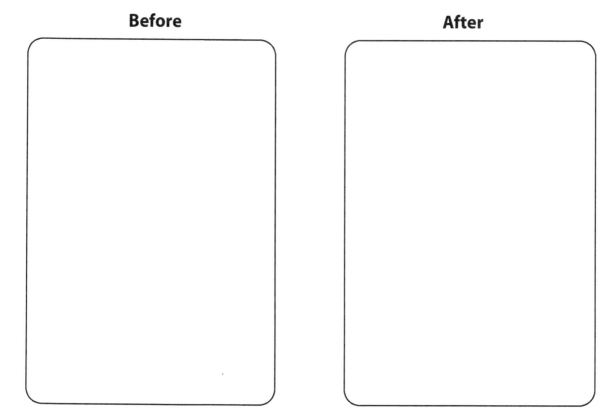

Before

After

Part 2

My Popsicle started out as a _____.
(*solid or liquid*)

My Popsicle got warmer and turned into a _____.
(*solid or liquid*)

Changing from a solid to a liquid is called _____.
(*freezing or melting*)

National Science Teaching Association

Changes in Matter

Reversible Changes

Heating or cooling matter can cause it to change. A reversible change is a change in matter that can be reversed, or undone. Melting and freezing are usually reversible changes. For example, if you add heat to solid butter, it can melt and change into a liquid. Once the butter is liquid, the change can be reversed. You can change it back into solid butter by cooling it.

Freezing and Melting

Different kinds of matter freeze and melt at different temperatures. For example, a piece of chocolate will begin to melt into a liquid at around 97°F. If it cools to below 97°F, it will begin to form a solid again. You can melt and freeze a piece of chocolate over and over again because it is a reversible change.

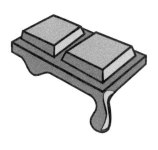

Liquid water freezes at 32°F and becomes ice. When the temperature of ice rises above 32°F, it begins to melt and become liquid water again. You can freeze and melt water over and over because it is a reversible change.

Are All Changes Reversible?

If you crack a raw egg, you will find that it is mostly liquid inside. When you add enough heat to cook the egg, it becomes a solid. But cooking an egg is NOT a reversible change. You can't make the egg liquid again!

If you burn a piece of paper, it changes. It turns into ashes and smoke. It is not paper anymore. It cannot go back to what it was before. So not all changes are reversible!

When the leaf of a plant gets too cold, it can freeze. It can become hard and stiff. When the leaf warms up, it cannot go back to what it was before. So this is NOT a reversible change.

You can cause changes in matter by heating or cooling it. Some of these changes can be reversed and some cannot. Can you think of more examples of reversible changes?

Name: _____

Reversible Change
Frayer Model

Definition	Drawings

Reversible Change

Examples	Nonexamples

How to Make
a Frozen Treat
in a Flash

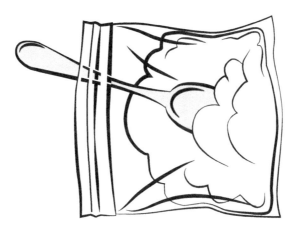

Name: _____

Last, take the treat out of the bag and eat it before
it _____.
 (melts or freezes)

Remember, this is _____
 (a reversible or not a reversible)
change.

If it melts, you can freeze it again!

First, place the _____ juice in
          (solid or liquid)
a small plastic bag.

Next, add _____ ice and salt to
         (solid or liquid)
the large plastic bag.

Then place the small bag into the large bag.
Shake to turn the liquid in the small bag into a
_____ .
(solid or liquid)

The salt lowers the temperature of the ice so the
treat can _____ faster.
           (melt or freeze)

National Science Teaching Association

Name: _____

STEM Everywhere

Dear Families,

At school, we have been learning about **melting and freezing**. We made Popsicle soup and a frozen treat. We learned that melting and freezing are reversible changes. We also learned that salt can be used to make things freeze faster. Why do we salt sidewalks? To find out more, ask your learner questions such as:

- What did you learn?
- What was your favorite part of the lesson?
- What are you still wondering?

At home, you can turn liquid coffee creamer into solid ice cream with the help of some ice and salt. Follow the instructions below.

Materials
2 vanilla coffee creamers (individual size)
Reusable water bottle or container with tight lid
Ice to fill container
¼ cup of salt
Water

Instructions
1. Place your creamer cups in the bottle.
2. Fill your bottle ½ full with ice.
3. Add ¼ cup salt.
4. Fill the rest of the bottle with ice.
5. Add water until about ½ full.
6. Place the lid tightly on your container.
7. Shake the bottle for five minutes. (You may want to wear gloves or oven mitts as the bottle will get very cold.)
8. Remove the creamer and, without opening it, check to see if it is solid by either squeezing the sides or shaking the cup near your ear. If you feel or hear liquid, place the creamer cups back in the bottle and shake for two more minutes.
9. Open and enjoy!

That Magnetic Dog

Description

Learners explore the phenomenon that some things are attracted to a magnet and others are not. They discover through exploration that not all metals are magnetic and communicate their findings in a poster session. Then they learn by reading a nonfiction book that magnets attract iron and iron-containing materials. Finally, they learn how different types of magnets are used for different purposes, and they design their own magnetic solution to a problem.

Alignment with the *Next Generation Science Standards*

Performance Expectation		
2-PS1-1: Plan and conduct an investigation to describe and classify different kinds of materials by their observable properties.		
Science and Engineering Practices	**Disciplinary Core Idea**	**Crosscutting Concept**
Analyzing and Interpreting Data Compare predictions (based on prior experiences) to what occurred (observable events). **Obtaining, Evaluating, and Communicating Information** Read grade-appropriate texts and/ or use media to obtain scientific and/or technical information to determine patterns in and/or evidence about the natural and designed worlds.	**PS1.A: Structure and Properties of Matter** Matter can be described and classified by its observable properties.	**Patterns** Patterns in the natural and human-designed world can be observed, used to describe phenomena, and used as evidence.

Note: The activities in this lesson will help students move toward the performance expectation listed, which is the goal after multiple activities. However, the activities will not by themselves be sufficient to reach the performance expectation.

Featured Picture Books

TITLE: **That Magnetic Dog**
AUTHOR: **Bruce Whatley**
ILLUSTRATOR: **Bruce Whatley**
PUBLISHER: **Angus & Robertson**
YEAR: **1994**
GENRE: **Story**
SUMMARY: *Skitty is a dog with "magnetic" qualities. She doesn't attract metal, like keys and spoons. She attracts food.*

TITLE: **Is It Magnetic or Nonmagnetic?**
AUTHOR: **Trudy Rising**
PUBLISHER: **Crabtree Publishing Company**
YEAR: **2012**
GENRE: **Non-Narrative Information**
SUMMARY: *From the What's the Matter? series, this book introduces magnetic and nonmagnetic as properties of matter that can be used to classify materials. It explains the "secret" to magnetic materials and explores the strength of different magnets as well as their uses.*

Time Needed

This lesson will take several class periods. Suggested scheduling is as follows:

Session 1: **Engage** with *That Magnetic Dog* Read-Aloud and **Explore** with Fishing with Magnets

Session 2: **Explain** with What Can You Catch with a Magnet? Poster, *Is It Magnetic or Nonmagnetic?* Read-Aloud, and Revisiting *That Magnetic Dog*

Session 3: **Elaborate** with Uses for Magnets

Session 4: **Evaluate** with Magnetic Solutions and The Day My Feet Were Magnets (Optional)

Materials

- Magnet warning signs page

For Fishing with Magnets (per team of 3 or 4 students):

- A container or tray with a large variety of both magnetic and nonmagnetic items to test for magnetic properties (see chart for suggestions)
- 1 30 cm piece of string
- 1 ceramic ring magnet or magnetic wand
- 1 pencil

Ceramic ring magnets and magnetic wands are available from

Educational Innovations Inc.
www.teachersource.com

Amazon
Amazon.com

Peel-and-stick adhesive business card magnets are available from

Amazon
Amazon.com

MAGNETIC ITEMS	NONMAGNETIC ITEMS
pipe cleaner	aluminum foil
steel paper clip	plastic paper clip
magnetite rock	small rock (other than magnetite)
stainless steel spoon	white plastic and silver-colored plastic spoons
steel bolt	toothpick or craft stick
steel washer	aluminum washer
steel wool	metallic-looking fabric or cotton ball
antique iron skeleton key	brass housekey
steel lid from a soda bottle	aluminum tab from a soda can
tumbled magnetic hematite stone	glass marble or tumbled glass pebble
magnetic foreign coins (such as UK copper-plated steel penny and 2 pence and UK nickel-plated steel 5 pence and 10 pence)	nonmagnetic coins (such as U.S. coins, including a penny—note that the vast majority of U.S. coins in circulation are nonmagnetic)

For What Can You Catch with a Magnet? (per team of 3 or 4 students)

- 1 piece of white card stock or poster paper, 9 x 12 or larger
- Crayons or markers
- Tape

For Revisiting That Magnetic Dog

- Assortment of keys
- Assortment of plastic and metal spoons
- Magnet

For Magnetic Solutions (per student)

- 1 magnet
  (Note: Additional materials will vary.)

For STEM Everywhere (per student)

- One 2 x 3 ½ in peel-and-stick adhesive business card magnet

Student Pages

- What Can You Catch with a Magnet?
- My Magnetic Solution
- STEM Everywhere

Background for Teachers

A *magnet* is an object or material that produces an invisible *magnetic field*. Within this field, a magnet attracts or repels other magnets and pulls on objects with iron in them. Magnetic force acts across distance—a magnet does not need to touch magnetic materials to act on them. A magnetic field is strongest around the *poles*, or ends, of a magnet. All magnets have a north pole and a south pole. If you hold two magnets so that their unlike (north and south) poles are close but not touching, you will feel the force of the magnets *attracting* each other. If you hold two magnets so that their like (north and north or south and south) poles are close but not touching, you will feel the force of the magnets *repelling* each other.

Although physicists consider "magnetic" materials to be those that can be magnetized, we are simplifying this classification for young learners. In the nonfiction book *Is It Magnetic or Nonmagnetic?*, any material that is attracted to a magnet is referred to as a *magnetic* material. Any material that is not attracted to a magnet is referred to as a *nonmagnetic* material. This lesson focuses on *magnetic* and *nonmagnetic* as properties of matter that can be used to sort, or classify, matter. A common misconception is that all metals are magnetic. In fact, only materials that contain iron, cobalt, or nickel are attracted to a magnet. We focus on the metals iron and steel (an iron *alloy*) as the most common magnetic materials because items made of cobalt and nickel are not nearly as familiar to students. After exploring these magnetic materials, students discover some uses for magnets and design a "magnetic" solution to a problem. In grades 3–5, students will learn more about magnetic force.

Students are engaged in several different science and engineering practices (SEPs) in this lesson. They use the SEP of asking questions and defining problems as they question why certain things are attracted to a magnet and others are not, and they define a simple classroom problem that can be solved using a magnet. Students are involved in planning and carrying out investigations as they test and sort materials by magnetic properties. The SEP of developing explanations and designing solutions is incorporated as students develop the explanation that not all metals are magnetic, and they design a solution to a problem using magnets and magnetic material. The crosscutting concept (CCC) of cause and effect is addressed as students learn that iron is the cause of some things sticking to a magnet.

> # WARNING
>
> Magnets are used in a wide variety of electronic equipment. Placing a magnet close to such equipment may cause damage. Before using magnets in your classroom, make students aware that magnets should be kept away from electronic equipment. Also, keep magnets away from credit cards, videotapes, and any other materials that have information on a magnetic strip.

Learning Progressions

Below are the disciplinary core idea (DCI) grade band endpoints for grades K–2 and 3–5. These are provided to show how student understanding of the DCIs in this lesson will progress in future grade levels.

DCI	Grades K–2	Grades 3–5
PS1.A: Structure and Properties of Matter	• Matter can be described and classified by its observable properties.	• Measurements of a variety of properties can be used to identify materials.

Source: Willard, T., ed. 2015. *The NSTA quick-reference guide to the* NGSS: *Elementary school.* Arlington, VA: NSTA Press.

engage

That Magnetic Dog Read-Aloud

> Connecting to the Common Core
> **Reading: Literature**
> INTEGRATION OF KNOWLEDGE AND IDEAS: 2.7

 Inferring

Show the book *That Magnetic Dog* to the class. Introduce the author and illustrator. *Ask*

? What do you think this book might be about? (Answers will vary.)

Next, read the book aloud, then *ask*

? Why does the author describe the dog as "magnetic"? (She attracts people and food.)

? Have you ever heard of someone having a "magnetic personality"? What does that mean? (People are drawn or attracted to them.)

? What does magnetic mean? (Answers will vary.)

Making Connections: Text to Self

Ask

? Have you ever explored with magnets? (Answers will vary.)

? What do you know about magnets? (Answers will vary.)

explore

Fishing with Magnets

Before you begin this phase of the lesson, copy the magnet warning signs on fluorescent paper and post them on computers and other electronic equipment in the classroom. Explain to students that magnets can damage electronic equipment like televisions and computers, so they must pay attention to the signs. Then *ask*

? What types of items do you think stick to a magnet? (Students may say that some or all metal items stick to a magnet.)

> **SEP: Analyzing and Interpreting Data**
> Compare predictions (based on prior experiences) to what occurred (observable events.)

Split students into teams of three or four. Give each team a container or tray with a variety of magnetic and nonmagnetic items (see materials list for suggestions). Invite students to take a close look at the items, pick them up, and feel them. Then have them sort the items into three piles:

- Items they predict will stick to a magnet
- Items they predict will not stick to a magnet
- Items they are not sure will stick to a magnet

"FISHING" WITH A MAGNET

Have students discuss their thinking as they are sorting. When they have finished sorting, ask them to pick up one item that they predict will stick to the magnet and hold it up. *Ask*

? Why did you predict that item will stick? (Answers will vary, but students will typically put all of the metal items in this pile.)

Next, ask them to pick up one item they predict will not stick to the magnet, and *ask*

? Why did you predict that item won't stick? (Answers will vary.)

> **CCC: Patterns**
> Patterns in the natural and human designed world can be observed, used to describe phenomena, and used as evidence.

Then ask them to pick up one item of which they are unsure whether it will stick to a magnet, and *ask*

? What makes you unsure about that item? (Answers will vary.)

MAKING A POSTER

Finally, *ask*

? How can we find out which items will stick to a magnet? (Test them!)

Tell students that they are going to take turns "fishing" with a fishing pole made out of a magnet to see which items in the box they can "catch." Show students how to make the fishing pole by tying one end of a string around the end of a ceramic ring magnet or magnetic wand and the other end of the string to a pencil. Students are now ready to use their fishing poles to see what items their magnets will catch. Tell students to create two new piles as they take turns fishing:

1. Things that stick to the magnet
2. Things that do not stick to the magnet

explain

What Can You Catch with a Magnet? Poster

In teams, have students create a poster to present their findings to the rest of the class. They can do so by drawing a line down the center of a large piece of white card stock or poster paper and writing "Things That Stick" on the left side and "Things That Don't Stick" on the right side. Then have them tape the items that stick to the magnet onto the left side and the items that do not stick to the magnet onto the right side.

Writing

> Connecting to the Common Core
> **Writing**
> RESEARCH TO BUILD KNOWLEDGE: 2.8

After students are finished making their posters, pass out the What Can You Catch with a Magnet? student page and have them answer questions 1–3. (They will answer questions 1–4 after the read-

aloud.) Questions and possible responses are as follows:

1. What items can you "catch" with a magnet? (Answers will depend on the materials in each set.)
2. What do those items have in common? (Students may notice that many, but not all, of the metal items stick to the magnet.)
3. Why do you think those items stick to the magnet? (Students may infer that those items stick to the magnet because they are metal.)

Next, have them share their posters and explain their responses to questions 1–3 on the student page with the rest of the class. As they share, you can ask clarifying questions, such as:

? Why do you think so?
? What is your evidence?
? What surprised you?

At this point, many students may have proposed that the items that stick to the magnet are metal and the items that don't stick are not metal. Although this conclusion is not entirely correct, they are getting closer to the secret of magnetic materials.

You may want to demonstrate that a penny does not stick to a magnet, even though it is metal. Some metals stick to a magnet, but not all. Students may hypothesize that there is something "special" about the items that stick to the magnet.

Is It Magnetic or Nonmagnetic? Read-Aloud

Connecting to the Common Core
Reading: Informational Text
Craft and Structure: 2.4, 2.5

Using Features of Nonfiction/ Chunking

Show students the cover of the book *Is It Magnetic or Nonmagnetic?*, and then show the table of contents and a few of the inside pages. *Ask*

? Is this a fiction or nonfiction book? (nonfiction)
? How can you tell? (Answers may include that it has a table of contents, photographs, bold-print words, and an index.)

Determining Importance

Explain that, because the book is nonfiction, you can enter the text at any point. You don't have to read the book from cover to cover if you are looking for specific information. Tell students that this book might be able to help them discover the secret of the materials that stick to a magnet. Ask students to signal (by giving a thumbs-up, touching their nose, or some other method) when they hear the answer to this question:

? What is "special" about the items that stick to a magnet?

Read the book aloud, stopping when the answer is revealed on page 7. Students should now understand that items stick to a magnet if they contain iron. That's the secret! *Ask*

? What do all of the items on the "Things That Stick" side of the poster have in common? (They all contain iron.)
? What do we call items that stick to a magnet? (magnetic)

SEP: Obtaining, Evaluating, and Communicating Information
Read grade-appropriate texts and/or use media to obtain scientific and/or technical information to determine patterns in and/or evidence about the natural and designed worlds.

Point out that many of the items that stick to a magnet are made of steel. Steel is a metal that contains iron. If they have a rock in their set of materials that sticks to the magnet, then the rock contains iron. If they have a spoon in their set that sticks to the magnet, then the spoon contains iron, and so on.

Then explain that objects that do not stick to a magnet are called nonmagnetic. These items do not contain iron. Students will notice that some of the metal items, such as aluminum, do not stick. That is because aluminum does not contain iron. The metal penny does not stick. That is because pennies do not contain iron. (Pennies are actually made of copper-coated zinc.)

Note: There are other metals, such as cobalt and nickel, that are magnetic, but iron is more common and more familiar to students.

Students can now use the scientific vocabulary to label their posters. They will label the side of the poster containing items that stick to a magnet with the word *magnetic* and the other side with the word *nonmagnetic.*

Determining Importance

Next, read the rest of the questions on the What Can You Catch with a Magnet? student page together, and ask students to listen for the answers as you continue reading the book through page 13.

**Writing**

Connecting to the Common Core
Writing
RESEARCH TO BUILD KNOWLEDGE: 2.8

Stop reading after page 13 and have students answer questions 4–7. Questions and possible responses are as follows:

4. What do properties of matter describe? (Page 6: Properties of matter describe how something looks, feels, tastes, smells, or sounds. Properties can also tell us how something acts.)

5. Fill in the blanks: Materials that have a magnetic property can pull, or _____, objects with _____ in them. (Page 7: attract, iron)

6. What else have you learned about magnets from the book so far? (Answers will vary.)

7. What are you still wondering about magnets? (Answers will vary.)

Revisiting *That Magnetic Dog*

Monitoring Comprehension

Tell students that there was a sentence in *That Magnetic Dog* that didn't make sense to you. Reread the first page of the book, which states, "Magnets attract metal objects like keys and spoons." Then *ask*

? What does the word *attract* mean? (pull)

? Does that sentence make sense to you? Is it entirely correct to say, "Magnets attract metal objects, like keys and spoons"? (Based on what students have learned through the explore and explain phases of this lesson, they should be able to identify the sentence as being incorrect.)

? Why? What is your evidence? (Students should be able to share evidence from their testing that not all keys and spoons stick to a magnet. You may want to have students retest the keys and

---

spoons in their sets with a magnet and share examples of exceptions to the statement that "Magnets attract metal objects, like keys and spoons.")

? Why don't all of the keys and spoons stick to a magnet? (Not all of the keys and spoons contain iron. There may be some old keys in their set that do contain iron, but most housekeys are now made of brass, which is an alloy, or mixture, of copper and zinc. Brass is often used for keys because it doesn't rust and is soft enough to easily be cut into the needed individual patterns.)

 Turn and Talk

Have students turn to a partner and discuss this question:

? How could we rewrite the sentence in the book to make it scientifically accurate, or correct?

(Possible answers include:

Magnets attract metal objects that contain iron.

Magnets attract some, but not all, metal objects.

Magnets attract keys and spoons that contain iron.)

Have pairs share their responses with the class.

elaborate

Uses for Magnets

Ask

? What are some uses for magnets? (Answers will vary.)

Show students the table of contents of *Is It Magnetic or Nonmagnetic? Ask*

? Which section do you think we should read to find out more about some of the uses for magnets? (Useful Magnets, page 14)

Read aloud pages 14–17 (you can skip the rest of the book or read it later if you wish), which share the different shapes and strengths of magnets as well as several different technologies that use magnets. For each of the technologies, *ask*

? What problem does the magnet solve?

Technology from the Book	Problem It Solves
Magnetic strip (page 14)	Holds and organizes cooking tools
Magnetic chess set (page 15)	Keeps the pieces from falling off the board
Magnetic can opener (page 15)	Holds the lid while the can is being opened
Scrapyard magnet (page 16)	Sorts the iron objects from the rest of the materials
Metal detector (page 17)	Finds metal objects underground

Next, *ask*

? Are there any useful magnets in our classroom? (Answers will vary.)

LOOKING FOR MAGNETS IN THE CLASSROOM

Give students time to walk around and discover any useful classroom magnets, then identify the problem that they solve. Some examples might include:

Classroom Magnet	Problem It Solves
Magnetic clip	Holds papers together on a whiteboard or other magnetic surface
Magnetic pouch	Holds and organizes objects
Magnetic cabinet latch	Keeps cabinet door closed
Refrigerator door magnet	Keeps refrigerator door sealed shut

Some students may know that motors and electronic devices like speakers, headphones, and computers also contain magnets.

evaluate

Magnetic Solutions

Tell students that they are going to have the chance to design a magnetic solution to a simple problem. *Ask*

? What does the word *solution* mean? (A solution is an answer to a problem.)

MAGNETIC SOLUTION

Explain that in this case, a solution is a device, toy, or game invented to solve a problem. *Ask*

? What "problem" does a toy or game solve? (A toy or game gives you something to do when you're bored, helps you have fun with your friends, entertains you, etc.)

Give each student a magnet (you can use the ring magnets from the explore phase or other magnets if you prefer). Students may choose to work together so that their solutions employ the use of multiple magnets.

Brainstorm some solutions together, such as:

- a magnetic pouch made of an envelope and a magnet that holds pencils or supplies in a student's locker or on the side of their desk
- a paper holder that holds a small stack of paper together between two magnets
- a magnetic metal detector made of a magnet attached to a pencil or a stick that can that pull out magnetic materials buried in sand or rice
- a magnetic picture frame that attaches a picture to a locker door
- a magnet-powered toy car that moves across a desk
- a magnetic metal collector that pulls paper clips out of a glass of water
- a magnetic toy sorter made of a magnet on a string that separates metal toy cars from other toys
- a magnetic paper clip maze made of a thin paper plate or aluminum pie pan with a maze drawn on it

Once you brainstorm a few solutions, students will get the idea!

After they have designed their solution (or toy or game), have them test and evaluate it, then redesign it if necessary. Next, pass out the My Magnetic Solution student page and have them draw and name their solution, describe how it works, identify which materials in their solution are magnetic and which materials are nonmagnetic, and explain why they chose those materials.

Writing

Connecting to the Common Core
Writing
TEXT AND PURPOSES: 2.3

Optional Writing Extension: The Day My Feet Were Magnets

Ask students to think about what would happen if they woke up one morning to find that their feet had mysteriously been turned into very strong magnets. Brainstorm ideas together by asking questions such as:

? When you woke up, how would you know that your feet were magnets?

? What would your feet look like or be made of?

? How would they feel?

? What things would be attracted to your feet? Why?

? What problems would you have if your feet were very strong magnets?

? What advantages or superpowers would you have if your feet were very strong magnets?

? How would your day be different if your feet were very strong magnets?

Then have them write a story on their own, or you may choose to write a class story.

MATERIALS FOR DESIGN A GAME ACTIVITY

STEM Everywhere

Give students the STEM Everywhere student page as a way to involve their families and extend their learning. They can do the activity with an adult helper and share their results with the class.

Opportunities for Differentiated Instruction

This box lists questions and challenges related to the lesson that students may select to research, investigate, or innovate. Students may also use the questions as examples to help them generate their own questions. These questions can help you move your students from the teacher-directed investigation to engaging in the science and engineering practices in a more student-directed format.

Extra Support

For students who are struggling to meet the lesson objectives, provide a question and guide them in the process of collecting research or help them design procedures or solutions.

Extensions

For students with high interest or who have already met the lesson objectives, have them choose a question (or pose their own question), conduct their own research, and design their own procedures or solutions.

After selecting one of the questions in the box or formulating their own question, students can individually or collaboratively make predictions, design investigations or surveys to test their predictions, collect evidence, devise explanations, design solutions, or examine related resources. They can communicate their findings through a science notebook, at a poster session or gallery walk, or by producing a media project.

Research

Have students brainstorm researchable questions:

? How are magnets made?

? What are magnetic poles?

? How is Earth like a magnet?

Investigate

Have students brainstorm testable questions to be solved through science or math:

? Can magnetic force pass through water?

? Can magnetic force pass through wood, plastic, or other materials?

? Are larger magnets stronger than smaller magnets?

Innovate

Have students brainstorm problems to be solved through engineering:

? Can you design a maze that uses magnets and magnetic items?

? Can you design a magic trick that uses magnets and magnetic items?

? Can you make a magnet?

More Books to Read

Branley, F. M. 2016. *What makes a magnet?* New York: HarperCollins.
Summary: This updated version of the Let's-Read-and-Find-Out Science book explains the basic principles of magnetism.

Enz, T. 2020. *Discover magnets*. North Mankato, MN: Pebble Books.
Summary: Clear text and colorful photographs describe magnets, how they work, and where they are used.

Rosinsky, N. 2003. *Magnets: Pulling together, pushing apart*. Minneapolis: Picture Window Books.
Summary: Simple text and illustrations, accompanied by fun facts, explain how magnets work, why Earth is really a giant magnet, how a compass works, and more. Includes simple experiments, table of contents and glossary, and a website with links to other safe, fun websites related to the book's content.

Weakland, M. 2011. *Magnets push, magnets pull*. Mankato, MN: Capstone Press.
Summary: This book explains the basics of magnetism with simple text and photographs.

NO MAGNET ZONE

KEEP MAGNETS AWAY

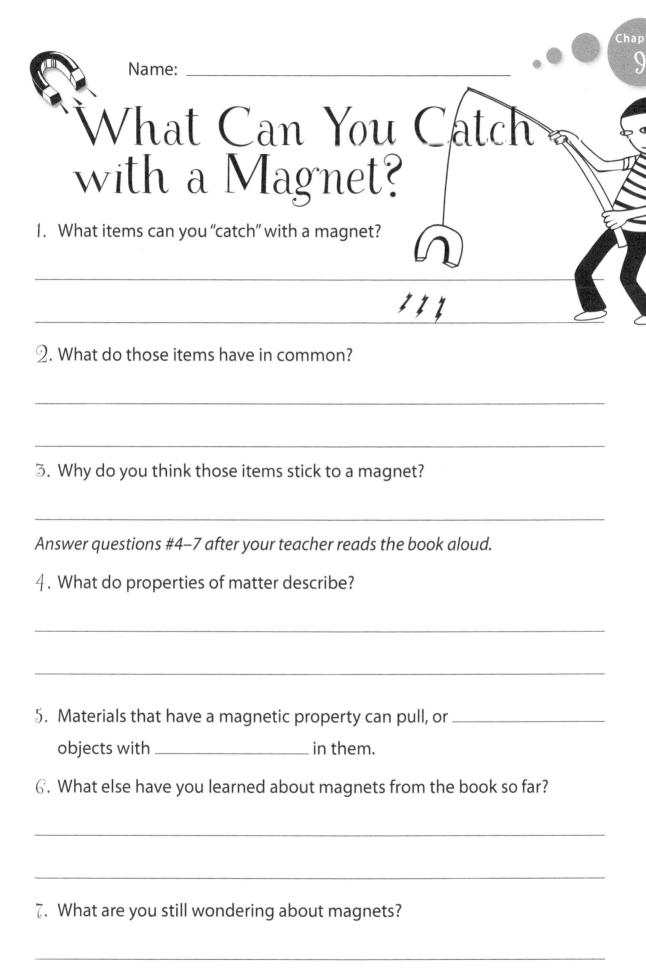

Name: _____

What Can You Catch with a Magnet?

1. What items can you "catch" with a magnet?

_____

_____

2. What do those items have in common?

_____

_____

3. Why do you think those items stick to a magnet?

_____

Answer questions #4–7 after your teacher reads the book aloud.

4. What do properties of matter describe?

_____

_____

5. Materials that have a magnetic property can pull, or _____
   objects with _____ in them.

6. What else have you learned about magnets from the book so far?

_____

_____

7. What are you still wondering about magnets?

_____

Name: _____

My Magnetic Solution

Name of solution: _____

How does it work? _____

_____

What parts are magnetic? _____

_____

Why did you use magnetic materials for those parts? _____

_____

What parts are nonmagnetic? _____

_____

Why did you use nonmagnetic materials for those parts?

_____

_____

STEM Everywhere

Dear Families,

At school, we have been learning about how **some materials are magnetic and other are nonmagnetic**. To find out more, ask your learner questions such as:

- What did you learn?
- What was your favorite part of the lesson?
- What are you still wondering?

At home, you can make your own refrigerator magnet, then use it to find magnetic materials around the house. Caution: Do not use magnets on electronic devices!

First, choose a template to color (or use the blank one and design your own). Then cut it out and attach it to a peel-and-stick adhesive business card magnet.

Use your magnet to test materials around the house. What materials are magnetic?

_____

_____

_____

_____

_____

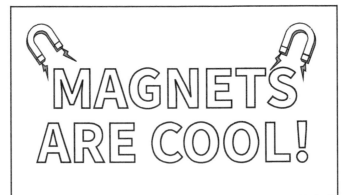

Crayons

Description

Crayons provide a fun and familiar context for learning about science and engineering. Students observe the phenomenon that crayons can be changed in many ways (breaking, melting, and cooling) and learn the many steps involved in manufacturing crayons. After designing their own process for recycling broken crayons, they demonstrate their understanding through a creative writing activity.

Alignment with the *Next Generation Science Standards*

Performance Expectations

2-PS1-4: Construct an argument with evidence that some changes caused by heating or cooling can be reversed and some cannot.

K-2-ETS1-1: Ask questions, make observations, and gather information about a situation people want to change to define a simple problem that can be solved through the development of a new or improved object or tool.

Science and Engineering Practices	Disciplinary Core Ideas	Crosscutting Concepts
Asking Questions and Defining Problems Ask questions based on observations to find more information about the natural and/or designed world(s). Ask and/or identify questions that can be answered by an investigation. **Planning and Carrying Out Investigations** With guidance, plan and conduct an investigation in collaboration with peers. **Obtaining, Evaluating, and Communicating Information** Read grade-appropriate texts and/or use media to obtain scientific and/or technical information to determine patterns in and/or evidence about the natural and designed world(s).	**PS1.B: Chemical Reactions** Heating or cooling a substance may cause changes that can be observed. Sometimes these changes are reversible, and sometimes they are not. **ETS1.A: Defining and Delimiting Engineering Problems** A situation that people want to change or create can be approached as a problem to be solved through engineering. Such problems may have many acceptable solutions.	**Energy and Matter** Objects may break into smaller pieces, be put together into larger pieces, or change shapes. **Cause and Effect** Events have causes that generate observable patterns.

Note: The activities in this lesson will help students move toward the performance expectations listed, which is the goal after multiple activities. However, the activities will not by themselves be sufficient to reach the performance expectations.

Featured Picture Books

TITLE: ***The Day the Crayons Came Home***
AUTHOR: **Drew Daywalt**
ILLUSTRATOR: **Oliver Jeffers**
PUBLISHER: **Philomel Books**
YEAR: **2015**
GENRE: **Story**
SUMMARY: *In this clever story of Duncan's crayons, a colorful bunch that have survived a series of misadventures, each color has a tale to tell and a plea to be brought home to the crayon box.*

TITLE: ***The Crayon Man: The True Story of the Invention of Crayola Crayons***
AUTHOR: **Natascha Biebow**
ILLUSTRATOR: **Steven Salerno**
PUBLISHER: **Clarion Books**
YEAR: **2019**
GENRE: **Dual Purpose**
SUMMARY: *This beautifully illustrated picture book biography tells the inspiring true story of Edward Binney, the inventor of the Crayola crayon.*

Time Needed

This lesson will take several class periods. Suggested scheduling is as follows:

Session 1: **Engage** with Mystery Object and *The Day the Crayons Came Home* Read-Aloud and **Explain** with Crayon Observations

Session 2: **Explore/Explain** with Melting Crayons Demonstration and Discussion

Session 3: **Explain** with *The Crayon Man* Read-Aloud and Card Sequencing

Optional Math Extension: Favorite Crayon Colors Graph

Session 4: **Elaborate** with Crayon Recycling Design Challenge

Session 5: **Evaluate** with Postcard from a Crayon

Materials

For Mystery Object

- Paper bag
- 1 crayon of any color

For Crayon Observations (per student)

- Crayon (Note: To make it easier for students to remove the wrapper, you can use a knife to prescore the paper.)
- Ruler

For Melting Crayons Demonstration and Discussion

- Hot glue gun (for teacher use only)
- Several unwrapped crayons of various colors
- 1 piece of card stock
- Hair dryer (for teacher use only)

For Card Sequencing (per group of 2–4 students)

- Precut How Crayons Are Made Cards in plastic sandwich bags

For Crayon Recycling Design Challenge

- Ovenproof, nonstick, or silicone candy or baking molds, ice cube trays, or silicone muffin cups
- Nonstick cooking spray
- Cookie sheet
- Oven or toaster oven (for teacher use only)

For STEM Everywhere (per student)

- 3 crayons of similar colors but different brands (include 1 Crayola crayon and two off-brand crayons such as the kind that can be purchased at a dollar store)

SAFETY

- Be careful when using hot appliances and hot or liquid wax in the classroom, and keep those items away from children.
- Melting crayons can produce irritating fumes. Before heating crayons, make sure the room has proper ventilation.

Student Pages

- Crayon Observations
- How Crayons Are Made Cards
- Postcard template
- STEM Everywhere

Background for Teachers

Crayons have been an important staple of the elementary classroom for many years. They were first invented to solve a problem voiced by many teachers in the late 19th century: the need for an affordable writing and drawing tool available in a wide variety of colors that was safe for classroom use. Wax crayons commonly used by artists were available, but many brands were expensive and often contained toxic pigments. Edwin Binney, who with his cousin C. Harold Smith owned and operated the Binney & Smith chemical company of Pennsylvania, came up with a solution. In 1903, they introduced the first box of Crayola-brand crayons for children. The crayons, made of paraffin wax and colorful, nontoxic pigments, were individually wrapped in paper and labeled with their colors. Each box of eight crayons

cost a nickel. Edwin Binney's wife, Alice Stead Binney, is credited with coming up with the name Crayola from the French words *craie*, meaning "chalk," and a shortened form of *oléagineux*, meaning "oily."

Although several crayon companies competed in the lucrative school market before Crayola did, the Crayola name is by far the most famous. The first box contained the colors red, orange, yellow, green, blue, violet, brown, and black. Now, there are 120 colors of Crayola crayons. Crayola has a team of chemists and chemical engineers who are in charge of developing new crayon colors. Their laboratory holds the secret formula to every crayon color! The engineers experiment with different color combinations to come up with new shades. When they discover a promising new color, they test it on hundreds of kids to see whether children like it. After extensive testing and further product development (including the invention of a catchy, descriptive name), a new crayon is ready for the box. Some of the improvements to the original 8-pack of Crayola crayons include a 48-color "stadium seating" box, a 64-color box with a built-in sharpener, washable and twistable versions, and glitter crayons.

The invention, design, and manufacture of crayons demonstrate the intersection of science, technology, and engineering. This lesson also demonstrates how science and art intersect. Students are inspired by a picture book to think about all of the ways crayons can be changed. The crosscutting concepts (CCCs) of cause and effect and matter and energy are explored as students observe that adding heat can change a crayon from a solid to a liquid and that allowing it to cool can change it back to a solid. Students learn that sometimes changes in matter are reversible, and sometimes they are not. Students observe how crayons are manufactured and design a process for creating crayons of mixed colors and different shapes out of crayon pieces. Finally, students creatively write about the changes their crayons experienced.

Students are engaged in several science and engineering practices (SEPs) in this lesson. They ask questions and define problems as they investigate the many ways crayons can be changed. They plan and carry out investigations together as they observe crayons breaking, melting, and becoming solid again, and they design a process for recycling broken crayons. Reading a nonfiction book and watching a video of crayons being made engages students in the CCC of obtaining, evaluating, and communicating information.

The concept of reversible change in K–2 falls under the disciplinary core idea (DCI) of chemical reactions and sets a foundation for students to later learn about chemical reactions and the conservation of matter. In learning about the lengthy process that Edwin Binney went through to invent and then mass produce Crayola crayons, second graders make sense of the complexities of engineering design. These ideas are built upon in the upper elementary grades when students begin to define the specific criteria and constraints when designing a solution.

Learning Progressions

Below are the DCI grade band endpoints for grades K–2 and 3–5. These are provided to show how student understanding of the DCIs in this lesson will progress in future grade levels.

DCIs	Grades K–2	Grades 3–5
PS1.B: Chemical Reactions	• Heating or cooling a substance may cause changes that can be observed. Sometimes these changes are reversible, and sometimes they are not.	• When two or more different substances are mixed, a new substance with different properties may be formed. • No matter what reaction or change in properties occurs, the total weight of the substances does not change
ETS1.A: Defining and Delimiting Engineering Problems	• A situation that people want to change or create can be approached as a problem to be solved through engineering. Such problems have many acceptable solutions.	• Possible solutions to a problem are limited by available materials and resources (constraints). The success of a designed solution is determined by considering the desired features of a solution (criteria). Different proposals for solutions can be compared on the basis of how well each one meets the specified criteria for success or how well each takes the constraints into account.

Source: Willard, T., ed. 2015. *The NSTA quick-reference guide to the* NGSS: *Elementary school.* Arlington, VA: NSTA Press.

engage

Mystery Object

*Inferring*

In advance, hide a crayon in a mystery bag (a paper bag with a question mark on it will do just fine). Tell students that you have a mystery item in the bag, and give them some clues about the item: It is red, you can draw with it, and so on. Allow students to guess after each clue. When they have guessed correctly, pull out the crayon and show it to them. Say, "You may think this crayon is ordinary, but by the end of this lesson, you might think that crayons are extraordinary!"

The Day the Crayons Came Home Read-Aloud

Connecting to the Common Core
Reading: Literature
KEY IDEAS AND DETAILS: 2.1

*Determining Importance*

Show students the cover of *The Day the Crayons Came Home.* Introduce the author, Drew Daywalt, and illustrator, Oliver Jeffers. Tell students that as you read the book, you would like them to notice all of the different things that happen to the crayons

and the ways the crayons in the book are changed. Then read the book aloud, using a different voice for each crayon (you will be discussing point of view later).

Questioning

After reading, *ask*

? Is this book fiction or nonfiction? (fiction)

? How can you tell? (It's a pretend story with characters, dialogue, setting, plot, etc. It doesn't have any of the features of nonfiction such as a table of contents, headings, bold-print words, or an index.)

> Connecting to the Common Core
> **Reading: Literature**
> CRAFT AND STRUCTURE: 2.6

Ask

? Who's telling the story? (The story opens and closes with a narrator, but each page in between is told from the points of view of the crayons.)

? How does the text show the crayons' points of view? (The first page of each two-page spread is a postcard written by a different color of crayon. The postcard is written using words such as *I*, *we*, *my*, and *me*, which tells us that the crayon wrote it.)

? Why do you think the author wrote the book this way? (It's funny, it gives the reader a different perspective on crayons, etc.)

? How does the illustrator help tell the story? (One page of each two-page spread features a handwritten postcard in the actual color of the crayon speaking. Each crayon has a different kind of handwriting to help show that a new character is being introduced. The other page is a drawing or collage illustrating the crayon's adventures.)

You may want to have students view the video "Oliver Jeffers: Picture Book Maker" to get a fascinating (and very funny!) behind-the-scenes view of how he writes and illustrates picture books (see "Websites").

Together, recount some of the ways the crayons were changed in the book: They were broken, melted by the Sun, chewed by a dog, sharpened, melted in the dryer, and so on. Tell students they are going to learn both science and engineering concepts by observing crayon properties, exploring how crayons can be changed, and learning how crayons are made.

OBSERVING AND MEASURING CRAYONS

explain

Crayon Observations

Connecting to the Common Core
Mathematics
MEASUREMENT AND DATA: 2.MD.2

First, hold up a crayon and *ask*

? After reading the book *The Day the Crayons Came Home*, what are you wondering about crayons? (Answers will vary.)

? What properties of this crayon could we observe? (color, length, shape, etc.)

Then give each student a crayon, a ruler, and a Crayon Observations student page. Using the crayon, students should first draw a detailed picture of the crayon. Next, have them remove the wrapper from the crayon, and ask them to use all of their senses (except taste!) to make and record observations of the crayon. Observations should include the color, shape, odor (smell), and texture (feel) of the crayon. Review how to measure objects with a ruler, and have students measure and record the length of the crayon. Then have them list some ways that they could change the crayon. *Ask*

? Do you think your crayon is a solid, a liquid, or a gas? (solid) Why do you think so? (Answers will vary, but students may mention that a solid keeps its shape.)

? What are some ways you could change your crayon? (breaking, melting, sharpening, etc.)

CCC: Energy and Matter
Objects may break into smaller pieces, be put together into larger pieces, or change shapes.

Have students break the crayon into three or four smaller pieces. Then *ask*

? How is your crayon different now? (more pieces, shorter lengths, different shapes, etc.)

? How it is the same? (still draws, same color, same odor, etc.)

? Is your crayon still a solid? (yes)

? Is it possible to change a crayon from a solid to a liquid? (Answers will vary.)

? How do you think you could change your crayon from a solid to a liquid? (Answers will vary.)

Note: Students should save their crayon pieces because they will be used in the elaborate activity.

explore/explain

Melting Crayons Demonstration and Discussion

In advance, hot glue several unwrapped crayons of various colors to a piece of card stock. Have a hair dryer available for the following activity. *Ask*

? What do you think will happen if we use the hair dryer to heat up the crayons? (Answers will vary, but students will likely say the crayons will melt.)

Have students watch and make observations as you use a hair dryer on high heat to melt the crayons. After the wax has cooled and dried (wait about 30 seconds), have students feel the hardened wax. You can find detailed instructions for this activity here:

 PBS Parents: How to Make Recycled Crayons.
www.pbs.org/parents/crafts-and-experiments/melt-your-own-crayon-art

MELTING CRAYONS DEMONSTRATION

> **CCC: Cause and Effect**
> Events have causes that
> generate observable patterns

Ask

? What changes did you observe? (The solid wax slowly started dripping down the paper as the crayons melted and turned into a liquid. Then more and more of the wax melted and dripped down the paper. Finally, the wax hardened after the hair dryer was taken away.)

? Once wax is hardened, can it be melted again? (yes, by applying heat)

? Could it be made into another shape? (Answers will vary, but students may suggest putting the hot wax into a mold.)

Explain that melting wax is an example of a *reversible change*. Write "reversible change" on the board, and explain that many things can change from one state of matter to another and back again. For example, water can change from a solid (ice) to a liquid and then back to a solid. *Ask*

? What can you do to ice to change it to a liquid? (heat it or melt it)

? How can you reverse the change and make water become solid again? (cool it or freeze it)

? What can you do to solid wax to change it to a liquid? (heat it or melt it)

? How can you reverse the change and make wax become solid again? (cool it or freeze it)

Explain that liquid wax differs from water in that it becomes a solid at room temperature. (You don't have to put it in a freezer to make it solid.) In the book, cooling with water makes the wax harden into a solid. *Ask*

? How does the demonstration of melting crayons show a reversible change? (Heat melted the solid wax into a liquid, but the change was reversible because the liquid wax hardened back into solid wax when it cooled.)

Challenge students to work with a partner and think of a change that is *not* reversible. For example, when you boil a raw egg (which contains mostly liquid material), it becomes a solid. Cooling the egg will not reverse the change; it remains solid.

 Questioning

Ask

? What questions do you have about crayons? (Answers will vary.)

> **SEP: Asking Questions and Defining Problems**
> Ask questions based on observations to find more information about the natural and/or designed worlds..

Turn and Talk

Have students share their wonderings with a partner, and then record some of their questions on a "Crayon Questions" class chart. Ask students how each question could be answered (e.g., by doing research, asking an expert, or conducting an experiment). Then add the following questions to the list (if they are not already on it):

? Where did this box of crayons come from?

? Who invented crayons?

? What are crayons made of?

? How do they get their shape?

? How do they get their wrappers?

? How did all of these colors end up in one box?

Discuss each question with your students, and allow them to share their ideas (responses will vary).

explain

The Crayon Man Read-Aloud

Tell students that you have a book that will answer many of their questions. Show them the cover of *The Crayon Man: The True Story of the Invention of Crayola Crayons.* Tell students that as you read the book aloud, you would like them to listen for any answers to their crayon questions that are written on the chart.

After reading "None of these inventions was any good for drawing in color" on page 12, *ask*

? What problems was Edwin Binney trying to solve? (The crayons at the time were big, dull, and clumsy. The ones used by artists were expensive, broke easily, and some were even poisonous.)

? What criteria did he have for a successful solution? (The crayons would need to be strong, cheap, safe, and colorful.)

> **SEP: Obtaining, Evaluating, and Communicating Information**
> Read grade-appropriate texts and/or use media to obtain scientific and/or technical information to determine patterns in and/or evidence about the natural and designed world(s).

After reading page 17, *ask*

? How did Edwin and his team create the colors for the crayons? (by grinding rocks and minerals into fine powders)

After reading page 21, *ask*

? Did the team get the crayons right on their first try? (No, they had to keep experimenting and making new discoveries.)

? Do you think most inventors get their inventions right on the first try? (no)

After reading page 31, *ask*

? How does the first box of Crayola crayons in 1903 compare to boxes of Crayola crayons today? (Answers will vary but may include the first box cost a nickel and only contained 8 crayons, now crayons are more expensive and come in sets of 64 colors or more.)

You may want to show students a photo of a 1903 box of Crayola crayons from the National Museum of American History (see "Websites").

After reading the last page of the story (not the end matter), *ask*

? What are some interesting things you learned about crayons from the book? (Answers will vary.)

? How do you think the process of making crayons then compares to how they are made now? (Answers will vary but might include using more high-tech factories, using robots, or making more crayons in a shorter amount of time.)

Card Sequencing

 Sequencing Before Reading

Tell students they are going to learn more about how crayons are made today. Before reading the section at the end of the book titled "How Crayola Crayons Are Made Today," give each group of two to four students a set of precut How Crayons Are Made Cards. Challenge them to work together to put the cards in order to show the steps needed to manufacture, or make, crayons in a factory. Tell them that they will have an opportunity to reorder the cards later. For now, they can just make their best guess on the order.

Have students compare their card sequences with those of other groups and explain their thinking.

Connecting to the Common Core
Reading: Informational Text
KEY IDEAS AND DETAILS: 2.1

 ## Sequencing After Reading

After students have sequenced their cards, read the section titled "How Crayola Crayons Are Made Today" and give students the opportunity to reorder their How Crayons Are Made Cards as you read. The cards should be sequenced in the following order:

1. Wax is heated and melted.
2. Colored powders are added.
3. Wax is pumped into a mold.
4. Wax cools and hardens into crayon shapes.
5. Crayons are pushed out and moved by a robotic arm.
6. The crayons are wrapped with labels.
7. Labeled crayons are sorted by color.
8. A chute drops one of each color onto a conveyor belt.
9. Robotic arms load the crayons into boxes.
10. The finished crayons are shipped to the store.

Connecting to the Common Core
Reading: Informational Text
INTEGRATION OF KNOWLEDGE AND IDEAS: 2.9

 ## Making Connections: Text to Text

Next, show the video titled "How People Make Crayons" (see "Websites"), so students can see the Crayola Crayon Factory in action. Then *ask*

? How does the video compare with the description of how crayons are made from the book? (The video had some of the same people that were pictured in the book. The book described the process, but the video showed the process in action. The video also showed various jobs involved in making crayons.)

Challenge students to think about all of the science and engineering involved in making an ordinary crayon! *Ask*

? How do you think scientists and engineers might be involved in making crayons? (Answers will vary, but students may mention that scientists test different types of wax and pigments, and engineers use that information to figure out how to turn the raw materials into the best crayons possible. Engineers design every step of the crayon-manufacturing process, from the tanks that heat and melt the wax to the packing machines and robotic arms that put the crayons into boxes.)

> **CCC: Energy and Matter**
> Objects may break into smaller pieces, be put together into larger pieces, or change shapes.

 ## Questioning

Revisit your class list of crayon questions and have the students use evidence from the text and video to answer the questions.

Connecting to the Common Core
Mathematics
MEASUREMENT AND DATA: 2.MD.10

Optional Math Extension: Favorite Crayon Colors Graph

Ask

? What is your favorite crayon color? (Answers will vary.)

Next, have students write their favorite crayon color on a sticky note or color a sticky note with their favorite color. Create a bar graph with "Favorite Colors" on the x-axis and "Number of Votes" on the y-axis. Have students place their sticky notes on the bar graph. Analyze the results together. Then share with students that most kids around the world choose blue or red as their favorite crayon color. *Ask*

? What color was most popular in our class?

? How do our results compare with the favorite crayon colors (blue or red) of kids around the world? (Answers will vary.)

elaborate

Crayon Recycling Design Challenge

> Connecting to the Common Core
> **Reading: Literature**
> KEY IDEAS AND DETAILS: 2.1

Tell students that you have an exciting challenge for them, but first you want to revisit *The Day the Crayons Came Home.*

Questioning

Refer to the pages of *The Day the Crayons Came Home* where the crayons melted. Reread pages 27–28 about the turquoise crayon that melted in the dryer. *Ask*

? Why would a crayon melt in a dryer? (It is hot in a dryer.)

? How did the turquoise crayon get in the dryer? (Duncan left it in his pocket.)

? Why it is a bad thing if a crayon gets in the dryer? (It melts and stains clothes.)

Next, revisit pages 13–14 about the orange and red crayons that melted together. *Ask*

? Why did the red and orange crayons melt? (They were left in the heat of the Sun.)

Students should realize that because crayons are made of wax, they will turn to liquid when heated and become solid again when they are cooled.

Next, have students look at the crayons they broke during the explore phase of the lesson. Tell them that broken crayons aren't very useful, which is why we often discard them. But perhaps there is a way to recycle the broken crayons! Tell students that you have a design challenge for them: Come up with a simple and safe way to recycle the crayons into new crayons. Remind students that engineers designed every component of the crayon-making process—from the tanks that heat and melt the wax to the packing machines that put the crayons into boxes. Tell students you would now like for them to think like engineers and brainstorm ways to turn their broken crayons into multicolored crayons of different shapes.

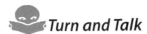Turn and Talk

Once engineers understand a problem, they think about all of the possible solutions. There are often many different solutions to a problem. Brainstorming is a good way to share ideas with others. Have students turn and talk to share their initial ideas with each other. Remind students that at this point in the design process, all ideas are acceptable.

> **SEP: Planning and Carrying Out Investigations**
> Plan and conduct an investigation in collaboration with peers.

MELTING CRAYONS IN A MOLD

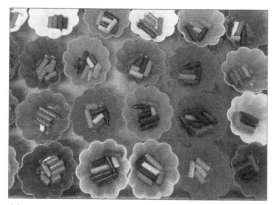

MELTING CRAYONS IN MUFFIN CUPS

CCC: Cause and Effect
Events have causes that
generate observable patterns.

Next, explain that you have some tools to share that might give them some ideas. Show students the nonstick or silicone candy or baking molds, ice cube trays, or muffin cups, and tell them that you will also be using an oven or toaster oven. Then let pairs or small groups of students discuss how they might design a step-by-step process for recycling the broken crayons into new crayons of different shapes and colors. For example, students could exchange crayon pieces with each other to mix up the colors and then place their broken pieces into the molds. The molds can then be heated to melt the pieces together. After pairs or groups have discussed different design process possibilities, dis-

cuss the variations as a class and come up with one way to try together. Write each step on the board. Detailed instructions for recycling crayons can be found on the PBS Parents website How to Make Recycled Crayons (see "Websites").

Treat the molds with nonstick cooking spray before adding the crayon pieces, so the recycled crayons will be easier to pop out once they have cooled and hardened. If they don't pop out easily, you can place them in the freezer for about 20 minutes. Place the molds on a cookie sheet and use an oven or toaster oven to melt the crayon pieces at low heat (250°F for about 20 minutes). (If you do not have access to an oven or toaster oven at school, you can complete this step at home.) After cooling, give each student a new crayon. Have students compare the properties of the new crayons with those of the original crayons.

Ask

? How are the crayons the same as they were before being recycled? (They are solid and can be used to write and color.)

? How are they different after being recycled? (They have mixed colors and different shapes.)

? Do you think this change could be reversed? (yes, but not easily)

RECYCLED CRAYONS

? How well did our recycling process work? (Answers will vary.)

? What would you change to make the process work better? (Answers will vary.)

You may want to have students test their recycled crayons by drawing a picture.

 evaluate

Postcard from a Crayon

Connecting to the Common Core
Writing
TEXT TYPES AND PURPOSES: K.3, 1.3, 2.3
Reading: Literature
CRAFT AND STRUCTURE: 1.6, 2.6

Writing

Give each student a postcard template student page copied on card stock. Tell students that they are going to write a friendly letter from the point of view of the crayon they observed at the beginning of the lesson. They will be using first person (*I*, *we*, *my*, and *me*) just as the author did in *The Day the Crayons Came Home*. Reread the first postcard in the book (from Maroon Crayon) as an example. Explain that, rather than describing an imaginative adventure the way Maroon Crayon did, they will be describing all of the things that happened to their crayon during the recycling process. Students can, however, think of a creative way their crayon may have been broken and begin their postcard with that event. They should end with the crayon being recycled into a new crayon with a new color and shape, with all of the steps of the recycling process described in between.

POSTCARD FROM A CRAYON

SEP: Obtaining, Evaluating, and Communicating Information
Read grade-appropriate texts and/or use media to obtain scientific and/or technical information to determine patterns in and/or evidence about the natural and designed world(s).

Encourage students to use temporal words such as *first* and *next* to signal event order. They should also use words such as *solid*, *liquid*, *heated*, and *cooled* in their writing. In the margins or on the back of their postcard, they can draw a scene showing one or more of the things that happened to the crayon during the recycling process.

Use the completed postcards to evaluate students' understanding of the core idea that heating or cooling a substance may cause changes that can be observed, and sometimes these changes are reversible. You may also want to evaluate English language arts objectives such as writing a friendly letter, expressing point of view, or using temporal words.

STEM Everywhere

Give students the STEM Everywhere student page as a way to involve their families and extend their learning. They can do the activity with an adult helper and share their results with the class. If students do not have access to these materials or the internet at home, you may choose to have them complete this activity at school.

Opportunities for Differentiated Instruction

This box lists questions and challenges related to the lesson that students may select to research, investigate, or innovate. Students may also use the questions as examples to help them generate their own questions. These questions can help you move your students from the teacher-directed investigation to engaging in the science and engineering practices in a more student-directed format.

Extra Support

For students who are struggling to meet the lesson objectives, provide a question and guide them in the process of collecting research or helping them design procedures or solutions.

Extensions

For students with high interest or who have already met the lesson objectives, have them choose a question (or pose their own question), conduct their own research, and design their own procedures or solutions.

After selecting one of the questions in the box or formulating their own question, students can individually or collaboratively make predictions, design investigations or surveys to test their predictions, collect evidence, devise explanations, design solutions, or examine related resources. They can communicate their findings through a science notebook, at a poster session or gallery walk, or by producing a media project.

Research

Have students brainstorm researchable questions:

? Where do the raw materials for crayons come from?

? What improvements has the Crayola company made to the crayon?

? What does a chemical engineer do?

Continued

Opportunities for Differentiated Instruction (*continued*)

Investigate

Have students brainstorm testable questions to be solved through science or math:

? Find out the price of a box of Crayola crayons and the price of the same-sized box of another brand. Which brand is more expensive? How much more does it cost? Can you design a test to compare the brands?

? Survey your friends and family: What is your favorite crayon color? Graph the results, then analyze your graph. What can you conclude?

? When you mix salt and water, the salt seems to disappear. Is this a reversible change? How could you get the salt back to its original form? Try it!

Innovate

Have students brainstorm problems to be solved through engineering:

? Can you design a new crayon color by mixing different colors together? Can you come up with a catchy and descriptive name for your new color?

? What happens if you add glitter to the crayon pieces before melting? How well do the glitter crayons work after melting and cooling?

? Can you design a crayon-recycling program for your school?

Websites

 "Oliver Jeffers: Picture Book Maker" (video)
*www.youtube.com/
watch?v=w-8ydwV45no*

 National Museum of American History: Crayola Crayons
*https://americanhistory.si.edu/
collections/search/object/
nmah_1196565*

 PBS LearningMedia: How People Make Crayons
*www.pbslearningmedia.org/
resource/959d7d86-78fa-
44e1-91a1-dcfa163ce7a0/
how-people-make-crayons*

 PBS Parents: How to Make Recycled Crayons.
*www.pbs.org/parents/
crafts-and-experiments/
melt-your-own-crayon-art*

 "The Life of an American Crayon" (video)
*www.crayola.com/splash/promos/the-
life-of-an-american-crayon.aspx*

More Books to Read

Daywalt, D. 2013. *The day the crayons quit*. New York: Philomel Books.

Summary: Poor Duncan just wants to color. But when he opens his box of crayons, he finds only letters, all saying the same thing: His crayons have had enough. They quit! Beige Crayon is tired of playing second fiddle to Brown Crayon. Black Crayon wants to be used for more than just outlining. Blue Crayon needs a break from coloring all those bodies of water. Orange Crayon and Yellow Crayon are no longer speaking—each believes he is the true color of the Sun.

Hall, M. 2015. *Red: A crayon's story*. New York: Greenwillow Books.

Summary: A blue crayon mistakenly labeled as "red" suffers an identity crisis until a new friend offers a different perspective. Red discovers what readers have known all along … he's blue! This witty and heartwarming book is about finding the courage to be true to your inner self.

Hansen, A. 2012. *Melting matter*. Vero Beach, FL: Rourke Publishing.

Summary: Simple text and full-color illustrations help explain what happens when everyday items such as ice cream and candles melt. This brief introduction to melting also introduces the idea that something that changes its state by melting or freezing remains matter and compares melting with dissolving and burning.

Nelson, R. 2013. *From wax to crayon*. Minneapolis: Lerner.

Summary: Simple text and full-color photographs describe each step in the production of crayons—from melting wax to coloring a picture.

Name: _____

Crayon Observations

1. Using your crayon, draw a picture of your crayon.

（blank drawing box）

2. Write down observations about your crayon. Do not taste it!

Color	Shape	Odor	Texture	Length

3. List some ways you could change your crayon.

_____

_____

_____

_____

How Crayons Are Made Cards

Colored powders are added.	Wax cools and hardens into crayon shapes.
The crayons are wrapped with labels.	Robotic arms load the crayons into boxes.
Wax is heated and melted.	A chute drops one of each color onto a conveyor belt.
Wax is pumped into a mold.	Labeled crayons are sorted by color.
The finished crayons are shipped to the store.	Crayons are pushed out and moved by a robotic arm.

POSTCARD

To:

Name: _____

Dear _____

Name: _____

STEM Everywhere

At school, we have been learning about crayons and how they can be changed. We broke them, melted them, and cooled them. We found out how crayons were invented and how they are manufactured. To find out more, ask your learner questions such as:

- What did you learn?
- What was your favorite part of the lesson?
- What are you still wondering?

At home, watch a video together called "The Life of an American Crayon" about how Crayola crayons are made.

 Search "Life of an American Crayon" to find the video at *www.crayola.com/splash/promos/the-life-of-an-american-crayon. aspx.*

After you watch the video, design a test to find out how Crayola crayons compare to other brands!

Brand	Crayon Observations
1. Crayola	
2.	
3.	

Conclusion:

_____

_____

_____

Science Mysteries

Description

After reading a story about an extraordinary young scientist, students are engaged in solving a mystery that involves exploring properties of matter. Students conduct an investigation, use science practices to gather evidence, and use that evidence to support their claim about the identities of two mystery mixtures.

Alignment with the *Next Generation Science Standards*

Performance Expectation		
2-PS1-1: Plan and conduct an investigation to describe and classify different kinds of materials by their observable properties		
Science and Engineering Practices	**Disciplinary Core Idea**	**Crosscutting Concepts**
Asking Questions and Defining Problems Ask and/or identify questions that can be answered by an investigation. **Planning and Carrying Out Investigations** Plan and conduct an investigation collaboratively to produce data to serve as the basis for evidence to answer a question. **Engaging in Argument From Evidence** Construct an argument with evidence to support a claim.	**PS I.A: Structure and Properties of Matter** Different kinds of matter exist and many of them can be either solid or liquid, depending on temperature. Matter can be described and classified by its observable properties.	**Energy and Matter** Objects may break into smalller pieces:, be put together into larger pieces, or change shape. **Patterns** Patterns in the natural and human-designed world can be observed, used to describe phenomena, and used as evidence.

Note: The activities in this lesson will help students move toward the performance expectation listed, which is the goal after multiple activities. However, the activities will not by themselves be sufficient to reach the performance expectation.

Featured Picture Books

TITLE: ***Ada Twist, Scientist***
AUTHOR: **Andrea Beaty**
ILLUSTRATOR: **David Roberts**
PUBLISHER: **Abrams Books for Young Readers**
YEAR: **2016**
GENRE: **Story**
SUMMARY: *In this charming story about a girl on a mission to use science to understand her world, young Ada discovers that her boundless curiosity can help her solve one smelly mystery!*

TITLE: ***Matter***
AUTHOR: **Abbie Dunne**
PUBLISHER: **Capstone Press**
YEAR: **2016**
GENRE: **Non-Narrative Information**
SUMMARY: *In this colorful, photo-packed book, young readers will learn about the properties of solids, liquids, and gases—how they can be mixed together and how they can change from one form to another.*

Time Needed

This lesson will take several class periods. Suggested scheduling is as follows:

Session 1: **Engage** with *Ada Twist, Scientist* Read-Aloud and Great Scientists Chart

Session 2: **Explore** with Properties of Matter and **Explain** with Our Results

Session 3: **Explain** with Properties of Matter Vocabulary and *Matter* Read-Aloud

Session 4: **Elaborate** with Mystery Mixtures

Session 5: **Evaluate** with Matter Quiz and Matter Mystery

Materials

For Great Scientists Chart (per student)

- 1 pack of sticky notes

For Properties of Matter (per student)

- Hand lens
- Safety goggles

For Properties of Matter (per group of 4 students)

- Small tray containing the following materials:
  - 4 plastic 3 oz cups, each half-filled with a different substance: salt, cornstarch, white sand, and baking soda (Use a permanent marker to label each cup with the name of the substance.)

- 1 small, plastic, lidded container filled with approximately ½ cup of water (labeled and closed)
- 1 small, plastic, lidded container filled with approximately ¼ cup of vinegar (labeled and closed)
- 2 plastic 5 ml eyedroppers (1 dedicated to each liquid)
- 4 teaspoons (1 dedicated to each solid)
- 16 wooden, noncolored craft sticks for stirring (4 per student)
- 16 plastic 3 oz bath cups (4 per student)

Note: The following quantities should provide enough for four classes

- 1 lb. of salt
- 1 box of cornstarch (12 oz)
- 1 lb. of white sand (Use a fine, crystalline sand for best results. Ashland decorative stone granules [1.75 lbs] are available in white at Michael's craft stores.)
- 1 box of baking soda (12 oz)

For Properties of Matter Vocabulary (per student)

- Vocabulary cards (1 strip of cards, precut)
- Tape or glue

For Mystery Mixtures (per student)

- Hand lens
- Safety goggles

For Mystery Mixtures (per group of 4 students)

- Small tray containing the following materials:
  - 2 plastic 3 oz bath cups, each half-filled with a different "mystery mixture": equal parts cornstarch and sand (mixture A), and equal parts salt and baking soda (mixture B) (Use a permanent marker to label each cup "Mystery Mixture A" or "Mystery Mixture B.")
  - 1 small, plastic, lidded container filled with approximately ½ cup of water (labeled and closed)
  - 1 small, plastic, lidded container filled with approximately ¼ cup of vinegar (labeled and closed)
  - 2 plastic eyedroppers (1 dedicated to each liquid)
  - 2 teaspoons (1 dedicated to each mystery mixture)
  - 8 wooden, non-colored craft sticks for stirring (2 per student)
  - 8 plastic 3 oz bath cups (2 per student)

For STEM Everywhere (if you wish to send the materials home with each student)

- Food coloring
- 2 cups cornstarch
- Aluminum foil pie pan

Student Pages

- Properties of Matter data sheet
- Properties of Matter testing mat
- Vocabulary Cards
- New Vocabulary List
- Mystery Mixtures data sheet
- Mystery Mixtures testing mat
- Matter Quiz
- Matter Mystery
- STEM Everywhere

Background for Teachers

Matter is all around us. Matter is defined as anything that has mass and takes up space. The paper this book is written on, the water in your bottle, the air you are breathing—they are all made of matter! So what is matter made of? All matter is made of tiny *atoms*. They are so small that you cannot see them with your eyes or even with a standard microscope. Atoms combine to form *molecules*, and these molecules make up a variety of substances. Matter can be described by its properties. Some properties of matter include color, texture, hardness, solubility (ability to dissolve in other substances), reactivity (ability to chemically react with other substances), and state.

Most matter on Earth is found in one of three states: solid, liquid, or gas. In this lesson, students find examples of all three states of matter as they observe common household substances such as salt, sand, baking soda, cornstarch, water, and vinegar. Each state of matter can be identified by its distinctive properties of shape and volume. A *solid* has a definite shape and a definite volume. Its molecules are the most tightly bound together of the three main states of matter. Solids can be poured only if they are made of very small particles such as salt crystals, grains of sand, or powdered substances. Up close, salt crystals look like tiny cubes. Their flat surfaces reflect light, so they look somewhat shiny. Sand, depending on its mineral composition, may be a mixture of different-shaped crystals and more irregular grains. A powder, such as baking soda or cornstarch, is a dry solid composed of a large number of very fine particles that may flow freely when tilted or poured.

A *liquid* has a definite volume, but its shape changes more readily because its molecules are more loosely bound together than those of a solid. A liquid, whether it is thick or thin, is a wet substance that can be poured and always takes the shape of its container. A *gas* has no particular shape or volume. It will expand to fill the space it is in. It can also be compressed to fit a smaller container. Gas has this property because the distances between the molecules of a gas are much greater than the distances between the molecules of a solid or a liquid. A bubble is a thin sphere of liquid enclosing air or another gas such as water vapor or carbon dioxide. Much of the universe is composed of a fourth state of matter known as *plasma*. Plasma has properties different from the other three fundamental states of matter. Scientists can generate plasma in a lab, and it naturally exists inside stars.

Matter can be combined in different ways. A *mixture* is made up of two or more different substances that are mixed but not combined chemically. Mixtures can be solids, liquids, or gases in any combination. Sand and salt stirred together is a mixture. Food coloring in water is a mixture. Air is a mixture of gases. One particular type of mixture is called a *solution*. In a solution, one substance is evenly mixed

with another, making the particles of the substance too small to be seen or filtered out. Salt [dissolved] in water is a solution. The salt disappears, but it is still there. If you tasted the solution, it would taste salty. This mixture could be separated by heating the water until it evaporates, leaving behind the salt crystals.

Matter can also be combined chemically. When two or more substances are mixed, a new substance with different properties may be formed. This process is called a *chemical change*. Chemical changes create entirely new substances. After a chemical change occurs, physical methods, such as drying or filtering, cannot undo the change. In a chemical change, the molecules of different materials rearrange to form entirely new *compounds*. The new compounds have different properties. For example, when vinegar and baking soda are mixed, a chemical change occurs and a new substance—carbon dioxide gas—is formed.

In this lesson, students perform tests on some common household substances to observe their properties. In the process, they learn that matter can be described and classified by its observable properties and that matter can be a solid, liquid, or gas. An equally important component of this lesson is students learning about the practices of scientists. By engaging in science and engineering practices (SEPs) to observe the properties of matter (and eventually solving a mystery), students learn firsthand how scientists ask questions, carry out investigations, and support their claims with evidence. Students are also introduced to the crosscutting concept (CCC) of energy and matter as they use their senses to make observations of different kinds of matter and the CCC of patterns as they recognize how patterns in certain substances appear and behave.

Learning Progressions

Below are the disciplinary core idea (DCI) grade band endpoints for grades K–2 and 3–5. These are provided to show how student understanding of the DCI in this lesson will progress in future grade levels.

DCI	Grades K–2	Grades 3–5
PS1.A: Structure and Properties of Matter	• Different kinds of matter exist and many of them can be either solid or liquid, depending on temperature. Matter can be described and classified by its observable properties.	• Measurements of a variety of properties can be used to identify materials.

Source: Willard, T., ed. 2015. *The NSTA quick-reference guide to the* NGSS: *Elementary school.* Arlington, VA: NSTA Press.

engage

Ada Twist, Scientist Read-Aloud

 Inferring

Show students the cover of *Ada Twist, Scientist* and introduce the author, Andrea Beaty, and illustrator, David Roberts. *Ask*

? Based on the cover, what do you think this book might be about? (a girl who likes science or is a scientist)

? How do you know? (from the title, the goggles she is wearing, or the pictures in the background)

? What do you think the tennis player on the cover has to do with the story? (Answers will vary.)

 Questioning

Connecting to the Common Core
Reading: Literature
KEY IDEAS AND DETAILS: 2.1

Read the book aloud, then *ask*

? Who is the tennis player on the cover? (Ada's brother)

? What mystery did Ada try to solve? (the source of the horrible stench)

? How did she try to solve it? (She wrote down lots of questions and then tested different smells with her homemade sniffing machine.)

? By the end of the story, did Ada solve the mystery? (no)

? Do you think scientists always find the answers to their questions? (Answers will vary.)

? The book says, "But this much was clear about Miss Ada Twist: She had all the traits of a great scientist." What are the traits of a great scien-

tist? In other words, what are great scientists like? (Answers will vary.)

? How was Ada a great scientist? (Answers will vary but may include being passionate about understanding the world around her, being curious or asking questions that lead to more questions, making observations, doing research, performing tests and experiments, persevering, etc.)

? Look back at page 18. What safety equipment does Ada wear to help her do science safely? (She wears safety goggles and gloves and also has her hair pulled up.)

? Look back at page 29. What other tools or equipment do you see in the picture that Ada might use to help her do science? (books, models, beakers and flasks, microscope, screwdriver, etc.).

? Ada is holding one of the most important tools of a great scientist. What is it? (pen, pencil, or marker)

Explain that great scientists use pencils (and technologies such as computers) to write down their

ENGAGING WITH ADA TWIST, SCIENTIST

Chapter 11

170

National Science Teaching Association

GREAT SCIENTISTS CHART

questions, plan their investigations, record their data and conclusions, draw sketches and diagrams, make claims supported by evidence, and compose research papers to share with other scientists. Good communication in all forms, not just writing, is one of the most important skills great scientists can have. Scientists also need to be team players!

Great Scientists Chart

Make a whole-class chart titled "Great Scientists…," and *ask*

? What great scientists do you know of? (Answers will vary.)

? What are some of the skills or characteristics of great scientists? (Answers will vary.)

 *Turn and Talk*

Next, have students turn and talk with a partner to come up with a few words that describe what great scientists are like or what they do in their work. Pass out sticky notes, and have each pair of students write their words or phrases on separate sticky notes and put them on the chart. Then

put similar words and phrases together and look for common themes such as "Great scientists… make observations," "Great scientists… are curious," "Great scientists… ask questions," or "Great scientists… use safety equipment."

Next, *ask*

? Would you like to be a great scientist? (Answers will vary, but many students will likely say yes!)

explore

Properties of Matter

Tell students that you have a problem: You mixed some household substances for a science activity, but you forgot to label your mixtures. Show them two containers of white mixtures. Explain that Mystery Mixture A contains two substances, and Mystery Mixture B contains two other substances. Tell them you need the help of some great scientists to figure out what's what. Like Ada Twist, they are going to use the skills of a great scientist to solve this mystery! Tell them that the first thing they will need to do is find out more about the four substances that you used in the mixtures by observing each substance's individual properties.

SEP: Asking Questions and Defining Problems
Ask questions that can be answered by an investigation.

Show students the labeled containers of salt, cornstarch, white sand, and baking soda. Tell them that these were the four household substances that you used in the mixtures. *Ask*

? What does "property of a substance" mean? (its characteristics or attributes)

? What properties of these substances could we safely observe? (what they look like [color, grains, etc.] and how they feel [texture, etc.])

? What are some ways that we can safely observe these substances? (look at them with a hand

OBSERVING MATTER

lens or microscope, touch them but do not taste them, etc.)

Arrange students into teams of four. Pass out a Properties of Matter data sheet student page, a Properties of Matter testing mat student page, a pair of goggles, and a hand lens to each student. Then review the safety guidelines for observing and testing the substances in this activity. Tell students to use their best powers of observation!

Now, have one person from each team go to the materials table and carefully carry a tray of materials back to his or her team. Tell students to wait until every team has its materials, and then you will go over the testing procedure together. Explain that their task is to be like Ada Twist, scientist, and ask questions and make observations while exploring the substances. Like Ada, they will also be following safety guidelines.

The first thing students should do is place a small plastic bath cup on each empty circle of their testing mat, which has circles labeled "salt," "corn-starch," "sand," and "baking soda." They should also place a craft stick next to each cup to use for stirring (stirring the water into the substance first, then stirring the vinegar into the substance and water). The purpose of the mat is to help the students identify the substance they are testing and allow for easy cleanup. After the activity, the

SAFETY
- Wear your safety goggles at all times.
- Do not taste or sniff any of the substances.
- Do not pour any of the substances out of the containers. Use only the spoon or eyedropper that is assigned to each substance to avoid contamination.
- You will be touching the substances with your fingers. Do not put your fingers near your face after touching them. When the activity is over, you must wash your hands with soap and water.
- You will be using a hand lens to observe the substances. Do not let the hand lens touch the substance. Put your eye as close to the lens as possible, and lean over the cup until the substance comes into focus. Try closing the eye that is not close to the lens to get a better view.

plastic cups, substances, craft sticks, and mat can be tossed into the trash.

> **SEP: Planning and Carrying Out Investigations**
> Plan and conduct an investigation collaboratively to produce data to serve as the basis for evidence to answer a question.

Tell students that you will all test the first substance together to learn the process. Have students take turns putting one *level* teaspoon of the salt from the plastic cup labeled "salt" into the corresponding cup on their testing mat. Remind them not to use this spoon for any other substance to avoid contamination. Tell students that they will record their observations on their Properties of Matter data sheet. Then begin the testing as follows:

Test 1: Rub the substance between your fingers. How does it feel? Record the texture. (Students may describe the salt as rough, hard, gritty, etc.)

Test 2: Use a hand lens to look more closely at the substance. Can you see any crystals? Write yes or no. (Explain that crystals can look like tiny cubes or other shapes with flat sides. Their flat surfaces reflect light, so they may look somewhat shiny. The sand, depending on its mineral composition, may be a mixture of different-shaped crystals and more rounded grains.)

Test 3: Use an eyedropper to add three full droppers of water (3 teaspoons or 15 ml) to the substance. (Remind students not to use this eyedropper with the vinegar to avoid contamination.) Stir with a craft stick for 30 seconds and observe if the salt appears to disappear, bubble, thicken, or do something else. (Most of the salt should eventually dissolve and disappear, but it is not important for students to use or understand the word *dissolve* at this point. They can also describe how the water appears [e.g., stays clear, turns cloudy, etc.].)

Test 4: Use an eyedropper to add 10 drops of vinegar to the same cup. (Remind students not to use this eyedropper with the water to avoid contamination.) Stir with a craft stick for 30 seconds and observe if more of the salt appears to disappear, bubble, thicken, or do something else. (A little more of the salt might eventually dissolve, but they

should not observe bubbling. Students will most likely observe nothing happening.)

After testing the salt, *ask*

? What else did you notice about the salt? (Answers will vary.)

? What questions do you have about the salt? (Questions will vary.)

Then have students test the other three substances following the same procedure. Remind them of the safety guidelines as they work. A sample completed data table is shown in Table 11.1 (observations may vary).

explain

Our Results

Turn and Talk

After students have finished testing all four substances, have them turn and talk with a partner to compare the results of their tests. Then *ask*

? What interesting observations did you make? (Answers will vary.)

Table 11.1. Sample Completed Data Table for Properties of Matter

Test	Salt	Cornstarch	Sand	Baking Soda
1. Texture (feel)	Rough and gritty	Slippery	Rough and gritty	Smooth
2. Crystals? (yes/no)	Yes	No	Yes	No
3. What happens with water?	Salt disappears, and water looks almost clear.	Water turns milky.	Sand does not disappear, and water looks cloudy.	Baking soda disappears, and water looks cloudy.
4. What happens with vinegar?	Nothing	Nothing	Nothing	Bubbles

? Were any of your results different from the other scientists' at your table? If so, why do you think so? (Answers will vary.)

? What do you think happened to the salt when you mixed it with the water? (Answers will vary.)

? What do you think happened to the cornstarch when you mixed it with the water? (Answers will vary.)

? What do you think happened to the sand when you mixed it with the water? (Answers will vary.)

? What did you notice when you added the vinegar to the baking soda? (It bubbled.)

? What else are you wondering about the substances? (Answers will vary.)

Explain that many of these questions will be answered through reading a nonfiction book during the next class period. Tell students to keep their Properties of Matter data sheets in a safe place because they will be referring to them later. Have students clean up by returning the tray of materials and stacking their cups. Then have students fold up their mats with the craft sticks inside and dispose of them in the trash. Students should wash their hands after they clean up.

Properties of Matter Vocabulary

New Vocabulary List

Tell students that they will be learning some new vocabulary that will help them learn more about properties of matter. Give each student a set of five precut Vocabulary Cards (*gas*, *solid*, *dissolve*, *matter*, and *liquid*). Explain that all of these vocabulary words relate to the things the students observed in the Properties of Matter activity. They may be familiar with some of the words, but some may be new. Have students read each word aloud, then give them time to discuss with a partner what they think each word means.

Next, pass out the New Vocabulary List student page to each student. A new vocabulary list is a "guess and check" type of visual representation. Students develop new vocabulary as they discuss or write their ideas about an unfamiliar word's meaning, read or hear the word in context, and then discuss or write their new understanding of the word. Read aloud each definition in the "What It Means" column, and then have students place each card where they think it belongs in the "Word" column. Tell them that at this point, it's OK to make a guess if they don't have much prior experience with the word. They will be able to find out if their prediction about each word's meaning is correct by reading the book *Matter*. During the read-aloud, they will be able to move their cards to the correct spot on the New Vocabulary List.

Matter Read-Aloud

Using Features of Nonfiction

Connecting to the Common Core
Reading: Informational Text
Craft and Structure: 2.4, 2.5

Tell students you would like for them to signal (by touching one of their ears) when they hear a word on their vocabulary list as you read the book aloud. Introduce the author, Abbie Dunne, as you show students the cover of the book. Then have them identify the table of contents, title page, glossary, index, and back cover as you flip through the book. *Ask*

? Is this book fiction or nonfiction? (nonfiction)

? How do you know? (It has photographs, a table of contents, glossary, index, etc.)

Read the book aloud, stopping at each page containing one of the new vocabulary words. After reading the word in context, read the glossary definition for the word as well. (The definitions on the New Vocabulary List are a combination of the in-text definitions and the glossary definitions.)

Table 11.2. Sample Completed Table for Matter *Read-Aloud*

Word	What It Means	Examples from The Text	Examples from The Activity
1. *Matter*	Anything that has weight and takes up space	Bed, books, me	Everything
2. *Solid*	Matter that holds its size and shape	Rocks, ice cubes, metal	Salt, cornstarch, sand, baking soda
3. *Liquid*	Matter that is wet and takes the shape of its container	Milk, water, shampoo	Water, vinegar
4. *Gas*	Matter that has no shape and spreads out to fill a space	Air	?
5. *Dissolve*	To mix a substance into a liquid until you can no longer see it	Salt dissolves in water.	Salt and baking soda dissolve in water.

Have students move their cards (if necessary) to the correct places on the New Vocabulary List. Then have them write a few examples from the text for each word in the "Examples from the Text" column. Refer students to their Properties of Matter data sheet and write one or more examples for each word in the "Examples from the Activity" column. When you get to *gas*, students will likely not know what kind of gas is inside the bubbles they observed, so leave that space blank until after the *Matter* read-aloud. Repeat these steps for each word. Table 11.2 shows the answers.

Questioning

Connecting to the Common Core
Reading: Informational Text
KEY IDEAS AND DETAILS: 2.1

Ask

? How did the book say you could tell if the salt is still in the water after it dissolves? (You could taste the water. The water would taste salty.)

Explain that when something dissolves, it seems to disappear. You can no longer see it, but it is still there. For example, if you stir salt into water and it dissolves completely, you would no longer be able to see the salt. The solution of salt and water would taste salty, although good scientists don't taste their experiments! If you stir sand into water, it would not dissolve. You would still be able to see the sand.

Then *ask*

? What did you notice when you added the vinegar to the baking soda? (It bubbled.)

? What kind of matter do you think was inside the bubbles? (Answers will vary.)

Explain that bubbles are filled with gas. For example, when you blow a bubble with chewing gum, you are filling it with a gas (your breath). When you blow a bubble with a bubble wand, you are filling it with a gas, too. Also, when you see bubbles inside boiling water, those are filled with gas (water vapor, which is an invisible form of water). In the activity, students dripped vinegar onto baking soda and saw bubbles. Explain that when vinegar and baking soda are mixed together, they combine to form a new substance with new properties—a gas called carbon dioxide, or CO_2. This gas forms bubbles. However, if you could pop the bubbles, the invisible carbon dioxide gas inside would have no shape and would spread out into the room. Carbon dioxide is one of the gases that make up the air we breathe. Have students add carbon dioxide (or CO_2) as an example of a gas to the "Examples from the Activity" column of their New Vocabulary List. Finally, have students tape or glue the Vocabulary Cards to the proper spaces on the student page.

elaborate

Mystery Mixtures

Tell students that now that they have made observations of the properties of each substance, they can use that information to figure out the contents of Mystery Mixture A and Mystery Mixture B! In other words, they can apply what they learned about the properties of the four different household substances to solve the mystery. They will be working with the same team they worked with for the Properties of Matter activity. Explain that they will need to refer to their Properties of Matter data sheet to compare the results of the tests on the known mixtures with those of the tests on these unknown mixtures. Then pass out a Mystery Mixtures data sheet student page, a Mystery Mixtures testing mat student page, a pair of goggles, and a hand lens to each student. Review the safety guidelines for observing and testing the mystery mixtures in this activity. Tell students to use their best powers of observation!

SAFETY

- Wear your safety goggles at all times.
- Do not taste or sniff any of the mixtures.
- Do not pour any of the mixtures or liquids out of the containers. Use only the spoon or eyedropper that is assigned to each substance to avoid contamination.
- You will be touching the mixtures with your fingers. Do not put your fingers near your face after touching them. When the activity is over, you must wash your hands with soap and water.
- You will be using a hand lens to observe the mixtures. Do not let the hand lens touch the mixture. Put your eye as close to the lens as possible, and lean over the cup until the mixture comes into focus. Try closing the eye that is not close to the lens to get a better view.

MYSTERY MIXTURES

Table 11.3. Sample Completed Data Table for Mystery Mixtures

Test	Mystery Mixture A	Mystery Mixture B
1. Texture (feel)	Rough, gritty, and slippery	Rough, gritty, and smooth
2. Crystals? (yes/no)	Yes (some)	Yes (some)
3. What happens with water?	Water turns milky, but crystals/grains remain	Water is a little cloudy, but crystals dissolve
4. What happens with vinegar?	Nothing	Bubbles

Have one person from each team go to the materials table and carefully carry a tray of materials back to their team. Tell students to wait until every team has its materials, and then you will go over the testing procedure together. Explain that their task is to be like Ada Twist, scientist, and ask questions and make observations to solve a science mystery! Like Ada, they will also be following safety guidelines. The first thing students should do is place a small plastic bath cup on each circle of their testing mat, which has circles labeled Mystery Mixture A and Mystery Mixture B. They should also place a craft stick next to each cup to use for stirring.

Next, review the procedure for testing the mystery mixtures by reading the directions at the top of the Mystery Mixtures data sheet together. Then have students begin testing the mixtures as they did in the Properties of Matter activity. A sample completed data sheet is shown in Table 11.3 (observations may vary).

Turn and Talk

After students have finished testing both mystery mixtures, have them turn and talk with a partner to compare the results and observations of their tests. Be sure they refer to their Properties of Matter data sheets to come up with logical conclusions that are based on the properties of the known substances. Explain that good scientists always provide *evidence* when they make a claim. So, on their student page, they need to write more than just what they think

the two substances in the mixture are. They must provide evidence to support their conclusions. Then have students work together to fill out the conclusions and evidence statements at the bottom of the page. The best answers are as follows:

I think Mixture A contains cornstarch and sand because it turned milky, the crystals or grains didn't dissolve, and it did not bubble.

I think Mixture B contains baking soda and salt because both substances dissolved in water and it bubbled.

> **SEP: Engaging in Argument from Evidence**
> Construct an argument with evidence to support a claim.

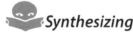

Synthesizing

Ask

? Which mystery mixture turned milky when mixed with water? (Mystery Mixture A)

? What do you think it must contain? (cornstarch)

? What is your evidence? (We observed the same thing happen with cornstarch in the Properties of Matter activity.)

? Which mixture had crystals that did not dissolve in water? (Mystery Mixture A)

? What do you think it must contain? (sand)

? What is your evidence? (We observed the same thing happen with sand in the Properties of Matter activity.)

? Which mixture had crystals that dissolved in water? (Mystery Mixture B)

? What do you think it must contain? (salt)

? What is your evidence? (We observed the same thing happen with salt in the Properties of Matter activity.)

? Which mixture bubbled when mixed with vinegar? (Mystery Mixture B)

? What do you think it must contain? (baking soda)

? What is your evidence? (We observed the same thing happen with baking soda in the Properties of Matter activity.)

? What are you still wondering? (Answers will vary.)

> **CCC: Patterns**
> Patterns in the natural world can be observed, used to escribe phenomena, and used as evidence.

Congratulate students on being great scientists and using their observations, knowledge, and skills to solve a mystery, just like Ada Twist did!

evaluate

Matter Quiz

You may want to review the three states of matter by showing the short (1:39 min.) PBS LearningMedia video called "What's the Matter?" (see the "Website" section), by having students quiz one another on vocabulary using their New Vocabulary List pages,

or by doing both. Then pass out the Matter Quiz student page. The answers are as follows:

1. Solid
2. Gas
3. Liquid
4. Liquid
5. Solid
6. C
7. D
8. E
9. B
10. A

Matter Mystery

As an additional evaluation activity, pass out the Matter Mystery student page, and have students work alone or with a partner to solve the mystery. The answers are as follows:

1. Cornstarch
2. Cornstarch does not have crystals. It turns water milky and does not bubble with vinegar.

Bonus: Students should draw a scientist on the back of their paper. Characteristics of a great scientist might include the following:

- Asks questions that lead to more questions
- Makes careful observations
- Uses tools
- Works safely
- Uses evidence to make claims
- Perseveres
- Communicates well

STEM Everywhere

Give students the STEM Everywhere student page as a way to involve their families and extend their learning. They can do the activity with an adult helper and share their results with the class. If students do not have access to these materials or the internet at home, you may choose to send the materials home or have students complete this activity at school.

Opportunities for Differentiated Instruction

This box lists questions and challenges related to the lesson that students may select to research, investigate, or innovate. Students may also use the questions as examples to help them generate their own questions. These questions can help you move your students from the teacher-directed investigation to engaging in the science and engineering practices in a more student-directed format.

Extra Support

For students who are struggling to meet the lesson objectives, provide a question and guide them in the process of collecting research or helping them design procedures or solutions.

Extensions

For students with high interest or who have already met the lesson objectives, have them choose a question (or pose their own question), conduct their own research, and design their own procedures or solutions.

After selecting one of the questions in the box or formulating their own question, students can individually or collaboratively make predictions, design investigations or surveys to test their predictions, collect evidence, devise explanations, design solutions, or examine related resources. They can communicate their findings through a science notebook, at a poster session or gallery walk, or by producing a media project.

Research

Have students brainstorm researchable questions:

? What kinds of scientists study matter?

? What kind of gas is in soda (or pop)?

? How do smells travel through the air?

Investigate

Have students brainstorm testable questions to be solved through science or math:

? Does salt dissolve faster in warm water or cold water?

? What combination of cornstarch and water makes the best oobleck?

? Survey your friends: If you could be a scientist, what kind would you be? Graph the results, then analyze your graph. What can you conclude?

Innovate

Have students brainstorm problems to be solved through engineering:

? Can you design a toy rocket that works with vinegar and baking soda?

? Can you build a model of a volcano that uses vinegar and baking soda to represent lava?

? Can you design a way to prove that air is matter (has weight and takes up space)?

Website

 "What's the Matter?" (video)
*https://ca.pbslearningmedia.org/
resource/evscps.sci.phys.matter/
whats-the-matter*

More Books to Read

Beaty, A. 2013. *Rosie Revere, engineer*. New York: Abrams.
Summary: Young Rosie dreams of being an engineer. Alone in her room at night, she constructs great inventions from odds and ends. Afraid of failure, Rosie hides her creations under her bed until a fateful visit from her great-great-aunt Rose, who shows her that a first flop isn't something to fear—it's something to celebrate.

Diehn, A. 2018. *Matter: Physical science for kids*. White River Junction, VT: Nomad Press.
Summary: From the Picture Book Science series, this book provides a simple definition of *matter*, information on the states of matter, and examples of things that are not matter.

Fries-Gaither, J. 2016. *Notable notebooks: Scientists and their writings*. Arlington, VA: NSTA Press.
Summary: Take a trip through time to discover the value of a special place to jot your thoughts, whether you're a famous scientist or a student. Engaging illustrations, photos, and lively rhyme bring to life the many ways in which scientists from Galileo to Jane Goodall have used a science notebook.

Mason, A. 2005. *Move it! Motion, forces and you*. Tonawanda, NY: Kids Can Press.
Summary: This lively and easy-to-understand book explores materials—their color, shape, texture, size, mass, magnetism, and more.

Zoehfeld, K. 2015. *What is the world made of?: All about solids, liquids, and gases*. New York: HarperCollins.
Summary: Part of the Let's-Read-and-Find-Out Science series, this book uses simple text and playful illustrations to explain the differences among the states of matter and includes a "Find Out More" section with experiments designed to encourage further exploration.

Name: _____

Properties of Matter

You can be like a scientist and explore the properties of matter!

Test 1: Rub the substance between your fingers. How does it feel? Record the texture.

Test 2: Use a hand lens to look more closely at the substance. Can you see any crystals? Write yes or no.

Test 3: Use an eyedropper to add three full droppers of water to the substance. Stir with a stick for 30 sec. What happens?

Test 4: Use an eyedropper to add 10 drops of vinegar to the substance and water mixture. Stir with a stick for 30 sec. What happens?

Test	Salt	Cornstarch	Sand	Baking Soda
1. Texture (feel)				
2. Crystals? (yes/no)				
3. What happens with water?				
4. What happens with vinegar?				

Properties of Matter

You can be like a scientist and explore the properties of matter!

Name: _____

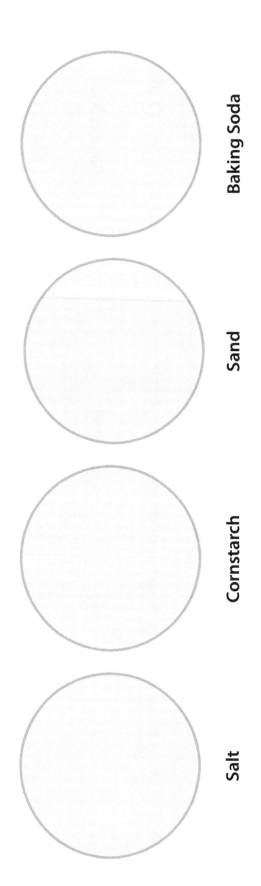

Salt Cornstarch Sand Baking Soda

Vocabulary Cards

Gas	Solid	Dissolve	Matter	Liquid

Gas	Solid	Dissolve	Matter	Liquid

Gas	Solid	Dissolve	Matter	Liquid

Gas	Solid	Dissolve	Matter	Liquid

Gas	Solid	Dissolve	Matter	Liquid

Gas	Solid	Dissolve	Matter	Liquid

Name: _____

New Vocabulary List

Word	What It Means	Examples From the Text	Examples From the Activity
1.	Anything that has weight and takes up space		
2.	Matter that holds its size and shape		
3.	Matter that is wet and takes the shape of its container		
4.	Matter that has no shape and spreads out to fill a space		
5.	To mix a substance into a liquid until you can no longer see it		

National Science Teaching Association

Name: _____

Mystery Mixtures

You can be like a scientist and use your observations to solve a mystery!

Test 1: Rub the mystery mixture between your fingers. How does it feel? Record the texture.

Test 2: Use a hand lens to look more closely at the mystery mixture. Can you see any crystals? Write yes or no.

Test 3: Use an eyedropper to add three full droppers of water to the mystery mixture. Stir with a stick for 30 sec. What happens?

Test 4: Use an eyedropper to add 10 drops of vinegar to the mystery mixture and water. Stir with a stick for 30 sec. What happens?

Test	Mixture A	Mixture B
1. Texture (feel)		
2. Crystals? (yes/no)		
3. What happens with water?		
4. What happens with vinegar?		

I think Mixture A contains _____ and _____ because _____ .

I think Mixture B contains _____ and _____ because _____ .

Mystery Mixtures

You can be like a scientist and use your observations to solve a mystery!

Mystery Mixture A

Mystery Mixture B

Name: _____

Matter Quiz

Write *solid*, *liquid*, or *gas* on the lines below.

| Block | Air | Water |

1. _____ 2. _____ 3. _____

Milk   Shoe

4. _____   5. _____

Write the letter of the definition next to each word.

6. ___ Matter   A. To mix a substance into a liquid until you can no longer see it

7. ___ Solid   B. Matter that has no shape and spreads out to fill a space

8. ___ Liquid   C. Anything that has weight and takes up space

9. ___ Gas   D. Matter that holds its shape

10. ___ Dissolve E. Matter that is wet and takes the shape of its container

Name: _____

Matter Mystery

Ada's teacher is filling jars with salt, cornstarch, sand, and baking soda, but she forgets to put labels on the jars! She asks Ada to help her identify what's inside one of the jars. Ada looks at the mystery substance with a hand lens and does not see any crystals. She takes a small sample of the substance and mixes it with water. The water turns a milky color. Then she takes another sample, places 10 drops of vinegar in it, and observes that nothing happens. Use the chart below to help Ada solve the mystery!

Test	Salt	Cornstarch	Sand	Baking Soda
1. Texture (feel)	Rough and gritty	Slippery	Rough and gritty	Smooth
2. Crystals? (yes/no)	Yes	No	Yes	No
3. What happens with water?	Salt disappears, and water looks almost clear	Water turns milky	Sand does not disappear, and water looks cloudy	Baking soda disappears, and water looks cloudy
4. What happens with vinegar?	Nothing	Nothing	Nothing	Bubbles

1. Which substance do you think it is? _____

2. What is your evidence? _____

_____

_____

_____

Bonus: Draw a picture of a scientist on the back of this page. Then write some characteristics of a great scientist around your picture!

STEM Everywhere

Dear Families,

At school, we have been learning about properties of matter. We used our observations of different kinds of matter to solve a mystery! To find out more, ask your learner questions such as:

- What did you learn?
- What was your favorite part of the lesson?
- What are you still wondering?

At home, you can watch a short video together about how to make oobleck, which is a substance that acts like both a solid and a liquid.

 Search for "How to Make Magic Mud Oobleck" on YouTube to find the video at *www.youtube.com/watch?v=WHLCYfwa36g.*

Make your own oobleck by mixing 1 cup of water, 5 drops of food coloring, and 2 cups of cornstarch in a foil pie pan. Next, you can do a simple experiment by observing what will happen if you drop a marble from a distance of 2 feet into the pan of oobleck.

What happens when a marble is dropped into oobleck? Predict, then try it!

_____

_____

How is oobleck like a solid?

_____

_____

How is oobleck like a liquid?

_____

_____

Build It!

Description

Children love to build. In this lesson, they use their creativity to build structures out of everyday materials. Next, they are introduced to a variety of iconic buildings and learn about the architects who designed them. Finally, students design and build architectural models of some of these famous structures.

Alignment with the *Next Generation Science Standards*

Performance Expectation

2-PS1-3: Make observations to construct an evidence-based account of how an object made of a small set of pieces can be disassembled and made into a new object.

Science and Engineering Practice	Disciplinary Core Idea	Crosscutting Concept
Developing and Using Models Develop a simple model based on evidence to represent a proposed object or tool.	**PS1.A: Structure and Properties of Matter** A great variety of objects can be built up from a small set of pieces.	**Scale, Proportion, and Quantity** Relative scales allow objects and events to be compared and described (e.g., bigger and smaller, hotter and colder, faster and slower).

Note: The activities in this lesson will help students move toward the performance expectation listed, which is the goal after multiple activities. However, the activities will not by themselves be sufficient to reach the performance expectation.

Featured Picture Books

TITLE: **Iggy Peck, Architect**
AUTHOR: **Andrea Beaty**
ILLUSTRATOR: **David Roberts**
PUBLISHER: **Abrams Books for Young Readers**
YEAR: **2007**
GENRE: **Story**
SUMMARY: *Iggy Peck spends every waking hour building things, until second grade, when his teacher forbids it. He finally wins her over by using his skills to save the day on his class field trip.*

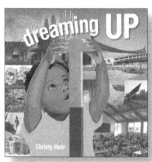

TITLE: **Dreaming Up: A Celebration of Building**
AUTHOR: **Christy Hale**
ILLUSTRATOR: **Christy Hale**
PUBLISHER: **Lee & Low Books**
YEAR: **2012**
GENRE: **Non-Narrative Information**
SUMMARY: *This book is a unique celebration of children's playtime explorations and the surprising ways childhood experiences find expression in the dreams and works of innovative architects. Each spread features illustrations of children building various structures as they play, paired with a photograph of an actual building that uses the same basic ideas and principles. Information on each featured building and its architect is contained in the end matter.*

Time Needed

This lesson will take several class periods. Suggested scheduling is as follows:

Session 1: **Engage** with *Iggy Peck, Architect* Read-Aloud and **Explore** with Free Build

Session 2: **Explain** with *Dreaming Up* Read-Aloud and Famous Buildings and Structures Video

Session 3: **Elaborate** with Iggy's Models and Architecture Journal

Session 4 and beyond: **Evaluate** with Build It! and Architecture Expo

Materials

For Free Build (per group of 3–6 students)

Each group receives a different set of building materials modeled after the book *Dreaming Up*, such as

- **Group 1:** Small paper or plastic cups and masking tape
- **Group 2:** Empty tissue or other small boxes and masking tape
- **Group 3:** Playing cards and painter's tape
- **Group 4:** Toothpicks and packing peanuts
- **Group 5:** Cardboard tubes, brown paper grocery or lunch bags, masking tape, and scissors
- **Group 6:** Craft sticks and masking tape

For Iggy's Models

- Images of the Gateway Arch, Golden Gate Bridge, Great Sphinx of Giza, Hōryū-ji temple, Leaning Tower of Pisa, and Neuschwanstein Castle

For Build It!

- Bins of the supplies used in the Free Build activity
- Pencils, crayons, and markers

SAFETY

- Use caution with scissors to avoid puncturing skin or eyes.
- Use eye protection when working with craft sticks.

Student Pages

- Architecture Journal
- STEM Everywhere

Background for Teachers

In this lesson, students are introduced to the fascinating world of architecture, a discipline that combines science, engineering, and art in the design of buildings. A Roman architect and engineer named Vitruvius, who lived in the first century BC, asserted that there were three principles of good architecture:

- **Durability**: Structures should be made of the right materials to stand up, be safe, and remain in good condition.
- **Utility**: Structures should be useful and function well for the people using them.
- **Beauty**: Structures should delight people and raise their spirits.

Although these principles originated thousands of years ago, they still hold true today. To achieve these goals, architects plan the overall appearance of buildings, while ensuring that they are safe, functional, and economical. Sketches, plans, elevation drawings, and architectural models are important tools in communicating an architect's ideas.

The *Framework* suggests that students in grades K–12 are engaged in the science and engineering practice (SEP) of developing and using models. In the early grades, these models progress from making diagrams and replicas to developing models to represent a new object or tool. This lesson uses models in the context of architecture. The lesson begins with a "free build" activity in which students work with building materials, such as cups, craft sticks, boxes, and cardboard tubes to create something new. Young children need time to tinker with a variety of materials to develop their understanding of how small pieces can be assembled into objects and structures and how objects and structures can be disassembled into smaller pieces.

Next, students are exposed to some iconic buildings from a range of historical periods, learn about famous architects and their inspirations, and reuse some of the materials they worked with during the explore phase to create sketches and design architectural models of buildings. Building models encourages children to test spatial relationships and mentally rotate objects, which can help them to develop better spatial abilities. It is important to note that models are not always physical. They can also be mental or conceptual. "Modeling can begin in the earliest grades, with students' models progressing from concrete 'pictures' and/or physical scale models to more abstract representations of relevant relationships in later grades, such as a diagram representing forces on a particular object or system" (Willard, 2015 p. 7). An architectural model is a type of scale model—a physical representation of a structure—that

is used to study aspects of architectural design or to communicate design ideas. Architects construct these models using a variety of materials, including blocks, paper, and wood, just as students do in the elaborate phase of the lesson. This activity provides opportunities for students to create drawings and physical models just as real architects do.

The crosscutting concept (CCC) of structure and function is highlighted throughout the lesson as students learn how the shape and stability of a structure, such as a building, bridge, or skyscraper, is related to its function.

Learning Progressions

Below are the disciplinary core idea (DCI) grade band endpoints for grades K–2 and 3–5. These are provided to show how student understanding of the DCIs in this lesson will progress in future grade levels.

DCI	Grades K–2	Grades 3–5
PS1.A: Matter and Its Interactions	• A great variety of objects can be built up from a small set of pieces.	• Measurements of a variety of properties can be used to identify materials.

Source: Willard, T., ed. 2015. *The NSTA quick-reference guide to the* NGSS: *Elementary school.* Arlington, VA: NSTA Press.

engage

Iggy Peck, Architect Read-Aloud

 **Inferring**

Show students the cover of *Iggy Peck, Architect* and introduce the author, Andrea Beaty, and the illustrator, David Roberts. *Ask*

? From looking at the cover and title, what do you think this book is about? (Answers will vary.)

? What do you think an architect does? (Students may know that architects are involved in designing buildings.)

Connecting to the Common Core
Reading: Literature
KEY IDEAS AND DETAILS: 2.1

 **Questioning**

Read the book aloud. Then *ask*

? What kinds of materials did Iggy Peck use to build the structures in the book? (chalk, pancakes, apples, dirt, etc.)

? How did Iggy's teacher feel about his passion for building? (She did not like it.) What evidence from the text makes you think that? (She would not allow him to build at school.)

? What happened to his teacher that made her dislike architecture? (She got lost on an architect's tour and was stuck in an elevator with a French circus troupe.)

? How did Iggy finally win his teacher over? (He used his building expertise to build a bridge to rescue the class.)

Making Connections: Text to Self

Ask

? Do you like to build things like the character Iggy Peck? (Answers will vary.)

? What materials have you used to build something? (Have students share with a partner.)

Tell students that the author, Andrea Beaty, was inspired to write this book because her son had a passion for building when he was young. He would build with anything he could get his hands on. He built towers out of soup cans from their pantry and houses out of jelly packets at restaurants.

explore

Free Build

Tell students that they are going to have the opportunity to be like Iggy Peck and use their imaginations and some everyday materials to create a structure. Divide students into groups of three to six, and explain that each group will receive different supplies for building. Each student will build his or her own structure, but the group will share the supplies. Afterward, students will have a chance to share their structures. Give each group a container with the supplies listed in the "Materials" section (p. 192). Set a time limit and let them build!

> **CCC: Scale, Proportion, and Quantity**
> Relative scales allow objects to be compared and described (e.g., bigger and smaller).

When students are finished, have them clean up their supplies and display their structures on their tables or desks. Invite students within each group to compare their structures. Pose the follow-

FREE BUILD

ing questions to move students' thinking toward the idea that although they all had the same set of pieces to work with, all of their structures were very different. *Ask*

? In your group, what shapes were the building materials?

? What shapes could you put together to make other shapes?

? How are your group's structures the same?

? How are they different?

? Which structure in your group is the tallest? Widest?

? Which uses the most materials?

? Which uses the least materials?

Point out that there was no right or wrong way to build these structures. Each person used their imagination and had a different vision for how to build the structures. A great variety of objects can be built from a small set of pieces.

You may want to set up an area to display each structure or take photographs of each one and hang them in the classroom to create a class display. You can refer to this display during the activities in the explain phase of the lesson.

explain

Dreaming Up Read-Aloud

Determining Importance

Show students the cover of *Dreaming Up: A Celebration of Building* and introduce Christy Hale, the author and illustrator of this book. Tell students that the supplies that were used in the free build activity were all inspired by this book. As you read the book aloud, have students signal (touch their noses) when you come to a two-page spread where the illustration on the left-hand page shows the supplies they used to build their structures. Compare the structures in the illustrations with the structures students made. Explain that these different structures are examples of how a great variety of objects can be made from a small set of pieces.

> Connecting to the Common Core
> **Mathematics**
> KEY IDEAS AND DETAILS: 2.7

Then compare each illustrated structure with the photograph of the actual building on the right-hand page. Have students notice similarities in lines and shapes among the structures the children built and the lines and shapes found in the actual buildings. Some examples are as follows:

COMPARING STRUCTURES

- Pages 3–4: The cups have a nearly cylindrical shape similar to the Petronas Towers.
- Pages 7–8: The box has a rectangular prism shape similar to the Box House.
- Pages 17–18: The playing cards are thin and straight, which is similar to the linear shapes on the Vitra Fire Station.
- Pages 19–20: The toothpicks and gumdrops form small triangles similar to the triangles that make up the large sphere of the Montreal Biosphere.
- Pages 25–26: The paper towel tubes are cylinders similar to the cylinders supporting the roofs and walls of the Paper Tube School.
- Pages 27–28: The shape of the craft sticks is similar to the wooden planks that make up the cylinder shape of Sclera Pavilion.

Next, *ask*

? Do you notice any patterns in this book? (Students may notice that on the left-hand side of each page is an illustration of kids building, and on the right-hand side is a photograph of an actual building. They may also notice that the way the text is arranged on the page is similar to the structures pictured.)

As an example, share pages 13–14, which show children building a sandcastle on the left-hand page and a photograph of La Sagrada Família on the right-hand page. Explain to students that Hale's poem compares children's building experiences (page 13) to real buildings (page 14).

**Synthesizing**

Then *ask*

? Why do you think the author of this book compared this famous building, La Sagrada Família, to a sandcastle? (It is the same color as sand and the same shape.)

? Why do you think the author and illustrator of this book, Christy Hale, decided to create the book this way? (Answers will vary.)

National Science Teaching Association

Features of Nonfiction

Connecting to the Common Core
Reading: Informational Text
CRAFT AND STRUCTURE: 2.5

Model how to find information about the author by looking at the back flap of the book jacket. Read the section that explains Hale's vision for this book:

Her inspiration for Dreaming Up *dates back to her first encounter with Barcelona's La Sagrada Família. "I'm sure I made the sandcastle connection way back then," says Hale. From then on, "it became a fun challenge to think of the many ways kids build, and then buildings that correspond to their building play."*

Explain that this cathedral, La Sagrada Família, was Hale's first inspiration for this book. After seeing how it resembled a child's sandcastle, she started to notice how other structures resembled things that children build.

Connecting to the Common Core
Reading: Informational Text
CRAFT AND STRUCTURE: 2.7

Questioning

Explain that the very different buildings featured in this book were designed by different architects. Show students the last four pages that discuss the architects for each building. Read a few of the sections aloud. You may want to begin with Cesar Pelli and the Petronas Towers. *Ask*

? Why do you think Cesar Pelli used this shape (tapered like graduated cups) for the Petronas

Towers? (Being wider at the bottom gives them more stability so they can reach higher.)

? Why do you think Pelli used concrete, steel, and glass to make the Petronas Towers? (Concrete and steel are strong; glass is lighter and lets light in.)

Allow students to suggest some other architects for you to read aloud about. After each one, go back to the page that shows the building that architect designed and *ask*

? Why do you think this architect used this shape for this structure? (Answers will vary but should reflect that the shape is related to the building's purpose or function.)

? What materials did the architect use on the building in the book? Why do you think they used those materials? (Answers will vary but should include that the materials are related to the stability and durability of the building as well as the overall shape.)

After reading about several architects, *ask*

? How are these architects different? (Some are men and some are women. They are different ethnicities, ages, and backgrounds. They have different inspirations. They designed with different materials and for different purposes.)

? What do all of these architects have in common? (They liked to build when they were young. They are creative.)

Synthesizing
Ask

? After reading both *Iggy Peck, Architect* and *Dreaming Up*, how have your ideas changed about what an architect does?

Famous Buildings and Structures Video

Making Connections: Text to Text

Tell students that you have a video to show them called "100 Most Famous Buildings/Structures of All Time" (see "Websites"). Explain that these particular buildings were chosen by the video's creator and that other people might have other ideas about the world's most famous buildings. Tell them that the video is set to music from the era, or historical time period, of each set of buildings. As you watch, have students signal when they see a building they recognize. It could be a building from *Dreaming Up*, a building they have visited, or a building they have seen in other books or videos. (Many students will likely recognize the Taj Mahal, Leaning Tower of Pisa, Eiffel Tower, and Gateway Arch.) After viewing, *ask*

? What buildings did you recognize from the book *Dreaming Up*? (Fallingwater, Habitat 67, Petronas Towers, Guggenheim Museum, and La Sagrada Família are all pictured.)

? What information was given for each building shown? (name, architect, and year built)

? What building materials did you recognize in the video? (stone, metal, concrete, etc.)

? Do you think those materials were the right choices for durability? (Yes, because all of these buildings are still standing.)

? Do all of the buildings look the same? (no)

? Why do you think the buildings look different? (They serve different purposes and were designed by different architects.)

? What are some of the uses for the different buildings in the video? (homes, churches, monuments, office buildings, etc.)

? Which buildings did you like the most? (Answers will vary.)

? Do you think that all of the buildings are beautiful? (Answers will vary.)

Explain that "beauty is in the eye of the beholder." Some people may criticize an architect's building, whereas other people may think the same building is very beautiful!

elaborate

Iggy's Models

Connecting to the Common Core
Reading: Informational Text
CRAFT AND STRUCTURE: 2.1

Revisit the book *Iggy Peck, Architect* and flip through the illustrations. Point out to students that Iggy is not just building random things in the book. He is actually creating models of famous buildings (some of which were in the video they just watched!). So, Iggy not only likes to build but also likes to study architecture.

Search online for photographs of famous buildings referenced in the book and have students compare Iggy's model with the actual building:

- Page 4: He uses diapers to create a model of the Leaning Tower of Pisa.
- Page 7: He uses dirt clods to make a model of the Great Sphinx of Giza.
- Pages 8–9: He uses modeling clay and pencils to make a model of Hōryū-ji temple.
- Pages 10–11: He uses pancakes and pie to make a model of the Gateway Arch.
- Page 18: He uses chalk to build a model of Neuschwanstein Castle.
- Pages 28–29: The bridge he builds is modeled after the Golden Gate Bridge.

Architecture Journal

Connecting to the Common Core
Writing
TEXT TYPES AND PURPOSES: 2.2

Writing

Give each student a copy of the Architecture Journal student pages. Tell students that they are going to have another opportunity to build something. However, unlike the first time, when their challenge was just to build something creative out of the materials they were given, this time they are going to build a model of an actual building. They will complete all the pages in the journal first, and then they will design and build a model of the building they chose.

> **SEP: Developing and Using Models**
> Develop a simple model based on evidence to represent a proposed object.

Architecture Journal Pages:

- Cover: Students write their name and decorate the journal cover any way they like.

- Pages 1–2: Students glue or tape pictures of some buildings they like. They can cut the pictures out of magazines or print them from images found online (search "famous buildings").

- Page 3: Students select the building they want to model and tape or glue a photo here. They also label the shapes they recognize in the building.

- Page 4: Students research some information about the building: the name, architect, location, and the materials used in the building.

- Page 5: Students think carefully about which materials would be best to represent their

building and then circle the materials they plan to use to make their model.

- Page 6: Students sketch a plan of how they will use those materials to make a model of the building they chose.

evaluate

Build It!

As students are working on their journals, review their sketches and provide feedback on their choice of materials for their models. *Ask*

? Why did you choose that building?

? Why did you choose those materials?

Next, they can build their model! Provide all of the building supplies from the Free Build activity (explore phase) in bins for students to access as they build. Encourage students to look closely at the photograph of their building. They may also use pencils, crayons, and markers to add details to their models.

Architecture Expo

Tell students that they are going to get to share their models with a visiting class at an architecture expo. Have students display their models on their desks. They should have their Architecture Journal open to pages 3–4 so that visitors can see a photograph of the building, its name, the architect, location, and materials used to build it. Have students do a gallery walk through the classroom, using sticky notes to post suggestions, questions, and positive feedback on the desks next to the models. Writing on sticky notes encourages interaction, and the comments provide immediate feedback for the "exhibitors."

A few guidelines for a gallery walk are as follows:

- All necessary information about the model should be provided in the display (pages 3–4 of the Architecture Journal) because students will not be giving an oral presentation.

- Like a visit to an art gallery, the gallery walk should be done quietly. Students should be respectful of the displays. You may even want to play soft, classical music to set the tone.

STEM Everywhere

Give students the STEM Everywhere student page as a way to involve their families and extend their learning. They can do the activity with an adult helper and share their results with the class. If students do not have access the internet at home, you may choose to have them complete this activity at school.

Opportunities for Differentiated Instruction

This box lists questions and challenges related to the lesson that students may select to research, investigate, or innovate. Students may also use the questions as examples to help them generate their own questions. These questions can help you move your students from the teacher-directed investigation to engaging in the science and engineering practices in a more student-directed format.

Extra Support

For students who are struggling to meet the lesson objectives, provide a question and guide them in the process of collecting research or helping them design procedures or solutions.

Extensions

For students with high interest or who have already met the lesson objectives, have them choose a question (or pose their own question), conduct their own research, and design their own procedures or solutions.

After selecting one of the questions in the box or formulating their own question, students can individually or collaboratively make predictions, design investigations or surveys to test their predictions, collect evidence, devise explanations, design solutions, or examine related resources. They can communicate their findings through a science notebook, at a poster session or gallery walk, or by producing a media project.

Research

Have students brainstorm researchable questions:

? What are the tallest buildings in the world, and who designed them?

? Who designed your school, and what year was it built?

? What materials were used to build your school, and why did the builder choose those materials?

Continued

Opportunities for Differentiated Instruction (continued)

Investigate

Have students brainstorm testable questions to be solved through science or math:

? What materials can hold the most weight without breaking: rubber bands, paper strips, or toothpicks?

? What materials could be used to make a model of a geodesic dome?

? Which shape can support the most weight: a triangular prism, a rectangular prism, or a cylinder?

Innovate

Have students brainstorm problems to be solved through engineering:

? What structure could you design for your school playground?

? What structure could you design to represent your school spirit?

? What would your dream house look like? What features would it have and what materials would you use?

Websites

 "100 Most Famous Buildings/Structures of All Time"(video)
www.youtube.com/watch?v=dA3Ak-FLk_A

 PBS: Style in Architecture (video)
www.pbs.org/video/artquest-style-architecture

More Books to Read

Ames, L. 2013. *Draw 50 buildings and other structures: The step-by-step way to draw castles and cathedrals, skyscrapers and bridges, and so much more …* New York: Watson-Guptill.
Summary: This step-by-step book filled with black-and-white line drawings reduces famous buildings such as the Taj Mahal and the Eiffel Tower (and other buildings such as igloos and castles) to basic lines and shapes. It then shows young artists how to put the shapes together and add details to represent each building.

Guarnaccia, S. 2010. *The three little pigs: An architectural tale*. New York: Abrams Books for Young Readers.
Summary: In this quirky retelling of the three little pigs, the pigs and their homes are nods to three famous architects—Frank Gehry, Philip Johnson, and Frank Lloyd Wright—and their signature homes. Each house is filled with clever details, including furnishing by the architects and their contemporaries. Of course, not all the houses are going to protect the pigs from the wolf's huffing and puffing. The wolf, and readers, are in for a clever surprise ending.

Harvey, J. 2017. *Maya Lin: Artist-architect of light and lines*. New York: Henry Holt and Company.
Summary: Elegant, simple writing paired with Dow Phumiruk's crisp, clean-lined illustrations tell the story of the inspiring American artist and architect who designed the Vietnam Veterans Memorial.

Hayden, K. 2003. *Amazing buildings*. New York: DK Children.
Summary: Simple text and vivid photographs depict how some of the world's most famous buildings were made.

Lyons, K. 2020. *Dream builder: The story of architect Phillip Freelon*. New York: Lee & Low Books.
Summary: This picture book biography celebrates a contemporary STEAM role model, an architect who overcame early struggles with reading to become a designer of schools, libraries, and museums that honor Black heritage and culture.

Ritchie, S. 2011. *Look at that building!: A first book of structures*. Tonawanda, NY: Kids Can Press.
Summary: Come along as the five friends from *Follow That Map!* start a whole new adventure. Max the dog needs a new doghouse to live in, so the gang is on a quest to find out all it can about buildings and how they are constructed.

Roeder, A. 2011. *13 buildings children should know*. New York: Prestel Verlag.
Summary: From the Great Pyramid of Giza to the Beijing National Stadium, this book presents 13 famous buildings from around the world. It includes information about the architect, location, materials, and special features of each building.

Stevenson, R. L. 2005. *Block city*. New York: Simon & Schuster Books for Young Readers.
Summary: This illustrated version of Robert Louis Stevenson's classic poem also includes folk songs, building projects, and math activities.

Van Dusen, C. 2019. *If I built a school*. New York: Dial Books
Summary: Chris Van Dusen's trademark rhymes and imaginative illustrations describe young Jack's dream school, including hover desks, skydiving wind tunnels, and a trampoline basketball court.

Winter, J. 2017. *The world is not a rectangle: A portrait of architect Zaha Hadid*. San Diego, CA: Beach Lane Books.
Summary: This picture book biography of famed Iraqi architect Zaha Hadid, known for her unconventional building design, describes the obstacles she had to overcome as well as the tremendous success she enjoyed throughout her career.

Architecture Journal

Name: _____

- -

Buildings I Like

Tape or glue some photographs of buildings you like.

Sketch

What will your model look like if you build it using only those materials? Make a sketch.

Materials

Cups

Tubes

Playing Cards

Index cards

Toothpicks

Craft sticks

Packing peanuts

Paper bags

Boxes

Other (draw):

Photo

Tape or glue a photograph of the building you want to model. Label the shapes you see in the building.

Research

Record some details about the building.

Name of Building:

_____

Architect:

_____

Location:

_____

This building is used for:

_____

_____

This building is constructed of these materials:

_____

_____

STEM Everywhere

At school, we have been learning about **how architects use different shapes and materials in their designs and that the shape of a building relates to the purpose of the building**. To find out more, ask your learner questions such as:

- What did you learn?
- What was your favorite part of the lesson?
- What are you still wondering?

 At home, watch a short video titled "Artquest: Style In Architecture" exploring different styles of architecture. *www.pbs.org/video/ artquest-style-architecture*

After you watch the video, look for the shapes that make up a building in your neighborhood.

Sketch of Building	Label the Shapes You Found
	Triangle Square Circle
	Arc Rectangle Cylinder

Seeds on the Move

Description

After observing the phenomenon of dandelion seeds being blown away by the wind, students investigate the various ways other plants disperse their seeds. They read about how wind and water help spread seeds, and they learn that some animals can even "plant" trees. Students take a "sock walk" in which they model one way that plants use animals to move their seeds around. Then they develop their own model that mimics an animal dispersing seeds.

Alignment with the *Next Generation Science Standards*

Performance Expectation

2-LS2-2: Develop a simple model that mimics the function of an animal in dispersing seeds or pollinating plants.

Science and Engineering Practice	Disciplinary Core Ideas	Crosscutting Concept
Developing and Using Models Develop a simple model based on evidence to represent a proposed object or tool.	**LS2.A: Interdependent Relationships in Ecosystems** Plants depend on animals for pollination or to move their seeds around. **ETS1.B: Developing Possible Solutions** Designs can be conveyed through sketches, drawings, or physical models. These representations are useful in communicating ideas for a problem's solutions to other people.	**Structure and Function** The shape and stability of structures of natural and designed objects are related to their functions.

Note: The activities in this lesson will help students move toward the performance expectations listed, which is the goal after multiple activities. However, the activities will not by themselves be sufficient to reach the performance expectations.

Featured Picture Books

TITLE: **_Flip, Float, Fly: Seeds on the Move_**
AUTHOR: **JoAnn Early Macken**
ILLUSTRATOR: **Pam Paparone**
PUBLISHER: **Holiday House**
YEAR: **2016**
GENRE: **Non-Narrative Information**
SUMMARY: _Colorful paintings and simple text explain many different methods of seed dispersal. The end matter includes information on plant parts and explains that not all seeds sprout._

TITLE: **_Who Will Plant a Tree?_**
AUTHOR: **Jerry Pallotta**
ILLUSTRATOR: **Tom Leonard**
PUBLISHER: **Sleeping Bear Press**
YEAR: **2010**
GENRE: **Narrative Information**
SUMMARY: _This engaging and informative book depicts the ways seeds are dispersed by various animals' behaviors and body structures._

Time Needed

This lesson will take several class periods. Suggested scheduling is as follows:

Session 1: **Engage** with Dandelion Observations and Wonderings

Session 2: **Explore** with Seed Observations and **Explain** with _Flip, Float, Fly_ Read-Aloud

Session 3: **Explain** with Seeds on the Move Lift-the-Flap Booklet

Session 4: **Elaborate** with _Who Will Plant a Tree?_ Read-Aloud and Sock Walk

Session 5: **Evaluate** with _Who Will Plant a Tree?_ Model

Materials

Note: Dandelions bloom in the spring and fall but most abundantly in the spring. If the season or location is not right for finding dandelions, you can use the videos and photographs in the "Websites" section.

For Dandelion Observations and Wonderings (per student)

• Dandelions (including buds, flowers, and seed heads)

For Seed Observations (per group of four students)

• Collection of seeds featured in the book _Flip, Float, Fly_, such as dandelion, maple, locust, coconut, acorn, burdock (burr), or whole fig cut in half to reveal the seeds (Optional: Use seed cards.)

• Hand lenses

For Sock Walk (per student)

- Adult-size white or light-colored sock
- Hand lens
- (Optional) Gallon-size zippered plastic bag

For Seeds on the Move Lift-the-Flap Booklet

- Crayons or colored pencils

For Who Will Plant a Tree? *Model*

- Tape
- Glue
- Scissors
- A variety of materials to make seed dispersal models, such as:
  - Play-Doh
  - Pipe cleaners
  - Construction paper
  - Paper towel tubes
  - Fur fabric
  - Craft feathers
  - Yarn
  - Velcro dots
  - Acrylic pom-poms

For STEM Everywhere (per student)

- Balloon
- Toilet paper tube
- About 1 tsp of small, lightweight seeds (such as grass seeds or wildflower seeds) in a zippered plastic bag

Note: The Elaborate phase of this lesson requires an outdoor area, preferably containing tall, unmown grass or weeds.

Student Pages

- Dandelion Observations and Wonderings
- Seed Cards
- What's on My Sock?
- Seeds on the Move
- Who Will Plant a Tree?
- STEM Everywhere

Background for Teachers

A Framework for K–12 Science Education suggests that by the end of grade 2, students should understand that plants have different parts that help them survive, grow, and produce more plants. One of those parts is a seed. Inside each seed is an embryo of a plant that, if conditions are right, will grow into a new plant. Multiple seeds often cannot survive if they are clustered too close to the parent plant because layers of leaves from the parent plant might block the light from reaching the seedlings, or too many roots would compete for water. Thus, it is key for the survival of many plant species that the seeds be moved to other places. The mechanism by which plant seeds are transported to new sites is called *seed dispersal*.

There are many ways that seeds are dispersed. For some seeds, like dandelion and maple seeds, wind simply blows them off the plant and carries them far away. These two seeds have parts that allow them to be easily carried by the wind. Dandelions have white seed heads containing fluffy seeds that catch in the wind and float easily. Maple seeds have winglike structures that allow them to sail on the wind and twist and twirl through the air. Sometimes water moves seeds from place to place. For example, ocean currents can carry coconuts to other pieces of land, where they sprout and grow into new coconut trees. Some plants depend on animals to move their seeds around. Many species of animals carry seeds from place to place without even knowing it. For instance, animals that eat plants will discard the seeds in their droppings. Seeds can also stick to animals' fur or feathers and fall off in another location. In these ways, new plants can grow far away from the tree or plant that produced the fruit.

In this lesson, students explore the crosscutting concept (CCC) of structure and function as they observe various seeds and identify structures that allow the seeds to be moved from place to place, like the hooks on a burdock seed that allow them to stick to fur and feathers, or the *pappus* (fluffy white tuft) of a dandelion seed that allows it to stay aloft. Students use the science and engineering practice (SEP) of developing and using models as they participate in a modeling activity in which they use a sock to mimic animal fur and take a "sock walk" to collect seeds. Next, they use various materials to develop their own model that mimics the function of an animal dispersing seeds. This lesson introduces seed dispersal as an interdependent relationship between plants and animals. This concept will serve as a foundation for the upper elementary grades when students will learn how multiple species are dependent on one another to maintain a healthy ecosystem. When students make their models, they engage in an engineering standard about how designs can be conveyed in drawings and models, which will be expanded upon in grades 3–5 to include researching and testing models.

Learning Progressions

Below are the disciplinary core idea (DCI) grade band endpoints for grades K–2 and 3–5. These are provided to show how student understanding of the DCIs in this lesson will progress in future grade levels.

DCIs	Grades K–2	Grades 3–5
LS2.A: Interdependent Relationships in Ecosystems	• Plants depend on animals for pollination or to move their seeds around.	• Organisms can survive only in environments in which their particular needs are met. A healthy ecosystem is one in which multiple species of different types are each able to meet their needs in a relatively stable web of life.

Continued

Learning Progressions (continued)

DCIs	Grades K–2	Grades 3–5
ETS1.B: Developing Possible Solutions	• Designs can be conveyed through sketches, drawings, or physical models. These representations are useful in communicating ideas for a problem's solutions to other people.	• Research on a problem should be carried out before beginning to design a solution. Testing a solution involves investigating how well it performs under a range of likely conditions

Source: Willard, T., ed. 2015. *The NSTA quick-reference guide to the* NGSS: *Elementary school.* Arlington, VA: NSTA Press.

engage

Dandelion Observations and Wonderings

Making Connections: Text-to-Self

Show students the cover of *Flip, Float, Fly*, which shows a girl blowing the seeds off a dandelion. *Ask*

? Have you ever seen these fluffy things?

? Where have you seen them? (growing in the ground)

? What do you think they are? (dandelions or dandelion seeds)

? Have you ever made a wish and blown on them? (Answers will vary.)

? What happened to the seeds? (They floated away.)

? What are you wondering about dandelion seeds? (Answers will vary.)

If the season and location are right, take students to an area where they can see dandelions growing, or bring some dandelions into the classroom for them to observe. It is best if you can bring in specimens at different stages of the dandelion life cycle, from the yellow flowers to the fluffy white seed heads. If you are not able to find dandelions, you can use videos and photographs for your observations (see "Websites").

Give students the Dandelion Observation and Wonderings student page. Whether they are observing actual dandelions, watching the videos, or both, have them complete the sketches and the Observations/Wonderings chart. Have students share some of their observations with a partner and then invite them to share with the class. Next, have them share their wonderings with a partner and then invite them to share with the class. *Ask*

? Could you see the seed part of the dandelions you observed? (Have students point out the seeds on their dandelion specimen or in a photograph of a dandelion [see "Websites"].)

? Why do you think dandelion seeds fly like they do? (Answers will vary.)

? What structures or parts of the dandelion seed help it float and fly? (The puffy, fluffy white part connected to the seed allows it to fly.)

explore

Seed Observations

In advance, collect some of the seeds featured in the book *Flip, Float, Fly*. Examples of these seeds are maple, locust, coconut, acorn, burr, and whole fig. (Figs should be cut in half to reveal the seeds.) Give each group of four students a collection of the seeds to observe. Have them use hand lenses to make careful observations of their size, shape, and other characteristics. Having students observe real seeds is preferred, but if you are not able to collect the seeds, you can use the Seed Cards student page.

After the students have observed the seeds, *ask*

? How do you think each of these seeds might be spread to other places? (Have students turn and talk about the characteristics of each seed and share ideas of how these seeds might be moved from place to place.)

? What parts do these seeds have that might help them move to other places? (Answers will vary.)

Observing seeds

SAFETY

- When working with seeds, use only sources that are pesticide/herbicide free.
- Check with the school nurse regarding student medical issues (e.g., allergies to pollen or tree nuts) and how to deal with them.

explain

Flip, Float, Fly Read-Aloud

Connecting to the Common Core
Reading: Informational Text
KEY IDEAS AND DETAILS: 2.1

 Determining Importance

Tell students that you are going to read the book *Flip, Float, Fly* to find out how each of the seeds they observed travels from its parent plant. Read the book aloud, stopping before the "Notes" section at the end. As you read, have students signal when they hear about each of the seeds they observed.

After reading, ask students to use evidence from the book to explain how the seeds they observed earlier move from place to place and discuss the parts of the seeds that allow them to do so. For example, the "wing" of a maple seeds allows it to fly far away from its parent tree. Have students toss a maple seed into the air and watch it fly. The open space inside a coconut allows it to float on the water and drift away on the waves. Demonstrate how a coconut floats by placing it in a bowl of water. Burdock seeds have hooks on them that stick to fur, feathers, and even our clothes. Demonstrate how a burdock seed sticks to fabric. *Ask*

? What do you think is the purpose of these seeds being moved away from their parent plant? (Answers will vary.)

Read the "Notes" section on the last page of the book, which explains that many seeds cannot sprout where they form. These seeds depend on animals, wind, and water to move them to another location. Tell students that the process of seeds being moved away from the parent plant is called *dispersal*.

> **CCC: Structure and Function**
> The shape of natural objects are related to their functions.

Seeds on the Move Lift-the-Flap Booklet

**Writing**

> Connecting to the Common Core
> **Writing**
> RESEARCH TO BUILD KNOWLEDGE: 2.8

Tell students that they are going to have an opportunity to show what they have learned about how seeds are moved. Give each student a copy of the Seeds on the Move student pages. To make a lift-the-flap booklet, have them fold each page on the dotted line and staple the pages. For each page, students should write the name of a seed that travels in that way and then draw the wind, water, or animal helping it move.

elaborate

Who Will Plant a Tree? Read-Aloud

> Connecting to the Common Core
> **Reading: Informational Text**
> KEY IDEAS AND DETAILS: 2.1

**Inferring**

Show students the cover of the book *Who Will Plant a Tree?* and *ask*

? What do you think this book is about? Why? (Answers will vary.)

Encourage students to explain their thinking by referring back to the cover's illustration and title.

Point out the bear, squirrel, and moose on the cover. *Ask*

? Do you think these animals can help to plant a tree? How? (Answers will vary.)

Determining Importance

Ask students to listen for the different ways that animals can help seeds travel from their parent plant to grow in other places as you read the book aloud.

Questioning

After reading, *ask*

? What were some of the ways the animals in the book planted trees? (Seeds stuck to their fur or feathers and then fell off later in a different place, they ate seeds and then pooped or spit them out, and so on.)

? Did these animals know they were planting trees? Did they do it on purpose? (no, except for the people at the end of the book)

**Making Connections: Text-to-Text**

> Connecting to the Common Core
> **Reading: Informational Text**
> INTEGRATION OF KNOWLEDGE AND IDEAS: 2.9

Ask

? How does this book compare with *Flip, Float, Fly?* (*Flip, Float, Fly* was about wind, water,

and animals moving seeds around. *Who Will Plant a Tree?* was about animals moving seeds around. The books both contained some of the same seeds such as maple, coconut, and fig.)

Sock Walk

Ahead of time, ask each student to bring in an adult-size sock (the fuzzier the better) that will easily fit over one of their shoes. Be sure to have some extra socks for any students who forget to bring them.

Ask

? Do you think animals around our school help to plant trees or other plants without knowing it?

? What kinds of seeds might they collect on their fur?

? How could you use the sock to make a model of an animal's fur?

> **SEP: Developing and Using Models**
> Develop a simple model based on evidence to represent a proposed object or tool.

Tell students that they will be taking a walk outdoors to see if they can collect any seeds. But they won't be using their hands to collect the seeds! Instead, they will be placing a sock over one of their shoes to make a model of an animal's fur-covered leg. As they walk around the school grounds, different kinds of seeds might stick to the socks, just like the seeds in the book stuck to the animals. After the sock walk, they will be examining their socks to see if they collected any seeds.

The best location for a sock walk would be a large unmown area of grass or weeds. Be sure to check for poisonous plants ahead of time. After the walk, have students carefully remove their socks before moving indoors to examine what was collected. Once inside, ask students to use hand lenses

Taking a sock walk

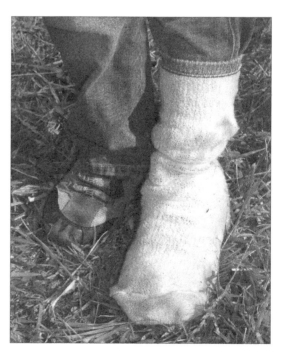

to observe what was collected on their socks. Have students draw and label what they observed on the What's on My Sock? student page.

Note: For an alternative activity, sprinkle an assortment of seeds on students' desks, then have each student put a sock on one hand and do the "sock walk" indoors.

After the sock walk, *ask*

? Which things on your sock do you think are seeds? Why do you think so?

? How could you know for sure? (plant the seeds)

You may want to see if the seeds will sprout by wetting the seed-covered socks with water, placing each in a zippered bag, and keeping them in a warm place for a few weeks.

SAFETY

- Students should wear long socks, long pants, long-sleeve shirts, hats, sunglasses, sunscreen, and safety glasses or goggles.
- Caution students against collecting ticks, mosquitoes, stinging insects, and other potentially hazardous insects.
- Check with the school nurse regarding student medical issues (e.g., allergies to bee stings) and how to deal with them.
- Find out whether outdoor areas have been treated with pesticides, fungicides, or any other toxins and avoid any such areas.
- Caution students against poisonous plants such as poison ivy or poison sumac.
- Bring some form of communication, such as a cell phone or two-way radio, in case of emergencies.
- Inform parents, in writing, of the field trip, any potential hazards, and safety precautions being taken.
- Have students wash their hands with soap and water upon completing the activity.

evaluate

Who Will Plant a Tree? Model

Remind students that the sock they used in the sock walk was a *model* of an animal's furry leg. Tell them that now they are going to be able to come up with their own model that mimics how an animal spreads seeds. Revisit the book *Who Will Plant a Tree?*, asking students to recall the various animals and the ways they move seeds. Provide students with a variety of supplies they can use to make their models. *Ask*

? How could you use these supplies to make a model that shows how a particular animal moves seeds?

? What could you use to represent the seeds?

? What could you use to represent the animal or part of the animal?

? How will you use the model to demonstrate a seed being moved from one place to another?

Give students the opportunity to look through the supplies, touch them, and think about how they might be used. Then invite them to share some of their ideas with partners or groups.

> **SEP: Developing and Using Models**
> Develop a simple model based on evidence to represent a proposed object or tool.

Writing

> Connecting to the Common Core
> **Writing**
> RESEARCH TO BUILD KNOWLEDGE: 2.8

Give students a copy of the *Who Will Plant a Tree?* student page. Have them fill in the sentence "A

_____ planted a _____." with the animal and plant they choose. In the box below, they can write and draw their description of how that animal moves that certain kind of seed. Then they can build their model. Ask students to demonstrate their models for you. Ask guiding questions such as:

? What represents the seeds in your model?

? How does your animal move the seed?

? What parts of the seed make this work?

? What parts of the animal make this work?

? Does the animal know the seed is being moved?

STEM Everywhere

Give students the STEM Everywhere student page as a way to involve their families and extend their learning. They can do the activity with an adult helper and share their results with the class. You will need to send home the following supplies with each student: a balloon (Before using balloons in the classroom, be sure that no one is allergic to latex.), a toilet paper tube, and about a teaspoon of small, lightweight seeds (such as wildflower or grass seeds) in a zippered plastic bag.

Opportunities for Differentiated Instruction

This box lists questions and challenges related to the lesson that students may select to research, investigate, or innovate. Students may also use the questions as examples to help them generate their own questions. These questions can help you move your students from the teacher-directed investigation to engaging in the science and engineering practices in a more student-directed format.

Extra Support

For students who are struggling to meet the lesson objectives, provide a question and guide them in the process of collecting research or helping them design procedures or solutions.

Extensions

For students with high interest or who have already met the lesson objectives, have them choose a question (or pose their own question), conduct their own research, and design their own procedures or solutions.

After selecting one of the questions in the box or formulating their own question, students can individually or collaboratively make predictions, design investigations or surveys to test their predictions, collect evidence, devise explanations, design solutions, or examine related resources. They can communicate their findings through a science notebook, at a poster session or gallery walk, or by producing a media project.

Research

Have students brainstorm researchable questions:

? How far can dandelion seeds travel from their parent plant?

? What kinds of seeds have "wings" other than a maple seed?

? What invention was inspired by the burdock seed?

Continued

Opportunities for Differentiated Instruction (continued)

Investigate

Have students brainstorm testable questions to be solved through science or math:

? How long does it take for a maple seed to fall from your hand to the ground? How long does it take if you break off the "wing"?

? Can you get maple seeds to sprout?

? Can you get dandelion seeds to sprout?

Innovate

Have students brainstorm problems to be solved through engineering:

? Can you design a model that mimics a maple seed's ability to fly?

? Can you design a model that mimics a dandelion seed's ability to fly?

? Can you design a way to spread grass seeds over a wide area?

Websites

Photos of Dandelion seeds from PBS
www.pbs.org/wgbh/nova/article/ dandelion-seed-flight

"The Dandelion" (video) from BBC's *The Private Life of Plants* documentary series
www.youtube.com/ watch?v=slUkyA2cy60

Time-Lapse Dandelion Flower to Seed Head (video)
www.youtube.com/ watch?v=UQ_QqtXoyQw

More Books to Read

Bodach, V. K. 2016. *Seeds.* Mankato, MN: Capstone Press.
Summary: Simple text and bold, close-up photographs present the seeds of different plants, how they grow, and their uses.

Gibbons, G. 1991. *From seed to plant.* New York: Holiday House.
Summary: This book provides a simple introduction to how plants reproduce. Topics include pollination, seed dispersal, and growth.

Jordan, H. 2015. *How a seed grows.* New York: Harper-Collins.

Summary: This updated Let's-Read-and-Find-Out Science book provides a simple introduction to how seeds grow into plants.

Page, R. 2019. *Seeds move!* San Diego, CA: Beach Lane Books.
Summary: Bright, colorful illustrations and simple text show many ways seeds are moved from place to place.

Robbins, K. 2005. *Seeds.* New York: Atheneum Books for Young Readers.
Summary: This book has stunning photographs and straightforward text that explains how seeds grow and how they vary in size, shape, and dispersal patterns.

Stewart, M. 2018. *A seed is the start.* Washington, DC: National Geographic Kids.
Summary: Illustrated with full-color photographs, this nonfiction book shares information on what a seed needs to grow as well as the many fascinating ways that seeds are dispersed.

Weakland, M. 2011. *Seeds go, seeds grow.* Mankato, MN: Capstone Press.
Summary: Simple text and photographs explain the basics of seed parts, how they are produced, and how they can be moved to different places by wind, water, and animals.

Dandelion Observations and Wonderings

Sketch a dandelion and label any parts you know.

Record your observations and wonderings below.

Observations	Wonderings

Seed Cards

Dandelion Seeds

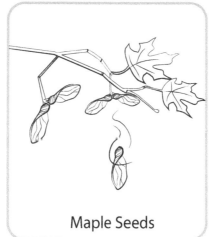

Maple Seeds

Tumbleweed Seeds

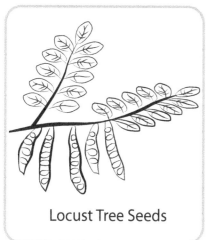

Locust Tree Seeds

Coconut Seeds

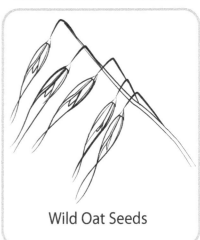

Wild Oat Seeds

Fig Seeds

Burdock seeds

Touch-Me-Not Seeds

Name: _____

What's on My Sock?

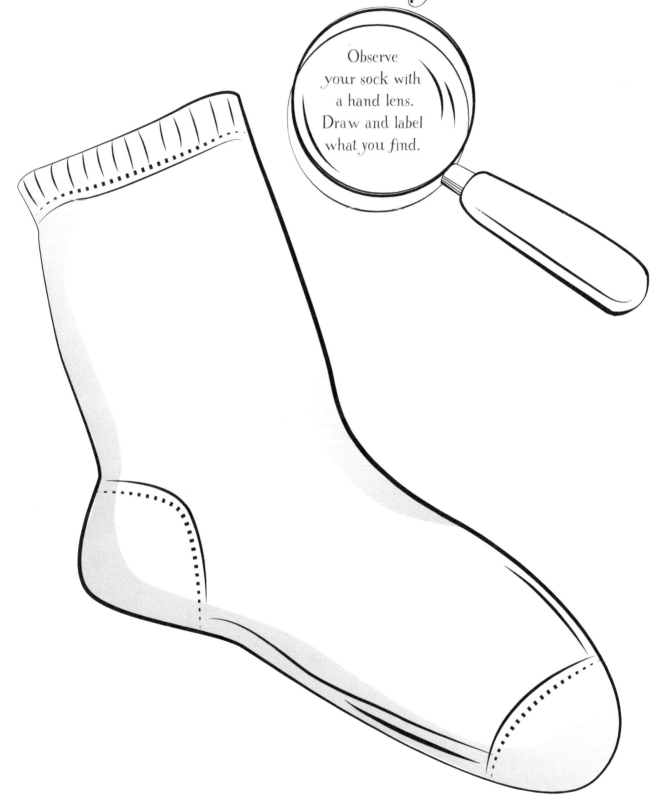

Observe your sock with a hand lens. Draw and label what you find.

Seeds on the Move

By_____

Water

Wind

Animals

Name:

Who Will Plant a Tree?

A _____ planted a _____ .

Show in words and pictures how this animal planted the seed.

Chapter 13

Picture-Perfect STEM Lessons, Grade 2, Expanded Edition

227

Name: _____

STEM Everywhere

At school, we have been learning how **many plants depend on wind, water, and animals to move their seeds**. To find out more, ask your learner questions such as:

- What did you learn?
- What was your favorite part of the lesson?
- What are you still wondering?

At home, you can watch a video about some amazing plants that are able to blast their seeds out of the seed pod with explosive force!

 "Seed Dispersal by Explosion" from Smithsonian Channel
www.youtube.com/watch?v=OB0P3mx_IxY

Next, you can make a model of an exploding seedpod. You just need a balloon, a toilet paper tube, tape, scissors, and some seeds.

1. Tie off the neck of a deflated balloon.
2. Cut off the tip of the balloon.
3. Wrap the balloon around one end of a toilet paper tube. Be sure it's snug.
4. Tape the balloon firmly in place.
5. Find a place where you would like to spread the seeds.
6. Sprinkle some of the seeds (not all) into the balloon and pull back the balloon as far as you can. Let go of the back end!
7. How far did your seeds go? Try again with more seeds and watch where they land.
8. Discuss how this model compares to the exploding seedpods in the video.

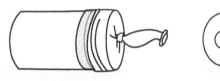
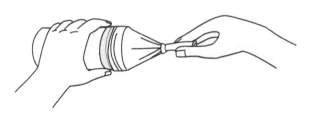

Activity adapted from https://pbskids.org/plumlanding/educators/activities/pdf/SeedBlast_Family_Activity.pdf

National Science Teaching Association

Flight of the Pollinators

Description

Students are introduced to the phenomenon that certain kinds of flowers are visited by certain kinds of animals. They dissect flowers to investigate what the animals are searching for inside the flowers and learn how both plants and animals benefit from the process of pollination. Finally, students develop a simple model that mimics a pollinator and use it to demonstrate plant pollination.

Alignment with the *Next Generation Science Standards*

Performance Expectations

K-2-ETS1-2: Develop a simple sketch, drawing, or physical model to illustrate how the shape of an object helps it function as needed to solve a given problem.

2-LS2-2: Develop a simple model that mimics the function of an animal in dispersing seeds or pollinating plants.

Science and Engineering Practices	Disciplinary Core Ideas	Crosscutting Concepts
Developing and Using Models Develop and/or use a model to represent amounts, relationships, relative scales (bigger, smaller), and/or patterns in the natural and designed world(s). **Obtaining, Evaluating, and Communicating Information** Read grade-appropriate texts and/or use media to obtain scientific and/or technical information to determine patterns in and/or evidence about the natural and designed world(s). Communicate information or design ideas and/or solutions with others in oral and/or written forms using models, drawings, writing, or numbers that provide details about scientific ideas, practices, and/or design solutions.	**LS2.A: Interdependent Relationships in Ecosystems** Plants depend on animals for pollination or to move their seeds around. **ETS1.B: Developing Possible Solutions** Designs can be conveyed through sketches, drawings, or physical models. These representations are useful in communicating ideas for a problem's solutions to other people.	**Structure and Function** The shape and stability of structures of natural and designed objects are related to their function(s). **Systems and System Models** Systems in the natural and designed world have parts that work together. Objects and organisms can be described in terms of their parts.

Note: The activities in this lesson will help students move toward the performance expectations listed, which is the goal after multiple activities. However, the activities will not by themselves be sufficient to reach the performance expectations.

Featured Picture Books

TITLE: **Flowers Are Calling**
AUTHOR: **Rita Gray**
ILLUSTRATOR: **Kenard Pak**
PUBLISHER: **HMH Books for Young Readers**
YEAR: **2015**
GENRE: **Narrative Information**
SUMMARY: *Beautiful artwork and poetry come together to introduce children to the wonders of pollination and the variety of pollinators.*

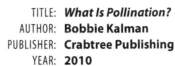

TITLE: **What Is Pollination?**
AUTHOR: **Bobbie Kalman**
PUBLISHER: **Crabtree Publishing**
YEAR: **2010**
GENRE: **Non-Narrative Information**
SUMMARY: *Photographs, diagrams, and straightforward text introduce a variety of pollinators and explain the importance of pollination for both the plants and the pollinators.*

Time Needed

This lesson will take several class periods. Suggested scheduling is as follows:

Session 1: **Engage** with *Flowers Are Calling* Read-Aloud and **Explore** with Look at a Flower—What Do You See?

Session 2: **Explain** with *What Is Pollination?* Read-Aloud

Session 3: **Elaborate** with Pollinator Model Design Challenge

Session 4: **Evaluate** with Pollination Presentations

Materials

For Look at a Flower—What Do You See? (per student or pair)

* Flower

  Note: Ask a local florist for flowers that are going to be discarded. Lilies, irises, daffodils, alstroemeria, tulips, or others with obvious pistils and stamens are best for this activity. Make sure that the flowers are mature so that the pistils and stamens are visible.

* Hand lens
* Cotton swab
* Piece of clear tape

For What Is Pollination? *Read-Aloud*

* Scissors
* Tape or glue

For Pollinator Model Design Challenge (per student)

- 5 multicolor acrylic pom-poms (0.19 in. or 5.0 mm size)
- 2 small paper cups
- 1 acrylic glove (Magic brand works well.)
- 5 Velcro dots (3/8 in. or 0.9 cm; just hooks, not loops)
- A variety of supplies to build and decorate models, such as construction paper, pipe cleaners, googly eyes, coffee filters, scissors, tape, and glue

Student Pages

- Look at a Flower—What Do You See?
- What Is Pollination?
- Pollinator Model Design Challenge
- 4-3-2-1 Pollination Presentation Rubric
- STEM Everywhere

Background for Teachers

The Natural Resources Conservation Service estimates that 75% of the world's plants and about 35% of the world's crops depend on animals for *pollination* (NRCS 2016). Some scientists estimate that animal *pollinators* are responsible for one in every three bites of food we eat! Pollination is critical to the sexual reproduction of flowering plants. Most flowers have male and female parts. The *stamen* (male part) makes a powder called *pollen*. The *pistil* (female part) must receive pollen to make seeds. The pistil has three parts: the *stigma*, *style*, and *ovary*. When pollen from a stamen reaches a stigma, the flower has been *pollinated*. The pollen travels down the style to the ovary. Inside the ovary are *ovules*. After pollination, the flower's petals fall off, the ovaries become fruit, and the ovules become seeds.

There are different ways flowering plants are pollinated. Some flowers can *self-pollinate*, which means pollen from the stamen moves to the pistil of the same flower. Flowers that self-pollinate have male and female parts close together. Sunflowers are an example of a flower that can self-pollinate. *Wind pollination* occurs when the wind carries pollen from one flower to another. Flowers that are pollinated by wind produce large amounts of tiny pollen grains, and much of the pollen does not make it to another flower. Wind-pollinated flowers are usually not fragrant and do not produce nectar because they do not need to attract pollinators. Many trees and grasses are pollinated by wind. *Cross-pollination* occurs when an animal moves pollen from one flower to another flower of the same species. Animals that move the pollen, such as insects, birds, and

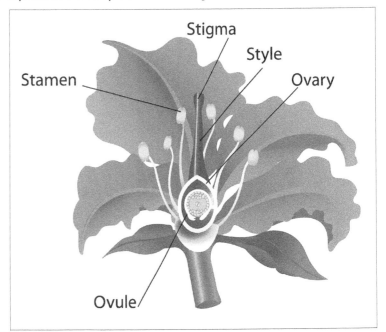

FLOWER DIAGRAM

bats, are called pollinators. Pollinators visit flowers to find food. Many of them eat the nectar produced by flowers. Some pollinators, such as bees, even eat the pollen itself. In their quest for nectar, these animals get pollen stuck on their bodies. When the animals visit other flowers of the same species, some of the pollen falls off their bodies onto the flowers. Thus, the animals unknowingly become pollinators.

Scientists have discovered that many pollinators are in danger. Strong evidence shows a decline in both the number and the diversity of some pollinators, including bees, butterflies, bats, and hummingbirds. Pesticides, disease, habitat loss, invasive plants, and climate change are thought to be the primary reasons these vital organisms are disappearing. One of the most important pollinators, the honeybee, is experiencing colony collapse disorder (CCD). CCD is a syndrome characterized by a nearly abandoned colony that includes dead bee bodies and lacks adult worker bees but still has a live queen and, usually, immature bees and honey. No cause for CCD has been scientifically proven, but some evidence points to a combination of factors, including parasitic mites and the overuse of a certain type of pesticide.

In this lesson, students are engaged in the crosscutting concept (CCC) of structure and function as they model the parts of plants and animals that make pollination possible. They also engage in the CCC of systems and system models as they learn that pollination is a system composed of parts that work together, benefitting both the animals and plants involved. They use the science and engineering practice (SEP) of developing and using models as they create a model that demonstrates this relationship. The SEP of obtaining, evaluating, and communicating information appears throughout the lesson as they read about pollination and then use what they have learned to explain how their model demonstrates the process.

Pollination is a key concept in understanding the interdependent relationships in ecosystems. The *Framework* suggests that students in grades K–2 learn that plants depend on animals for pollination. This understanding is crucial to comprehending the impact of pollinators on our ecosystems. The factors that make up a healthy ecosystem are addressed in more depth in grades 3–5.

Learning Progressions

Below are the disciplinary core idea (DCI) grade band endpoints for grades K–2 and 3–5. These are provided to show how student understanding of the DCIs in this lesson will progress in future grade levels.

DCIs	Grades K–2	Grades 3–5
LS2.A: Interdependent Relationships in Ecosystems	• Plants depend on animals for pollination or to move their seeds around.	• A healthy ecosystem is one in which multiple species of different types are each able to meet their needs in a relatively stable web of life.
ETS1.B: Developing Possible Solutions	• Designs can be conveyed through sketches, drawings, or physical models. These representations are useful in communicating ideas for a problem's solutions to other people.	• At whatever stage, communicating with peers about proposed solutions is an important part of the design process, and shared ideas can lead to improved designs.

Source: Willard, T., ed. 2015. *The NSTA quick-reference guide to the* NGSS: *Elementary school.* Arlington, VA: NSTA Press.

engage

Flowers Are Calling **Read-Aloud**

Connecting to the Common Core
Reading: Informational Text
CRAFT AND STRUCTURE: 2.5

 Inferring

Show students the cover of *Flowers Are Calling* and introduce the author, Rita Gray, and the illustrator, Kenard Pak. *Ask*

? What do you think the title *Flowers Are Calling* means? Whom or what do you think the flowers are calling? (Answers will vary.)

? Do you notice any animals on the cover? (Students will likely notice the bee, butterfly, and hummingbird on the cover.)

? What do you notice about the colors and shapes of the flowers on the cover? (The flowers are different colors and shapes.)

? Why do you think flowers are different colors and shapes? (Answers will vary.)

Synthesizing

Tell students that, as you read, you would like them think about what the title *Flowers Are Calling* means. Read the book aloud, stopping after the page that says, "They're calling some children to look again." Then *ask*

? Have your ideas changed about what the title *Flowers Are Calling* means? (Students should realize that the flowers are attracting different animals in different ways.)

? What animals were the flowers "calling" in the book? (butterfly, bumblebee, hummingbird, honeybee, beetle, bee fly, pollen wasp, moth, and bat)

? What do all of these animals have in common? (They all fly, they are attracted to flowers, they eat nectar, etc.)

? Have you ever seen any of the animals in the book in the wild? (Answers will vary.)

? Why do animals visit flowers? (Animals eat the flowers' nectar.)

? Why would flowers need to attract animals? (Answers will vary.)

OBSERVING FLOWER STRUCTURES IN THE CLASSROOM

explore

Look at a Flower—What Do You See?

Connecting to the Common Core
Reading: Informational Text
INTEGRATION OF KNOWLEDGE AND IDEAS: K.7, 1.7, 2.7

Give each student or pair of students a flower, a hand lens, a cotton swab, and the Look at a Flower—What Do You See? student page. Have students draw a detailed sketch of the flower. (Students do not necessarily need to know the vocabulary associated with the different flower parts at this time.) Turn to pages 28–30 in *Flowers Are Calling*, which are titled "Look at a Flower—What Do You See?" As you read the sections aloud, have students listen for what each characteristic has to do with "calling" animals to visit the flower. Point out the illustrations that accompany each section, and explain that the illustrator provided this art to help the reader better

understand each characteristic. After reading each section, have students observe the colors, patterns, shape, and smell of their own flowers and fill in their observations in the table. (*Note*: Time of opening is not on the student page because that characteristic cannot be observed during class time. However, read the paragraph and discuss so students know that time of opening is also an important factor in attracting certain animals.) Later, you may want to take students outside to observe flower structures on flowering plants found in your schoolyard. In this way, students can compare how the same flower structures may look different on different plants.

SEP: Obtaining, Evaluating, and Communicating Information
Read grade-appropriate text to obtain scientific information and determine patterns about the natural world.

COLLECTING POLLEN

OBSERVING FLOWER STRUCTURES IN THE SCHOOLYARD

Tell students that the reason the flowers were "calling" to the animals has to do with a special powdery substance inside the flower. Encourage them to look carefully to find the powder. When they find it, they should rub some off with a cotton swab and smear it in the corresponding box on the paper. Then have students place a piece of clear tape over the powder to hold it in place. Tell students that, in the next part of the lesson, they will find out what this mysterious powder is and why it is so important. (Some students may know that the powder is called *pollen*, but assure them that there is much to learn about why it is there and what it does.)

> **CCC: Systems and System Models**
> Organisms can be described in terms of their parts

explain

What Is Pollination? Read-Aloud

Connecting to the Common Core
Language
VOCABULARY ACQUISITION AND USE: 2.6

Cloze

Show students the cover of *What Is Pollination?* by Bobbie Kalman. Tell them this book can help them discover what that mysterious powder is and what it has to do with the flowers and the animals in *Flowers Are Calling*. Give students the *What Is Pollination?* student page. Directions for students are as follows:

1. Cut out the cards in the boxes.
2. Read the paragraph, and fill in each blank with the card you think belongs there.

3. Listen carefully while your teacher reads the book *What Is Pollination?*
4. After reviewing the paragraph as a class, move the cards if necessary. Then glue or tape them on the page.
5. On the back, draw a picture of what *pollination* means.

> **SEP: Obtaining, Evaluating, and Communicating Information**
> Read grade-appropriate text to obtain scientific information and determine patterns about the natural world.

The paragraph should read as follows:

Pollen is the fine powder at the center of most flowers. When it moves from one flower to another flower of the same kind, **pollination** takes place. Flowers must be pollinated to make **fruits** and **seeds**. Animals that carry pollen from one flower to another are called **pollinators**. They are not pollinating flowers on purpose. Most animals visit flowers because they are looking for **nectar**!

Connecting to the Common Core
Reading: Informational Text
CRAFT AND STRUCTURE: 2.5

Questioning

Ask

? Do pollinators know that they are helping the plants? (no)

? Why do pollinators visit flowers? (to get nectar or food for themselves)

? How do both the plants and pollinators benefit from pollination? (The plants get their pollen moved to other flowers, which allows them to make new plants, and the pollinators get food.)

Explain that pollinators and plants work together as a system. Systems in the natural world have parts that work together. For example, on page 11 of *What Is Pollination?*, students can see how the shape of a hummingbird's beak works with the shape of tubular flowers. On page 17, they can see how the furry body of a bumblebee works to carry sticky pollen produced by the plant.

On page 31, the author writes, "Each time you bite into an apple, pear, or vegetable, say a silent 'Thank you' to the pollinators that made it possible." *Ask*

? Why should we thank pollinators? (If plants were not pollinated, fruits and vegetables would not grow.)

? Why are pollinators in danger? (People are building in wilderness areas, which causes animals, including pollinators, to lose their homes and food. Pesticides and diseases are killing many pollinating insects.)

? What can we do to help pollinators? (Tell people why pollinators are important. Grow native flowers at home or school. Plant a vegetable or other garden.)

elaborate

Pollinator Model Design Challenge

Tell students that you have a challenge for each of them—to design and build a model that helps demonstrate how pollinators move pollen from one place to another. They will be using the following materials to build their models:

- 5 small pom-poms to represent pollen
- 2 small paper cups to represent two of the same type of flower

MODEL OF A POLLINATOR

- 1 acrylic glove on which they can tape or glue the following materials to make their models (see photo):
  - 5 small Velcro dots to represent the structures on the pollinator that pollen sticks to
  - Other materials to add more structures and details to their model: construction paper, pipe cleaners, googly eyes, coffee filters, tape, and glue

Their models will need to transfer pom-poms (pollen) from one cup (flower) to the other cup (flower). They may decorate the cups (e.g., add petals) if they would like to make them look more like flowers.

Tell students that before they begin, you want to give them the opportunity to see some pollinators in action. Explain that you have a clip from a movie called *Wings of Life* (see "Websites") that a filmmaker named Louis Schwartzberg made to teach people about pollination. Tell them that as they watch, you would like them to look for different types of pollinators, observe their different body parts, and watch how the pollinators interact with flowers.

Connecting to the Common Core
Reading: Informational Text
KEY IDEAS AND DETAILS: 2.1

 **Questioning**

After watching the video, *ask*

? What pollinators were featured in the video? (hummingbirds, bees, butterflies, and bats)

? How did they get from flower to flower? (by flying)

? Why were these animals visiting the flowers? (to get nectar)

? What body parts help them get to the nectar (Wings help them fly to the flowers, hummingbirds' long beaks can go deep inside flowers, bats and butterflies have long tongues to slurp nectar, bees' bodies are small enough to go inside many flowers, etc.)

SEP: Developing and Using Models
Develop and use a model to demonstrate relationships in the natural world.

CCC: Structure and Function
The shape of structures of natural objects are related to their functions.

Then give each student the Pollinator Model Design Challenge student page. Some suggestions for pollinators to model are bees, wasps, butterflies, moths, flies, beetles, hummingbirds, and bats. Have each student look through an online photo gallery (see "Websites") to choose a pollinator to model, record it online, print out a photo, and attach it to the student page. The photos will be used for reference as students make their models.

Next, they will describe how the real pollinator gets food from the flower and how the model pol-

linator will show this. They will also describe the parts of the real pollinator's body that the pollen sticks to and how the model pollinator will show this. Finally, they will explain how both plants and pollinators benefit from their interaction and how humans benefit from pollination. Students will use the photo and this information to help them design and build their models.

evaluate

Pollination Presentations

Connecting to the Common Core
Speaking and Listening
PRESENTATION OF KNOWLEDGE AND IDEAS: 2.4

 **Synthesizing**

After students have completed their models, pass out the 4-3-2-1 Pollination Presentation Rubric student page. Students should use the information from the Pollinator Model Design Challenge student page to help them with their presentations. You may consider having students present their models to an outside audience such as a local park official or nature expert.

Give students time to practice, then have them either give their presentations live or record them to be shown later. They must include the following information:

- A demonstration of how the pollinator moves pollen from one flower to another

- A description of the body parts that the pollinator uses to get food from the flower and the body parts that the pollen sticks to

- An explanation of how both plants and pollinators benefit from pollination

- An explanation of how humans benefit from pollination

Students can also share what they might do to improve their models. Use the rubric to evaluate their presentations.

> **SEP: Obtaining, Evaluating, and Communicating Information**
> Communicate information or design ideas with others in oral and written forms using models, drawings, writing, or numbers that provide details about scientific ideas.

STEM Everywhere

Give students the STEM Everywhere student page as a way to involve their families and extend their learning. They can do the activity with an adult helper and share their results with the class. If students do not have access to the internet at home, you may choose to have them complete this activity at school.

Opportunities for Differentiated Instruction

This box lists questions and challenges related to the lesson that students may select to research, investigate, or innovate. Students may also use the questions as examples to help them generate their own questions. These questions can help you move your students from the teacher-directed investigation to engaging in the science and engineering practices in a more student-directed format.

Extra Support

For students who are struggling to meet the lesson objectives, provide a question and guide them in the process of collecting research or help them design procedures or solutions.

Extensions

For students with high interest or who have already met the lesson objectives, have them choose a question (or pose their own question), conduct their own research, and design their own procedures or solutions.

After selecting one of the questions in the box or formulating their own question, students can individually or collaboratively make predictions, design investigations or surveys to test their predictions, collect evidence, devise explanations, design solutions, or examine related resources. They can communicate their findings through a science notebook, at a poster session or gallery walk, or by producing a media project.

Research

Have students brainstorm researchable questions:

? What kinds of plants would attract pollinators to your yard or schoolyard?

? Which crops in our area depend on pollinators?

? Which pollinators are in danger, and what can we do to help?

Continued

Opportunities for Differentiated Instruction (continued)

Investigate

Have students brainstorm testable questions to be solved through science or math:

? What are some common pollinators that visit our schoolyard?

? How many of the foods that I eat in a day require animal pollinators? (Keep a tally of how many times you eat vegetables, fruits, or nuts—or foods made using those products—in a day.)

? Which plants seem to attract the most pollinators in our schoolyard?

Innovate

Have students brainstorm problems to be solved through engineering:

? Can we build a feeder to attract hummingbirds to our schoolyard?

? Can we design a flower garden (either on a plot of land or in pots) to attract butterflies?

? Can we design a vegetable garden (either on a plot of land or in pots) to help pollinators?

Reference

 NRCS (Natural Resources Conservation Service). 2016. Insects and pollinators. U.S. Department of Agriculture. *www.nrcs.usda.gov/wps/portal/nrcs/main/national/plantsanimals/pollinate*

Websites

 National Geographic "Gold Dusters" Pollinator Photo Gallery
www.nationalgeographic.com/magazine/article/pollinators

 Penn State University Department of Entomology: Pollinator Image Gallery
https://ento.psu.edu/research/centers/pollinators/resources-and-outreach/pollinator-media

 U.S. Department of Agriculture: "Bee a Friend to Pollinators" (brochure)
https://nrcspad.sc.egov.usda.gov/distributioncenter/product.aspx?ProductID=849

"The Beauty of Pollination: Wings of Life" (video)
https://video.disney.com/watch/the-beauty-of-pollination-wings-of-life-4da84833e06fd54fff590f49

More Books to Read

Bersani, S. 2015. *Achoo! Why pollen counts.* Mount Pleasant, SC: Arbordale Publishing.
Summary: A cute storyline about a baby black bear that is allergic to pollen not only teaches readers about pollen allergies but also explains how vital this fine powder is to the animals and plants in the forest.

Fleming, C. 2020. *Honeybee: The busy life of apis mellifera.* New York: Neal Porter Books.
Summary: This detailed introduction to the life of a honeybee is full of intriguing facts about one of our most important pollinators.

Konicek-Moran, R. 2016. *From flower to fruit.* Arlington, VA: NSTA Kids.
Summary: Rich illustrations and an engaging narrative draw the reader into the world of botany. The book introduces the parts of a flower, the process of pollination, and the production of fruit. It includes activities and background information for parents and teachers.

Chapter 14

Marsh, L. 2016. *National Geographic Readers: Bees.* Washington, DC: National Geographic Kids.
Summary: A straightforward nonfiction book about bees, illustrated with stunning National Geographic photos.

Morgan, E. 2019. *Next time you see a bee.* Arlington, VA: NSTA Press.
Summary: Simple text and gorgeous photographs reveal the physical features that allow bees to collect and spread pollen. In addition to honeybees, this book describes many North American native bees and discusses why they are threatened (and how readers can help).

Pattison, D. 2019. *Pollen: Darwin's 130-year prediction.* Little Rock, AR: Mims House.
Summary: This fascinating true story reveals how Charles Darwin's prediction that a certain species of orchid on Madagascar was pollinated by giant moths would not be tested until a century later.

Pryor, K. 2019. *Bea's bees.* Chesapeake Bay, MD: Schiffer Kids.
Summary: Beatrix discovers a wild bee nest on her walk home from school. When the nest goes silent, Bea is determined to find out how she can help. End matter includes information on conserving bees.

Rich, S. 2014. *Mrs. Carter's butterfly garden.* Arlington, VA: NSTA Press.
Summary: In this story of how former First Lady Rosalynn Carter started a front-yard project that grew into a butterfly-friendly trail through her hometown of Plains, Georgia, students will learn why having welcoming spaces for butterflies is good for people and how to create their own butterfly gardens at home or school.

Slade, S. 2010. *What if there were no bees?: A book about the grassland ecosystem.* North Mankato, MN: Picture Window Books.
Summary: Part of the Food Chain Reactions series, this book highlights the importance of bees to the ecosystem. By addressing the question "What if there were no bees?," the reader learns these insects are a keystone species because many other species would likely become extinct without them.

Name: _____

Look at a Flower— What Do You See?

1. Observe the flower carefully. Draw a picture that shows its shape, colors, patterns, and parts.

[ ]

2. Listen as your teacher reads about each characteristic of a flower, then record the observations for your flower.

Characteristic	Observation
Color	
Pattern	
Shape	
Smell	

3. Look for the powdery substance in the center of your flower. Use a cotton swab to smear some in the box below and tape it in place.

[ ]

Name: _____

What Is Pollination?

_____ is the fine powder at the center of most flowers. When it moves from one flower to another flower of the same kind, _____ takes place. Flowers must be pollinated to make _____ and _____. Animals that carry pollen from one flower to another are called _____. They are not pollinating flowers on purpose. Most animals visit flowers because they are looking for _____!

Directions: Cut out the cards below and place them in the paragraph above. Then listen as your teacher reads the book *What Is Pollination?*

		nectar
	pollen	pollinators
	seeds	
fruits		
pollination		

Name: _____

Pollinator Model Design Challenge

Challenge: Design a model of a pollinator that can be used to demonstrate how it moves pollen from one flower to another while getting food.

Directions: Choose a real pollinator as an inspiration for your model. Then design your model using the materials provided.

Real Pollinator	Model Pollinator
Name and photo	Labeled sketch
How does the pollinator get food from the flower?	How will your model show this?
What parts of the pollinator's body does the pollen stick to?	How will your model show this?

1. How do both plants and pollinators benefit from pollination?

    Plants get _____

    Pollinators get _____

2. How do humans benefit from pollination?

_____

Name: _____

4~3~2~1
Pollination Presentation Rubric

Demonstrate the model of a pollinator that you designed. Your presentation should include the following:

4 Points: A demonstration of how your model pollinator moves pollen from one flower to another

4   3   2   1   0

3 Points: A description of the body parts that your model pollinator uses to get food from the flower and the body parts that the pollen sticks to

3   2   1   0

2 Points: An explanation of how both plants and pollinators benefit from pollination

2   1   0

1 Point: An explanation of how humans benefit from pollination

1   0

Score: _____/10

STEM Everywhere

At school, we have been learning about **pollination**. We learned that plants depend on animals to move their pollen. These animals are called **pollinators**. Both plants and pollinators benefit from this relationship. To find out more, ask your learner questions such as:

- What did you learn?
- What was your favorite part of the lesson?
- What are you still wondering?

At home, you can watch a video together called "RoboBees to the Rescue" about how **roboticists,** or engineers who design robots, at Harvard University are designing a robotic bee to pollinate plants.

 Search "RoboBees to the Rescue" on *www.pbslearningmedia.org* to find the video at *www.pbslearningmedia.org/resource/arct14.sci. nvrobobee/robobees-to-the-rescue.*

After you watch the video, you can design your own robot that is based on a different pollinator, such as a butterfly, hummingbird, beetle, moth, or bat.

Sketch of Real Pollinator	Sketch of Robot Pollinator

If You Find a Rock

Description

Learners observe the phenomenon that there are many different kinds of rocks with different properties. They observe, describe, and sort a variety of rocks and are introduced to various ways that rocks form. Then they explore different uses of rocks based on their properties.

Alignment with the *Next Generation Science Standards*

Performance Expectations

2-ESS1-1: Use information from several sources to provide evidence that Earth events can occur quickly or slowly.

2-PS1-1: Analyze data obtained from testing different materials to determine which materials have the properties that are best suited for an intended purpose.

Science and Engineering Practices	Disciplinary Core Ideas	Crosscutting Concept
Analyzing and Interpreting Data Record information (observations, thoughts, and ideas.) Use and share pictures, drawings, and/or writings of observations. **Obtaining, Evaluating, and Communicating Information** Read grade-appropriate texts and/or use media to obtain scientific and/or technical information to determine patterns in and/or evidence about the natural and designed world(s). Obtain information using various texts, text features (e.g., headings, tables of contents, glossaries, electronic menus, icons), and other media that will be useful in answering a scientific question and/or supporting a scientific claim.	**ESS1.C: The History of Planet Earth** Some events happen very quickly; others occur very slowly over a period of time much longer than one can observe. **PS1.A: Structure and Properties of Matter** Different properties are suited to different purposes.	**Stability and Change** Things may change slowly or rapidly.

Note: The activities in this lesson will help students move toward the performance expectations listed, which is the goal after multiple activities. However, the activities will not by themselves be sufficient to reach the performance expectations.

Featured Picture Books

TITLE: *If You Find a Rock*
AUTHOR: **Peggy Christian**
PHOTOGRAPHER: **Barbara Hirsch Lember**
PUBLISHER: **Harcourt**
YEAR: **2000**
GENRE: **Story**
SUMMARY: *Soft, hand-tinted photographs and simple, poetic text celebrate the variety of rocks that can be found, including skipping rocks, chalk rocks, and splashing rocks.*

TITLE: *Rocks: Hard, Soft, Smooth, and Rough*
AUTHOR: **Natalie Myra Rosinky**
ILLUSTRATOR: **Matthew John**
PUBLISHER: **Picture Window Books**
YEAR: **2002**
GENRE: **Non-Narrative Information**
SUMMARY: *Simple text and cartoonish illustrations provide information on igneous, sedimentary, and metamorphic rocks.*

Time Needed

This lesson will take several class periods. Suggested scheduling is as follows:

Session 1: **Engage** with *If You Find a Rock* Read-Aloud

Session 2: **Explore** with I Found a Rock and Rock Sorting

Session 3: **Explain** with *Rocks: Hard, Soft, Smooth, and Rough* Read-Aloud and Volcano Video

Session 4: **Elaborate** with Comparing Rocks Venn Diagram and If Rocks Could Talk Interviews

Session 5: **Evaluate** with Pet Rock Posters

Materials

For I Found a Rock (per student)

- Rock (brought in by student)
- Hand lens
- Centimeter ruler

For Rocks: Hard, Soft, Smooth, and Rough *Read-Aloud*

- One of each of the following rock samples: obsidian, granite, sandstone, limestone, and marble (per group of 5 students)
- Hand lens (1 per student)

For Comparing Rocks Venn Diagram

- 1 obsidian and 1 granite rock (per group of 4–6 students)
- Hand lens (1 per student)

For If Rocks Could Talk Interviews

- Tape or glue

For Pet Rock Posters

- Colored pencils, crayons, or markers
- Poster board
- Highlighter
- Glue stick
- Optional: Photo of the original Pet Rock packaging

Rock specimens in packs of 10 are available from *www.carolina.com*

Rock	Order Number
Obsidian, Black	GEO1112B
Granite, Gray	GEO1080B
Sandstone, Red	GEO2012B
Limestone, Fossil	GEO1198B
Marble, White	GEO2054B

Student Pages

- I Found a Rock
- Comparing Rocks Venn Diagram
- If Rocks Could Talk
- Pet Rock Advertising Poster Rubric
- STEM Everywhere

Background for Teachers

Children are naturally curious about the world around them, including the rocks beneath their feet. Learning about the properties and uses of Earth's materials, such as rocks, helps young children build a foundation for understanding the interactions of Earth's *geosphere* (crust, mantle, and core), *hydrosphere* (water), *atmosphere* (air), and *biosphere* (living things). Earth materials have different physical and chemical properties that make them useful in different ways. This lesson focuses primarily on the phenomenon that there are many different kinds of rocks with different properties. Students learn how to identify and describe these properties (shape, size, color, texture, and luster—but not hardness, which is a property used to identify minerals only) and explore how properties of rocks, including the presence of crystals, can be used to sort them. They learn that the properties of color, texture, and luster are useful for identifying different rock types, but the properties of size and shape are not. They also explore how a rock's properties and its uses are related.

Through observation and reading, students learn that rocks can be classified as igneous, sedimentary, or metamorphic depending on how they are formed. *Igneous* rock occurs when hot, molten rock, or *magma*, cools and solidifies. Magma originates deep within Earth near active plate boundaries or hot spots, then rises toward the surface. Most magma remains trapped underground and cools very slowly over many thousands or millions of years until it solidifies. This process forms *intrusive* igneous rock. These rocks typically cool so slowly that they have time to develop large crystals. Examples of intrusive igneous rock include *granite* and *gabbro*. Extrusive igneous rock is formed when magma exits Earth's surface through cracks or erupting volcanoes. Magma, called lava when it reaches the surface, cools and solidifies very quickly when it is exposed to water or to the atmosphere. Mineral crystals don't have much time to grow, so extrusive igneous rocks, such as *basalt*, have a very fine-grained texture. *Obsidian* is a volcanic glass that forms when a particular type of lava cools almost instantly.

Rocks can also form when *sediments*, such as sand, mud, pebbles, bones, shells, and plants, settle into layers on the bottoms of lakes, oceans, or rivers. Over millions of years, the top layers press down on the bottom layers and the bottom layers become *sedimentary* rock. *Sandstone* and *limestone* are examples of sedimentary rock. Limestone often contains the fossilized remains of animals that lived millions of years ago.

The third type of rock is *metamorphic* rock—rock that was formed when another kind of rock was exposed to tremendous heat and pressure over a long period of time. For example, *marble* is a metamorphic rock formed when limestone is "squeezed and cooked" inside Earth. The minerals within metamorphic rock are often arranged in stripes or swirls caused by heat and uneven pressure.

Although the rock cycle is not a focus of this lesson, students learn that rocks can melt inside Earth. They also read about some of the other processes that can create and transform the types of rocks in Earth's crust. Students are introduced to the concept of fast and slow changes to Earth's surface by learning about volcanoes and comparing how different igneous rocks are formed. Some volcanic igneous rocks can form very quickly but most types of rock are formed over thousands or millions of years. Students will build on these concepts in later grades when they learn how patterns of rock formations can reveal changes over time and how the presence and location of certain fossil types indicate the order in which rock layers were formed.

In this lesson, students apply the science and engineering practice (SEP) of analyzing and interpreting data as they record and share their observations of different types of rocks. They use the SEP of obtaining, evaluating, and communicating information as they read about different types of rocks and how they are formed, as well as the properties of rocks and their uses. Students apply the crosscutting concept (CCC) of stability and change as they discuss how some events on Earth, such as volcanic eruptions, happen very quickly, whereas others occur over a time period much longer than one can observe.

Learning Progressions

Below are the disciplinary core idea (DCI) grade band endpoints for grades K–2 and 3–5. These are provided to show how student understanding of the DCIs in this lesson will progress in future grade levels.

DCIs	Grades K–2	Grades 3–5
ESS1.C: The History of Planet Earth	• Some events happen very quickly; others occur very slowly; over a time period much longer than one can observe.	• Local, regional, and global patterns of rock formations reveal changes over time due to Earth forces such as earthquakes. The presence and location of certain fossil types indicate the order in which rock layers were formed.
PS1.A: Structure and Properties of Matter	• Different properties are suited to different purposes.	• Measurements of a variety of properties can be used to identify materials..

Source: Willard, T., ed. 2015. *The NSTA quick-reference guide to the* NGSS: *Elementary school.* Arlington, VA: NSTA Press.

engage

If You Find a Rock Read-Aloud

Hold a piece of obsidian and a piece of granite behind your back. Then announce to the class that you have found some things that are older than them, older than the school building, even older than you … things that could even be millions of years old! Have students guess what they are. Reveal the rocks, and then tell students that rocks are probably the oldest things that they will ever touch. Pass around the rocks, and ask students to share observations. *Ask*

- ? How can you describe the rocks?
- ? How are they alike? How are they different?
- ? Do you think they are the same kind of rock?
- ? How do you think the rocks formed?
- ? How long do you think it takes rocks to form?
- ? What could these rocks be used for?
- ? What other questions do you have about the rocks?

Then tell students that you have a book to read to get them thinking about rocks.

Making Connections: Text to Self

Introduce the author and photographer of the book *If You Find a Rock*. The author, Peggy Christian, is a rock hound who was born in the Rocky Mountains of Colorado and loves skiing, camping, and reading. Build connections to the author by *asking*

- ? What is a *rock hound*? (a person who likes to collect rocks)
- ? Is anyone here a rock hound? (Answers will vary.)
- ? What do you call a scientist who studies rocks to learn about Earth? (a geologist)
- ? Would you like to be a geologist? (Answers will vary.)

Explain that there are many people, both men and women, who choose geology as a career and devote their entire lives to studying it. Tell students that Peggy Christian's father was a geologist and maybe that is why she loves rocks so much.

Determining Importance

Explain that, while you are reading the book aloud, you would like students to think about what some of the rocks in the book are used for and what properties, or characteristics, make them suited for those uses.

Read aloud *If You Find a Rock*. (For fun, stop after reading the page about the wishing rock and invite students to close their eyes and make a wish.)

If You FIND A ROCK *READ-ALOUD*

After reading, *ask*

- ? What are some of the uses for the special rocks in the book? (Answers might include wishing rock, skipping rock, chalk rock, resting rock, splashing rock, and worry rock.)

? Have you ever owned a special rock?

? What made it special to you?

Tell students that they are going to be rock hounds on the hunt for their own special rock. They can select a rock from their own collection or, with adult supervision, find one outside. They should bring their special rock to school the next day. Send a letter home to inform parents of the assignment. Include these rules for students to follow: *Your rock must be smaller than a tennis ball. You are not allowed to throw your rock.* You may want to have extra rocks available for students who don't bring one in.

explore

I Found a Rock

The next day, have students place their rocks on their tables or desks. Ask them to observe their own rock and then look around at some of the rocks near them. Discuss the following questions:

? How are the rocks alike?

? How are the rocks different?

Encourage students to notice that rocks come in a wide variety of colors, shapes, sizes, and other characteristics. Then explain that a scientific tool called a hand lens can help them get an even closer look at their rocks. Demonstrate the proper way to use a hand lens (holding the lens close to one eye while bringing the rock toward the hand lens until it comes into focus), and caution them that touching the rock to the surface of the hand lens can scratch the lens. Pass out hand lenses to all students, and have them use the lenses to observe their rock more closely.

Next, revisit the book *If You Find a Rock*. Ask students to recall the rocks described in the book. List some of the rocks on the board, such as:

• skipping rock

• chalk rock

• resting rock

• wishing rock

• worry rock

• climbing rock

Then *ask*

? What makes each rock in the book suited for its special use? (Answers might include its shape, its color or size, and how it feels.)

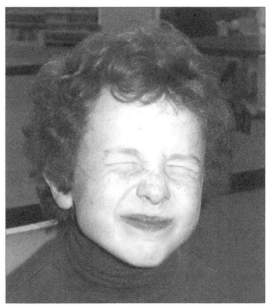

MAKING A WISH

Explain that these things—shape, color, size, texture (how it feels)—are called *properties* of rocks. Discuss how the properties of each rock in the book make it suited for a different purpose. For example, a skipping rock is used for skipping across water. The properties that make it suited for that purpose are its flat, rounded *shape* and its small *size*. Shape and size are properties of rocks. A chalk rock is used to draw pictures on pavement. The properties that make it suited for that purpose are its white *color* and its soft, dusty *texture*. Color and texture are also properties of rocks. Another property students may notice as they observe their rocks is *luster*, or how the rocks reflect light. Words that describe luster include *shiny*, *dull*, and *sparkly*.

Explain that shape, size, color, texture, and luster are different properties of rocks that make each one unique. Geologists who study rocks use some of these properties to identify different types of rocks. Tell students that they are going to observe and record the properties of their own special rock.

MEASURING A ROCK

Connecting to the Common Core
Mathematics
MEASUREMENT AND DATA: 2.MD.A.1

Pass out the I Found a Rock student page and centimeter rulers. Make sure students understand how to record the properties listed on the data table (color, texture, luster, size) by *asking*

? What are some words that might describe a rock's *color*? (Answers might include *black*, *white*, and *reddish-brown*.)

? What are some words that might describe a rock's *texture*? (Answers might include *bumpy*, *smooth*, and *rough*.)

? What are some words that might describe a rock's *luster*? (Answers might include *shiny*, *dull*, and *glassy*.)

? What is one way to measure a rock's *size*? (Use a ruler to measure the longest side in centimeters.)

> **SEP: Analyzing and Interpreting Data**
> Record information (observations, thoughts, and ideas.)Use and share pictures, drawings, and/or writings of observations.

Discuss how observations of size, such as big or small, are not scientific observations because they are not exact. Using measurements to describe the size of a rock is more scientific. Then have students

make careful observations of their rocks and complete their data tables.

Next, have students think about the unique properties of their rocks and fill in this cloze sentence: "I found a rock that would be good for _____ because it is _____."

Rock Sorting

This activity is a fun way to show that rocks can be identified by their unique properties. The object is to end with one student standing, holding his or her rock. Collect all of the I Found a Rock student pages. Randomly select one from the stack, but don't let students see it. Have all the students stand, holding their rocks. Then read the first observation on the page, for example, "I found a rock, and it is gray. If your rock is gray, stay standing." Students whose rocks are not gray should sit. Then read the second observation on the page, for example, "I found a rock, and it is smooth. If your rock is smooth, stay standing." Students whose rocks are not smooth should sit. Continue reading the obser-

vations, including the cloze sentence at the bottom, until only one student is standing. Repeat the process with several more student pages. Then *ask*

? What have you learned about rocks? (Students should recognize that rocks have different properties.)

? What are you still wondering about rocks? (Answers will vary.)

explain

Rocks: Hard, Soft, Smooth, and Rough Read-Aloud and Volcano Video

Connecting to the Common Core
Reading: Informational Text
KEY IDEAS AND DETAILS: 2.3

USING THE ROCK IDENTIFICATION CHART

Form groups of five students. Give each student a hand lens and one of the following rocks: obsidian, granite, sandstone, limestone, or marble. Have each student observe his or her rock and compare it to the other rocks in their group. *Ask*

? Are the five rocks all the same kind of rock? (no)

? How are they different? (They have different properties: shape, size, color, texture, and luster.)

? Is it possible to look at a rock and tell what kind of rock it is? (Answers will vary. The following activity will help students understand how geologists identify rocks by their properties.)

> **SEP: Obtaining, Evaluating, and Communicating Information**
> Read grade-appropriate texts to obtain scientific information to determine patterns in and/ or evidence about the natural world. Obtain information using various texts, text features (e.g. headings, tables of contents, glossaries, electronic menus, icons that will be useful in supporting a scientific claim.

Next, tell students that the picture book *Rocks: Hard, Soft, Smooth, and Rough* can give them clues about their rock's identity. Each one of the rocks they have been observing is described in the book. Read the book aloud, being sure to read the "fun facts" that are inset on some of the pages. Pause after reading each rock description and ask students to hold up their rock if they think it is the one being described.

After reading, use the rocks chart on page 21 to help students identify their rocks correctly. Explain that many different kinds of scientists use these kinds of charts, also called keys, to identify

unknown objects. After reading, use the following questions to help students understand how size and shape might not be good properties to use to identify rocks. *Ask*

? What properties did you use to identify your rock? (Answers might include color, texture, luster, swirls, stripes, or specks.)

? Were you able to identify your rock based on its size or shape alone? (no)

? Is size a good property to use to identify a type of rock? Why or why not? (No, because rocks are all different sizes depending on how they formed or broke apart from larger rocks.)

? Is shape a good property to use to identify a type of rock? (No, for the same reason as in the previous question.)

? What are the basic building blocks of rocks called? (minerals)

Next, have students use hand lenses to see if they can find any swirls, stripes, or shiny specks called crystals in their rock samples. These features are made by the minerals that make up their rocks. Some rocks are made of a single mineral, but most are made of several minerals. (A student who is observing a very fine-grained rock may not be able to see any minerals. Geologists often use special microscopes to look at very thin slices of rocks so they can determine mineral content and thus rock type.) Then *ask*

? How do scientists identify unknown rocks? (They can observe their properties and use a key.)

? What are the three main types of rocks you learned about in the book? (igneous, sedimentary, and metamorphic)

? How are rocks classified into these three groups? (Rocks are classified based on how they are formed.)

Making Connections: Text-to-Text

Revisit page 10 of *Rocks: Hard, Soft, Smooth, and Rough*. Point to the picture of the volcano and *ask*

? Does anyone know what this is called? (a volcano)

? What is the melted rock that comes out of a volcano called? (Answers will vary.)

Explain that when melted rock comes to Earth's surface it is called lava, but when it is *underground*, it is called magma. Point out the pool of magma below the picture of the volcano on page 10. Then *ask*

? Have you ever seen a volcano erupting?

? Would you like to see a video of a real volcanic eruption?

Show students the video titled "Iceland Volcano: Drone footage captures stunning up-close view of eruption" (see "Websites") or another video of an erupting volcano. Tell students that there are more than 1,500 active volcanoes on Earth and that this one is located in Iceland. Point out Iceland on a map. After watching the video, *ask*

? How do you think this video was taken? (by a drone, an aircraft without a human pilot)

? Why do you think a drone was used? (It would not be safe for a person to be that close to an erupting volcano.)

? What did you notice? (Answers will vary, but students may notice that lava is shooting from the volcano and pouring down the sides. They may also notice that the sides and base of the volcano are made of black rock.)

? What do you wonder? (Answers will vary.)

? Where do you think all the black rock on the volcano came from? (It came from the hot lava that cooled and turned into rock.)

Explain that an erupting volcano is an example of rock forming quickly. The hot lava is liquid rock that can instantly turn into solid rock when it hits the air. *Ask*

? Does all rock form this quickly? (no)

> **CCC: Stability and Changee**
> Things may change slowly or rapidly.

Students may remember from the book, *Rocks: Hard, Soft, Smooth, and Rough* that some rocks take a long time to form. Revisit the following pages that share these examples:

- Page 13 says that sedimentary rock can take millions of years to form.

- Page 17 says that fossils are made from plants and animals that died thousands or millions of years ago. Over time, they turned into rock.

- Page 18 says that over time, heat and pressure can turn a metamorphic rock into a new metamorphic rock.

Explain that some rocks form quickly and others form very slowly, over a period of time longer than one can observe. Tell students that in the next activity, they will be comparing two different kinds of rocks in order to learn more about how some rocks form quickly and others form slowly.

elaborate

Comparing Rocks Venn Diagram

*Venn Diagram*

Show students the two rocks you shared in the engage phase of the lesson—obsidian and granite. Give each group of 4–6 students a sample of each and the Comparing Rocks Venn Diagram student page. Tell students that one tool they can use to compare how things are alike and different is a Venn diagram. Have students observe the two rocks again with hand lenses. Then cut out each statement at the bottom of the student page and

COMPARING ROCKS

work with a partner to place the statements in the Venn diagram. Explain that if they are not sure at this point, that is OK. They will have a chance to resort the statements after doing some reading.

After students have had a chance to cut and sort the statements, *ask*

? If these rocks could talk, what do you think they could tell you? (Answers will vary.)

Tell students that every rock has a "story" to tell—its age, where it formed, how it formed, what it is made of, what it could be used for, etc. Geologists observe and test rocks to figure out their "stories." *Ask*

? Wouldn't it be fun to interview a rock to find out its story?

If Rocks Could Talk Interviews

1. Divide the class into groups of 4–6 students.

2. Give each student a copy of the If Rocks Could Talk student page. Have them quickly scan the text and notice the text features.

3. Ask, "What do you notice about the text?"

(It is about rocks, the rocks can talk, it is written as a script/interview/reader's theater/play, it is mostly dialogue, it has a cast of characters, there are different characters or roles, it is divided into two parts or episodes, etc.)

4. Ask, "Who are the different characters in the cast?" (Announcer, Geologist, Obsidian, Quartz)

5. Explain that each student in a group will have a speaking part. If there are four students in their group, each student will be either the Announcer, the Geologist, Obsidian, or Quartz. If there are five students, they will have a different Geologist for each episode. If there are six students, they will have a different Geologist and a different Announcer for each episode.

6. Have the students in each group divide up the speaking parts, or assign them yourself. (Note that the Announcer has the fewest lines.)

7. Ask students to read the script silently, paying close attention to any information that can help them complete their Venn diagrams.

8. Have students highlight and practice their own speaking part.

9. Have students perform the script within their own groups.

10. Optional: Choose a group or invite a group to volunteer, and have the students perform a reader's theater for the whole class. A reader's theater is a style of theater in which the actors read aloud from a script without costumes, scenery, or much movement. Actors rely on vocal expression to tell the story.

> **CCC: Stability and Change**
> Things may change slowly or rapidly.

After the If Rocks Could Talk activity, have students return to their Venn diagrams and work with their group or a partner to check their answers using information from the scripts. They may need to move the statements to the correct place. After they complete the Venn diagram, have them tape or glue the statements onto the paper. Answers are as follows:

Obsidian	Both	Granite
smooth texture	Formed from melted rock	rough texture
Cooled quickly from lava above ground		Cooled slowly from magma underground
Used for knives and arrowheads	Has many uses	Used for gravestones and countertops

IF ROCKS COULD TALK READER'S THEATER

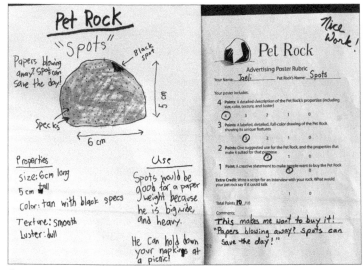

PET ROCK ADVERTISEMENT

evaluate

Pet Rock Posters

Connecting to the Common Core
Writing
TEXT TYPES AND PURPOSES: 2.2

Ask students if they have ever heard of a Pet Rock. Explain that way back in 1975, a businessman in California came up with the idea of selling rocks as pets. He considered dogs, cats, and birds too messy and expensive to keep and instead advertised his Pet Rock as the ideal pet. The Pet Rock was packaged in a box that looked like a pet carrying case, and it even came with a "Pet Rock Training Manual." Topics included "How to Make Your Pet Rock Roll Over and Play Dead" and "How to House-Train Your Pet Rock." Believe it or not, the Pet Rock became a huge hit and the salesman became rich. (Optional: Show students a photo of the original Pet Rock and its packaging.) *Ask*

? Would you have bought your own Pet Rock if you lived in the 1970s?

? Why do you think this businessman was able to sell so many Pet Rocks? (Answers might include: He had an original idea, and he used creative packaging and advertising.)

? What are some ways that advertisements help sell products? (Answers might include: They describe them, they make them sound useful, and they make them seem fun.)

Pass out the Pet Rock Poster Rubric student page and challenge students to create an advertisement for a Pet Rock. You may want to have them use either their own special rock or the rock they identified using the book *Rocks: Hard, Soft, Smooth, and Rough.* Have them give their rock a clever name ("Dusty," "Rocky," and "Cliff" come to mind!) and then design an ad to sell the rock. The advertisement should show what they have learned about properties of rocks, including:

• **4 Points:** A detailed description of the Pet Rock's properties (including size, color, texture, and luster)

• **3 Points:** A labeled, detailed, full-color drawing of the Pet Rock showing its unique features

• **2 Points:** One suggested use for the Pet Rock and the properties that make it suited for that purpose

• **1 Point:** A creative statement to make people want to buy the Pet Rock

• **Extra Credit:** Write a script for an interview with your rock. What would your Pet Rock say if it could talk?

Have students share their advertisements with the rest of the class or have a gallery walk.

STEM Everywhere

Give students the STEM Everywhere student page as a way to involve their families and extend their learning. They can do the activity with an adult helper and share their results with the class. If students do not have the internet at home, you may choose to have them complete this activity at school.

Opportunities for Differentiated Instruction

This box lists questions and challenges related to the lesson that students may select to research, investigate, or innovate. Students may also use the questions as examples to help them generate their own questions. These questions can help you move your students from the teacher-directed investigation to engaging in the science and engineering practices in a more student-directed format.

Extra Support

For students who are struggling to meet the lesson objectives, provide a question and guide them in the process of collecting research or helping them design procedures or solutions.

Extensions

For students with high interest or who have already met the lesson objectives, have them choose a question (or pose their own question), conduct their own research, and design their own procedures or solutions.

After selecting one of the questions in the box or formulating their own question, students can individually or collaboratively make predictions, design investigations or surveys to test their predictions, collect evidence, devise explanations, design solutions, or examine related resources. They can communicate their findings through a science notebook, at a poster session or gallery walk, or by producing a media project.

Research

Have students brainstorm researchable questions:

? What are some common rocks that can be found in your state? What are they used for?

? What are some different kinds of geologists? What do they do?

? What technologies help geologists explore volcanoes?

Investigate

Have students brainstorm testable questions to be solved through science or math:

? Can you use Moh's Hardness Scale to test different minerals for hardness? (See *Rocks: Hard, Soft, Smooth, and Rough* page 23)

? How can you measure the volume of a rock (how much space it takes up)?

? Can you make your own sandstone brick? (See *Rocks: Hard, Soft, Smooth, and Rough* page 22)

Innovate

Have students brainstorm problems to be solved through engineering:

? Can you design a display case for a rock collection?

? Can you design and create a mosaic, balanced rock sculpture, birdhouse, etc. using small rocks?

? Can you design a robot that could explore an active volcano? Draw it!

Websites

 "Iceland volcano: Drone footage captures stunning up-close view of eruption" (video)
www.youtube.com/watch?v=b9Hq6bTBF2A

 If Rocks Could Talk (interviews adapted from American Museum of Natural History Website)
www.amnh.org/explore/ology/earth/if-rocks-could-talk2/obsidian

More Books to Read

Baylor, B. 1985. *Everybody needs a rock*. New York: Aladdin.
Summary: Everybody needs a rock—at least that's the way this particular rock hound feels about it in presenting her own highly individualistic rules for finding just the right rock for you.

Hooper, M. 2015. *The pebble in my pocket: A history of our Earth*. New York: Viking Juvenile.
Summary: A girl finds a pebble on the ground and wonders where it came from. The answer unfolds through scientifically accurate text, colorful illustrations, and a helpful timeline that follows the pebble's long journey from the inside of a volcano to the day the girl picks it up off the ground.

Miller, P. 2021. *What can you do with a rock?* Naperville, IL: Sourcebooks.
Summary: Simple text and colorful illustrations answer the question, what can you do with a rock?

Salas, L. 2015. *A rock can be…* Minneapolis: Millbrook Press.
Summary: From Salas and Dabija, the team who created *A Leaf Can Be…* and *Water Can Be…*, this book sparks the reader's imagination by sharing some of the many things a rock can be: a tall mountain, a park fountain, a food grinder, a path winder, and so on.

Wenzel, B. 2019. *A stone sat still*. San Francisco: Chronicle Books.
Summary: This beautifully illustrated book tells the story of a stone that seems ordinary. But to the animals that encounter the stone, it serves many purposes.

I Found a Rock

Color	Texture	Luster	Size
What colors or patterns does it have?	How does it feel?	How shiny or dull is it?	What is the longest length in cm?

Labeled Drawing of My Rock

I found a rock that would be good for _____

because it is _____ .

Name: _____

Comparing Rocks Venn Diagram

Directions: Observe the two rocks with a hand lens. Then cut out the statements at the bottom of the page, and place each statement below Obsidian, Granite, or Both.

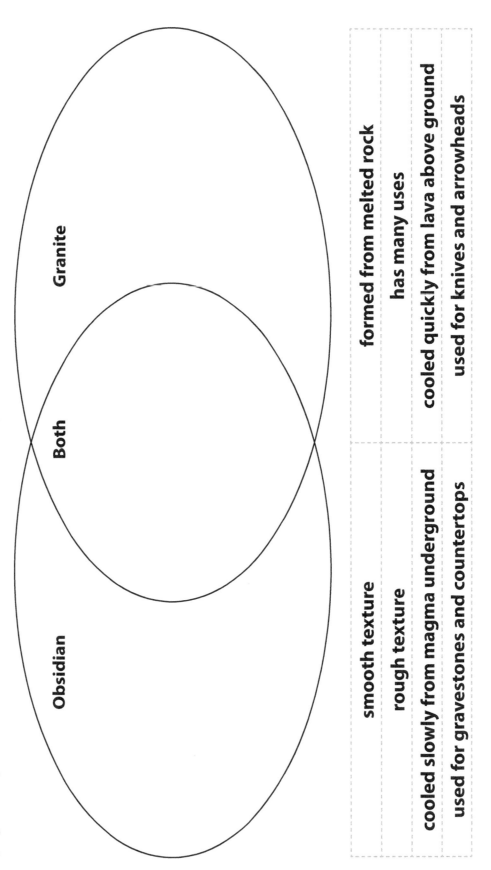

Obsidian   Both   Granite

smooth texture

rough texture

cooled slowly from magma underground

used for gravestones and countertops

formed from melted rock

has many uses

cooled quickly from lava above ground

used for knives and arrowheads

If Rocks Could Talk

Episode 1

Cast: Announcer, Geologist, Obsidian

ANNOUNCER: Welcome to the show "If Rocks Could Talk!"

ALL: (*clapping*)

ANNOUNCER: Can rocks talk? Of course not! But if they could, we're here to find out what they would say.

GEOLOGIST: My name is Dr. _____. I'm a geologist.

ANNOUNCER: A geologist is a scientist who studies the Earth's surface.

GEOLOGIST: Indeed. I'll be your geologist on this episode of "If Rocks Could Talk." Today we're going to meet a rock with a very interesting story.

OBSIDIAN: Can we get started already? I don't have all day!

GEOLOGIST: Sorry folks, Obsidian is a bit hot-tempered. I guess that's what happens when you erupt from a volcano.

OBSIDIAN: Very funny.

GEOLOGIST: So, tell us how you formed.

OBSIDIAN: Well, it all began deep underground. There's so much heat and pressure down there that rocks can melt!

ANNOUNCER: You heard it here first, folks. Rocks can melt!

OBSIDIAN: They sure can. Did you know there are pools of hot melted rock called magma miles below the Earth's surface?

GEOLOGIST: I knew that. But go on.

OBSIDIAN: And if there's a crack or weak zone above it, that magma is gonna blow!

GEOLOGIST: Indeed it is.

OBSIDIAN: Next thing you know, you've got yourself a volcanic eruption!

If Rocks Could Talk, Episode 1, Continued

GEOLOGIST: What happens then?

OBSIDIAN: Well, when the magma reaches the surface, it's called lava. The lava flows out and cools off. I formed above ground when some of that lava cooled.

GEOLOGIST: Well, I "lava" your smooth texture.

ANNOUNCER: Let's take a short break to observe Obsidian's texture! (*Everyone looks at obsidian using hand lenses.*)

ALL (*Except Obsidian*): Ooohhh, pretty!

OBSIDIAN: Pretty sharp, too. In fact, Native Americans used to carve obsidian into knives and arrowheads.

GEOLOGIST: Why are you so smooth and sharp? I don't see any crystals at all!

OBSIDIAN: I don't know if you've ever seen a volcano erupt –

GEOLOGIST: No, but it would really "mag-ma" day!

OBSIDIAN: Very funny. Anyway, some events on Earth, like volcanic eruptions, happen very quickly. And hot lava can cool off quickly when it hits air or water.

GEOLOGIST: And?

OBSIDIAN: When a certain type of lava cools very quickly, obsidian can form!

GEOLOGIST: And?

OBSIDIAN: When you cool and harden that fast, you don't have time to form big, shiny crystals like some rocks. You're just...glass. (*looks sad*)

GEOLOGIST: Don't be sad! Your properties may be different, but they make you special. I mean, not all rocks can be used for arrowheads!

ANNOUNCER: And there you have it, folks! Rocks have different properties!

ALL: (*clapping*)

Adapted from www.amnh.org/explore/ology/earth/if-rocks-could-talk2

National Science Teaching Association

If Rocks Could Talk

Episode 2

Cast: Announcer, Geologist, Granite

ANNOUNCER: Welcome to the second episode of "If Rocks Could Talk!"

ALL: (*clapping*)

GEOLOGIST: My name is Dr. _____. I'm a geologist. On our last episode, we spoke with Obsidian. Obsidian is a smooth, shiny volcanic rock that can form when lava cools very quickly above ground. Our next guest will answer the question "What happens when magma cools very slowly underground?" (*looks around for Granite*)

GRANITE: Yo. I'm right here.

GEOLOGIST: Oh, sorry, Granite, I didn't see you there. You're not quite as flashy as Obsidian.

GRANITE: I may not be flashy, but don't just take me for "granite."

GEOLOGIST: You're a real joker, aren't you?

GRANITE: Yeah, I had like, thousands of years to think of jokes while I was cooling off.

GEOLOGIST: Thousands of years indeed. Anyway, on our last episode, we learned that some changes on Earth happen very quickly. Volcanic eruptions. The cooling of lava into obsidian. But other events happen very slowly, over a period of time much longer than any human can observe. The formation of the Grand Canyon. The cooling of magma into —

GRANITE: Yo, you want me to tell my story or what?

GEOLOGIST: Oh, so you're a tough guy.

GRANITE: You could say that. I mean, haven't you ever seen gravestones made of granite? Countertops? Buildings? You ever been to Mount Rushmore?

If Rocks Could Talk, Episode 2, Continued

GEOLOGIST: OK, I get it, you're strong.

GRANITE: I sure am. So here's my story. A few billion years ago, I formed from melted rock.

GEOLOGIST: Like Obsidian did.

GRANITE: Yeah, but not quite like that. I didn't shoot out of a volcano like Obsidian. I took my time, kept it on the "down low."

GEOLOGIST: Are you saying you formed in a pocket of hot, liquid magma deep underground?

GRANITE: Yeah, sure. Took thousands of years for that magma to cool down. In fact, I cooled so slowly I had plenty of time to grow all these shiny specks.

GEOLOGIST: Crystals? Mind if we take a closer look?

ANNOUNCER: Let's take a short break to look at Granite's crystals! (*Everyone looks at Granite using hand lenses.*)

ALL (*Except Granite*): Ooohhh, pretty crystals!

GRANITE: Aw, shucks!

GEOLOGIST: You know, Granite, even though you have a rough texture, you are pretty cool.

GRANITE: Yeah, well, sorry we got off to a rocky start.

GEOLOGIST: No hard feelings.

ANNOUNCER: And there you have it, folks! Rocks can form quickly or rocks can form slowly. Rocks have different properties. Annnnd...rocks can be very useful!

ALL: (*clapping*)

GRANITE: Rocks rock!

GEOLOGIST: Indeed!

Adapted from www.amnh.org/explore/ology/earth/if-rocks-could-talk2

Pet Rock

Advertising Poster Rubric

Your Name: _____ Pet Rock's Name: _____

Your poster includes:

4 **Points**: A detailed description of the Pet Rock's properties (including size, color, texture, and luster)

    4   3   2   1   0

3 **Points**: A labeled, detailed, full-color drawing of the Pet Rock showing its unique features

         3   2   1   0

2 **Points**: One suggested use for the Pet Rock and the properties that make it suited for that purpose

               2   1   0

1 **Point**: A creative statement to make people want to buy the Pet Rock

                        1   0

Extra Credit: Write a script for an interview with your rock. What would your pet rock say if it could talk?

                        1   0

Total Points_____/10

Comments:

_____

_____

Name: _____

STEM Everywhere

Dear Families,

At school, we have been learning about rocks. We learned that rocks have different properties and can be used for different purposes. We also learned that some rocks form quickly and others form slowly. To find out more, ask your learner the following questions and discuss their answers:

- What did you learn?
- What was your favorite part of the lesson?
- What are you still wondering?

You can watch a video together called "Scientist Profile: Rock Scientist," which features a geologist working in the field and lab.

 To watch the video, scan the QR code, go to *www.pbslearningmedia.org* and search for "Rock Scientist," or go to *www.pbslearningmedia.org/resource/46106c1c-0ed0-4887-af0e-fcc523739dfd/46106c1c-0ed0-4887-af0e-fcc523739dfd*

After you watch the video, look around your neighborhood and notice rocks being used for different purposes (building materials, decorations, landscaping, etc.). Draw or write the ways you see rocks being used below.

Wind and Water

Description

Students explore the phenomenon that wind and water can change the shape of the land and remove soil. They explore natural solutions that can help control erosion, such as planting trees and grass, as well as technologies, such as building levees and installing erosion control fabric. Finally, they compare multiple solutions to an erosion problem and describe one that they think will be the best.

Alignment with the *Next Generation Science Standards*

Performance Expectations

2-ESS1-1: Use information from several sources to provide evidence that Earth events can occur quickly or slowly.

2-ESS2-1: Compare multiple solutions designed to slow or prevent wind or water from changing the shape of the land.

K-2-ETS1-3: Analyze data from tests of two objects designed to solve the same problem to compare the strengths and weaknesses of how each performs.

Science and Engineering Practices	Disciplinary Core Ideas	Crosscutting Concept
Analyzing and Interpreting Data Use observations (firsthand or from media) to describe patterns and/or relationships in the natural and designed world in order to answer scientific questions and solve problems. **Constructing Explanations and Designing Solutions** Compare multiple solutions to a problem.	**ESS1.C: The History of Planet Earth** Some events happen very quickly; others occur very slowly over a time period much longer than one can observe. **ESS2.A: Earth Materials and Systems** Wind and water can change the shape of the land. **ETS1.C: Optimizing the Design Solution** Because there is always more than one possible solution to a problem, it is useful to compare and test designs.	**Stability and Change** Things may change slowly or rapidly.

Note: The activities in this lesson will help students move toward the performance expectations listed, which is the goal after multiple activities. However, the activities will not by themselves be sufficient to reach the performance expectations.

Featured Picture Books

TITLE: ***Kate, Who Tamed the Wind***
AUTHOR: **Liz Garton Scanlon**
ILLUSTRATOR: **Lee White**
PUBLISHER: **Schwartz and Wade Books**
YEAR: **2018**
GENRE: **Story**
SUMMARY: *A resourceful girl named Kate has a neighbor who lives at the top of a very steep hill. The wind is blowing everything away, including the clothes on his clothesline, the shutters on his house, and even his words. Kate solves the man's problem with the wind by designing an environmentally sound solution: planting trees.*

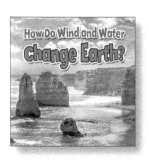

TITLE: ***How Do Wind and Water Change Earth?***
AUTHOR: **Natalie Hyde**
PUBLISHER: **Crabtree Publishing**
YEAR: **2015**
GENRE: **Non-Narrative Information**
SUMMARY: *This nonfiction book defines* weathering *and* erosion, *describes fast and slow changes that build up and wear down landforms, and identifies ways that water changes Earth through rivers, tides, landslides, freeze/thaw cycles, and glaciers.*

Time Needed

This lesson will take several class periods. Suggested scheduling is as follows:

Session 1:   **Engage** with *Kate, Who Tamed the Wind* Read-Aloud and **Explore** with Wind and Water Change Earth's Surface Media Gallery

Session 2:   **Explore** with Wind and Water Model

Session 3:   **Explain** with *How Do Wind and Water Change Earth?* Cloze and Read-Aloud and Erosion Problems

Session 4:   **Elaborate** with Erosion Solutions Journal and **Evaluate** with Comparing Solutions

Session 5 and beyond: **Evaluate** with A Local Erosion Problem

Materials

Note: Throughout the lesson, a computer and a whiteboard or projector will be needed to display images.

For Wind and Water Model (per class)

• Large, shallow, clear plastic tub or container, approx. 40 qt. capacity
• Approx. 10 lbs. of clean, damp play sand
• Small toy house or upside-down plastic cup

- 6 plastic hand pumps
- 6 plastic squeeze bottles (12–16 oz.)
- 24 miniature plastic trees (the kind used for cupcake décor or crafts)
- 6 safety goggles
- Water supply
- (Optional) Stopwatch or cell phone timer

SAFETY
Students should wear safety goggles when using sand.

For How Do Wind and Water Change Earth? *Cloze and Read-Aloud*

- Scissors
- Tape or glue

Student Pages

- Wind and Water Cloze
- Erosion Solutions Journal (stapled)
- STEM Everywhere

Background for Teachers

Scientists have evidence that Earth is at least 4.5 billion years old. During this long span of time, Earth's surface has been in a state of constant change. Both constructive and destructive forces of nature have changed Earth's surface throughout its history. *Constructive forces*, such as volcanic eruptions, crustal deformation, and deposition, build up mountains and landmasses. *Destructive forces*, such as weathering and erosion, wear away Earth's surface. *Weathering* refers to the physical breakdown of rock caused by factors such as water, wind, freeze-thaw cycles, and plant roots, or chemical breakdown such as the wearing away of rock surfaces by acid rain. *Erosion* occurs when weathered rock and soil fragments are transported to another place by wind, water, or ice. *Deposition* occurs when the materials are dropped in another place.

Most changes to Earth's surface caused by weathering and erosion happen very slowly over many years. For example, slow-moving glaciers can take hundreds or thousands of years to create valleys and other landforms through erosion. Geologists estimate it took the Colorado River 5–6 million years to carve out the Grand Canyon. However, some changes can occur in a matter of minutes, hours, or days. Riverbank erosion can happen quickly during a flood or storm surge. A rapidly moving landslide or mudslide, triggered by heavy rain, wind, or earthquakes, can change the surface of Earth in minutes. The powerful waves, wind, and heavy rainfall caused by a strong hurricane can move massive amounts of sand away from beaches, reshaping the coastal landscape quickly. Sandstorms and dust storms can lift large amounts of sand and dust from bare, dry soils and deposit them miles away in a matter of hours.

Wind affects landscapes through a process called *wind erosion*, in which wind breaks up land and carries soil, sand, and bits of rock to other places. Wind erosion can have a devastating effect on farmland by removing fertile topsoil. Eroded soil can be deposited in waterways where it affects water quality. It can also be emitted into the air where it affects air quality.

There are a variety of methods that can control both wind and water erosion, with many more being developed. Erosion control methods protect farmland and residential landscapes from soil loss, prevent water pollution caused by stormwater runoff, reduce habitat loss, and diminish human property damage. A natural way to prevent erosion is by planting vegetation. Plant roots hold the soil together and prevent excess movement. Tree trunks, leaves, and branches protect soil from wind. Examples include planting dune grass to protect sand dunes, planting trees in strategic places to act as windbreaks, planting cover crops, and inserting live willow stakes into the ground to hold soil in place along streambanks. Mulching with plant materials is another natural but short-term erosion control method.

Other erosion control methods include structural solutions such as earthen or concrete levees, floodwalls, retaining walls, terraces, fences, gravel, and riprap (large rocks installed in mesh where a structure or shoreline is exposed to rushing water). There are also many technologies that have been developed to control erosion, such as *erosion control fabrics* made of materials like coconut fiber, straw, or geotextiles. These fabrics protect loose soil from short-term erosion while promoting germination and plant growth for long-term erosion control. Ideally, native plants should be used in combination with erosion control fabric.

The advantages and disadvantages of any solution must be considered when planning erosion control. For example, many plastics used in erosion control are not biodegradable. Wildlife can get entangled in plastic netting, which is especially deadly to snakes. The application of larger-sized riprap makes it difficult for wildlife to move along a shoreline. Levees can fail, causing catastrophic damage. Some erosion control methods may not be aesthetically pleasing, and people often avoid adopting any solution that reduces profits, takes too long to work, or is too labor-intensive or expensive.

In this lesson, students use the science and engineering practice (SEP) of obtaining, evaluating, and communicating information as they read about the effects of wind and water erosion on soil and landforms. Then they apply the SEP of constructing explanations and designing solutions as they compare solutions to slow or prevent wind and water erosion. Students recognize the crosscutting concept (CCC) of stability and change as they learn how some changes to Earth's surface occur slowly, over many years, or rapidly, over hours or days. The idea that wind and water can change the shape of land is a foundational concept that students will build upon in later grades.

Learning Progressions

Below are the disciplinary core idea (DCI) grade band endpoints for grades K–2 and 3–5. These are provided to show how student understanding of the DCIs in this lesson will progress in future grade levels.

DCIs	Grades K–2	Grades 3–5
ESS1.C: The History of Planet Earth	• Some events happen very quickly; others occur very slowly, over a time period much longer than one can observe.	• Local, regional, and global patterns of rock formations reveal changes over time due to Earth forces such as earthquakes. The presence and location of certain fossil types indicate the order in which rock layers were formed.

Continued

Learning Progressions (continued)

DCIs	Grades K–2	Grades 3–5
ESS2.A: Earth Materials and Systems	• Wind and water can change the shape of the land..	• Rainfall helps to shape the land and affects the types of living things found in a region. Water, ice, wind, living organisms, and gravity break rocks, soils, and sediments into smaller particles and move them around.
ETS1.C: Optimizing the Design Solution	• Because there is always more than one possible solution to a problem, it is useful to compare and test designs.	• Different solutions need to be tested in order to determine which of them best solves the problem, given the criteria and the constraints.

Source: Willard, T., ed. 2015. *The NSTA quick-reference guide to the* NGSS: *Elementary school.* Arlington, VA: NSTA Press.

engage

Kate, Who Tamed the Wind
Read-Aloud

Connecting to the Common Core
Reading: Literature
KEY IDEAS AND DETAILS: 2.1

**Inferring**

Show students the cover of *Kate, Who Tamed the Wind* and share the names of the author and illustrator. *Ask*

❓ What do you think the title means? (Answers will vary.)

❓ What does the word *tame* mean? (Answers will vary, but students may make analogies to taming an animal or use words such as *control, tone down, conquer*, etc.)

❓ Can you see wind? (no)

❓ How can you tell from the cover that it's windy there? (there are leaves in the air, the trees are bent)

**Making Connections: Text to Self**

❓ Have you ever lost anything to the wind? (Answers will vary.)

❓ Can you stop the wind from blowing? (no)

❓ How could you keep the wind from carrying away your things? (Answers will vary, but students may have tied things down, used rocks as paperweights, or used windbreaks such as umbrellas.)

Tell students that as you read, you would like them to listen for what the author means by "taming the wind." Read the book aloud, then *ask*

❓ What did the man lose to the wind? (clothes from the clothesline, shutters, boards, his hat, even his words)

❓ How did Kate make her plan to help the man? (She drew her ideas on the ground with chalk.)

❓ What was Kate's plan? (to carry trees in a wagon to the top of the hill, plant them around the man's house, and wait for them to grow)

? How did the illustrator show that much time had passed by the end of the story? (the man's beard had turned gray, Kate had grown up)

? Did Kate's plan work? How do you know? (Yes, because the neighbor's things were no longer lost to the wind.)

 ## Synthesizing

? Now that you have heard the story, what do you think the title means? (Kate did something to "tame," or control, the wind in order to help her neighbor.)

explore

Wind and Water Change Earth's Surface Media Gallery

 ### Turn and Talk

After reading, have students turn to a partner and discuss this question:

? What can wind do? (Answers may include damage homes, move or carry objects, blow down trees, and so on.)

 Then project this photo of a field in Kansas: *https://agriculture.ks.gov/images/ default-source/default-album/wind-erosion.jpg?sfvrsn=f8a78ac1_0*

Ask

? What do you think is happening in the picture? (Wind is blowing away the soil from the field.)

? Why do you think that is happening? (The soil is dry, it is windy, there are no trees to block the wind, there is nothing covering the soil, there are no plants holding the soil in place, etc.)

? How do you think that affects the farmer? (The farmer's crops would not grow, or grow as well, without the topsoil.)

> **SEP: Analyzing and Interpreting Data**
> Use observations (firsthand or from media) to describe patterns and/or relationships in the natural and designed world in order to answer scientific questions and solve problems.

Tell students you are going to show some more videos and photographs of wind changing Earth's surface. Have students make observations and share them with a partner as you project the media collection called "Wind Changes Earth's Surface."

This collection features videos and photos of the following phenomena:

- Wind blowing sand on sand dunes
- Sand covering a bench
- A tornado forming
- Trees knocked down by the wind

 www.pbslearningmedia.org/resource/ buac20-k2-sci-ess-windandwaterchanges/ wind-and-water-change-earths-surface

Stop after sharing each example from the media collection, and *ask*

? What did you notice? (Answers will vary.)

? What do you wonder? (Answers will vary.)

? What can wind do? (move sand or soil, form a tornado, knock down trees)

? Do those things happen quickly or slowly? (Some happen quickly, some happen more slowly. Some occur in seconds, like the tornado. Others can take hours or days, like the wind blowing the sand to cover the bench. Some changes can even take many years to happen.)

Then *ask*

? What other things can change Earth's surface? (Answers will vary, but students may know about water erosion, earthquakes, volcanoes, landslides, glaciers, etc.)

Tell students that you are going to show some videos and photographs of water changing Earth's surface. Have students make observations and share them with their partner as you project the media collection called "Water Changes Earth's Surface." (Use the same web address as before, but scroll to find the "Water" gallery.)

This collection features videos and photos of the following phenomena:

• Water moving small rocks and sand along a riverbed

• A riverbank that has been worn away by water

• A mudslide caused by extreme rainfall

• Waves breaking off large pieces of land from a coastline

• Waves wearing away the underside of a coastal cliff

Stop after sharing each example from the media collection, and *ask*

? What did you notice? (Answers will vary.)

? What do you wonder? (Answers will vary.)

? What can water do? (move rocks or sand, wear away the bank of a river, cause a mudslide, break off large pieces of land from a coastline, wear away the underside of a cliff)

? Do those things happen quickly or slowly? (Some happen quickly; some happen more slowly. Some occur in seconds, like the mudslide. Others can take hours or days, like the riverbank being worn away by water. Some changes can even take many years to happen.)

Wind and Water Model

Note: This activity can be messy and is best done outside.

Pour about 10 lbs of clean, damp play sand into a long, clear plastic tub (the bigger, the better) and form it into a steep hill. Place a small toy house or an upside-down plastic cup at the peak of the hill to represent the house where Kate's neighbor lives. Press the house firmly into the sand so it doesn't move easily. Have hand pumps, squirt bottles, and a water source nearby.

Then gather students around the container, and tell them that scientists and engineers often build models to help them understand phenomena such as the effects of wind and water on Earth's surface. Have students think back to the book *Kate, Who Tamed the Wind*, and *ask*

? What does the pile of sand represent in this model? (the hill where the neighbor lived)

DEMONSTRATING THE POWER OF WIND

DEMONSTRATING THE POWER OF WATER

MODELING KATE'S SOLUTION

? What do the grains of sand represent? (soil)

? What does the model of a house represent? (the neighbor's house)

? What problem did the neighbor have? (There was too much wind.)

? How could we represent wind in our model? (Blow on the sand and the house.)

Demonstrate the power of wind by having no more than six students at a time put on safety goggles and use hand pumps to blow on the mound of sand (you may want to set a timer for 10 seconds). Make sure no one is standing "down wind." For fun, have the rest of the class make "wind sounds"!

Have the class make observations after each group of students has blown on the sand. Then *ask*

? What did you notice? (Students should notice that the "wind" blows sand away.)

? What can wind do? (blow sand/soil, carry sand/soil away, destroy landforms)

Next, demonstrate the power of water by having no more than six students at a time put on safety goggles and use squeeze bottles to squirt water on the mound of sand (you may want set a timer for 10 seconds). For fun, have the rest of the class make "rain sounds"!

Have the class make observations after each group of students has squirted water on the sand. Then *ask*

? What did you notice? (Students should notice that the water moves the sand aside to form trenches or channels and that some of the sand is carried away to the bottom of the hill by the water.)

? What can water do? (move sand/soil, carry sand/soil away, destroy landforms)

Next, ask students to think back to Kate's idea in the book *Kate, Who Tamed the Wind. Ask*

? What could we do to protect our sand hill from wearing away? (Plant something on it.)

SEP: Analyzing and Interpreting Data
Use observations (firsthand or from media) to describe patterns and/or relationships in the natural and designed world in order to answer scientific questions and solve problems.

Tell students that you can use plastic trees to represent the trees planted by Kate. (*Note*: You may need to reform the sand dune before moving forward.) Have students press the trees firmly into the sand. Then have a few more students take turns blowing air and squirting water on the sand. *Ask*

? What did you notice? (Answers will vary.)

? What was different this time? (Answers will vary.)

? Did the solution work? (Answers will vary.)

Students should be able to recognize that the addition of the plastic trees helped keep some of the sand from moving when they blew or squirted water on it.

explain

How Do Wind and Water Change Earth? Cloze and Read-Aloud

Connecting to the Common Core
Reading: Informational Text
CRAFT AND STRUCTURE: 2.4, 2.5

**Using Features of Nonfiction**

CCC: Stability and Change
Things may change slowly or rapidly.

Tell students that you are going to read a book that will help them learn more about how wind and water change Earth's surface. Share the cover of *How Do Wind and Water Change Earth?* and introduce the author. Then flip through the book to show the table of contents and some of the interior pages. *Ask*

? Is this book fiction or nonfiction? (nonfiction)

? How can you tell? (Answers may include it has a table of contents, photographs, bold-print words, and an index.)

Connecting to the Common Core
Language
VOCABULARY ACQUISITION AND USE: 2.6

Cloze
Pass out the Wind and Water Cloze student page. Student directions are as follows:

1. Cut out the cards at the bottom of the page.

2. Read the cloze, and fill in each blank with the card you think belongs there.

3. Listen carefully while your teacher reads the book *How Do Wind and Water Change Earth?*

CLOZE ACTIVITY

4. After reviewing the cloze as a class, move the cards if necessary. Then glue or tape them on the page.

5. On the back, draw an example of *erosion*.

After reading pages 4–19 of the book aloud, discuss the cloze and give students the opportunity to move the cards if necessary. Bring attention to the words *quickly* and *slowly* and how they are used in the cloze paragraph. Explain that some changes, like the ones caused by floodwaters (page 11), can be observed within hours. Other changes, like flowing water carving deep valleys (page 14), occur over a period of time much longer than one person could observe.

When students are satisfied with their choices, they can tape or glue the cards to the page.

CCC: Stability and Change
Things may change slowly or rapidly.

Next, have students draw an example of erosion on the back of their papers, and then have a few students share and discuss their drawings.

The completed cloze should read as follows:

Wind and Water

1. Wind, water, and ice can break large landforms into small pieces. This is a slow process called <u>weathering</u>. (page 4)

2. Air that moves is called <u>wind</u>. (page 4)

3. Moving material from one place to another is called <u>erosion</u>. (page 7)

4. Almost three-quarters of Earth is covered by <u>water</u>. (page 10)

5. <u>Floodwaters</u> can make big changes to Earth's surface quickly by moving rocks and carving out new channels. (page 11)

6. Rivers and streams can slowly carve out deep valleys with steep sides called <u>canyons</u>. (page 14)

7. When too much rain hits soil or sand, it can begin to slide away. This is called a <u>landslide</u>. (page 17)

8. Slow-moving rivers of ice are called <u>glaciers</u>. (page 18)

Erosion Problems

Questioning

Connecting to the Common Core
Reading: Informational Text
KEY IDEAS AND DETAILS: 2.1

Explain that erosion and weathering are happening to Earth's surface all the time. Sometimes these processes produce interesting and beautiful landforms, such as the Grand Canyon pictured on page 14. However, many times these processes are harmful to the land and people living on it. *Ask*

? What are some examples of harmful effects of weathering and erosion from the book? (floods, landslides)

? Have you ever seen any of the harmful effects of weathering and erosion in your neighborhood? (Students may have noticed flooded baseball fields, eroded streambanks, bare spots in their yards, etc.)

You may want to share some examples of erosion you have seen in your own neighborhood or around the school. Then show erosion time-lapse images from the internet (such as the ones at the following link) and have students discuss their observations and wonderings.

 www.usgs.gov/media/images/ coastal-erosion-san-francisco-3

Ask

? What could be done to repair this damage and prevent further erosion? (Answers will vary. Students will learn more about erosion control methods in the elaborate phase.)

 For more examples of erosion problems, project the following gallery: *https://lakeshoreguys.com/shoreline-erosion-photos*

elaborate

Erosion Solutions Journal

Explain that thankfully, there are many solutions available for erosion problems. Pass out the Erosion Solutions Journal student pages. It has space for drawing and writing about four different types of solutions for controlling erosion:

- Using **plants**
- Covering soil with **fabric**
- Installing **rock** or building retaining **walls**
- Constructing earthen or concrete **levees**

  (*Note:* These solutions are often used in combination with one another.)

For each page of the journal, read the solution together, then show a variety of examples using photos and videos. (Suggestions are in the chart that follows, but local examples would be ideal!)

> **SEP: Constructing Explanations and Designing Solutions**
> Compare multiple solutions to a problem.

LOCAL EROSION PROBLEM AND SOLUTION

Table 16.1 Erosion Solutions

Type	Examples	
Use **plants** to hold sand or soil in place	How Do Plants Prevent Erosion? (diagram) *https://socratic.org/questions/how-do-plants-prevent-erosion*	
	Willow Cuttings for Stream Erosion Control *https://bygl.osu.edu/sites/default/files/inline-images/Willow%20 Erosion%20Control%20-%20JB.jpg*	
	"How to Plant Dune Grass for Coastal Sustainability" (video) *www.youtube.com/watch?v=kDRuaF1H7XU*	
	"Wind Break" (video) *www.youtube.com/watch?v=95Slo2Fv3og*	
Cover soil with **fabric** to hold soil in place while plants grow through it	Jute Erosion Control Fabric *www.fisherbag.com/wp-content/uploads/2015/09/fisherbag-Jute-Erosion-Control.jpg*	
	Salmon River Bank Stabilization (erosion control fabric and plants) *www.intermountainaquatics.com/salmonriver*	
	The Kawainui Watershed Permanent BMP Project (plastic erosion control fabric over mulch and grass seeds) *www.stormwaterhawaii.com/portfolio/ kawainui-watershed-permanent-bmp-project*	
	Backyard Stream Repair (installation of erosion control matting) *www.youtube.com/watch?v=_qUWLMVBYY4*	

Continued

Table 16.1 Erosion Solutions *(continued)*

Type	Examples	
Install **rocks** or build retaining **walls** to hold soil in place	Riprap Shoreline Restoration (riprap rock over fabric) *https://lakeshoreguys.com/our-work*	
	Creek Bank Erosion Control (riprap rock over fabric) *https://reynoldscontractingva.com/creek-bank-erosion-control*	
	Rocks *https://tdhlandscaping.com/wp-content/uploads/2019/06/Internal-page-Erosion-Control-Drainage.jpg*	
	Retaining Walls *https://bythewall.com/retaining-walls*	
Construct earthen or concrete **levees** on riverbanks to control flooding	"What Are Levees?" (video) *https://www.youtube.com/watch?v=X-pxokpBDvk*	
	Wikipedia Media File: Levees (click through gallery) *https://en.wikipedia.org/wiki/Levee#/media/File:Sacramento_River_Levee.jpg*	
	A New Orleans Levee *https://image.cnbcfm.com/api/v1/image/102945760-GettyImages-482149280.jpg?v=1529469328&w=630&h=354*	
	Earthen Levee on the Ohio River *https://kgs.uky.edu/kgsweb/download/misc/landuse/UNION/unionissues_files/image016.jpg*	

As you show examples for each type of solution, discuss the following:

? How does the solution control erosion? (Answers will vary.)

? What do you think are some advantages, or positive things, about the solution? (Students may note that the solution seems safe for people, animals, and the environment; uses natural materials; seems inexpensive or easy to use; is nice to look at; and so on.)

? What do you think are some disadvantages, or negative things, about the solution? (Students may note that the solution could harm people, animals, or the environment; seems expensive or difficult to use; would take a long time to work; is not nice to look at; and so on.)

Next, have students draw a picture to represent an example of the solution and record their observations and wonderings in their journal.

Encourage students to look for erosion solutions in their own neighborhoods. Maybe they have seen people putting down fabric or noticed retaining walls. Perhaps they live near a levee or have heard of one nearby. They may even have erosion solutions, such as wind breaks, rock walls, and drainage ditches filled with gravel, around their own homes.

evaluate

Comparing Solutions

Writing

Connecting to the Common Core
Writing
RESEARCH TO BUILD KNOWLEDGE: 2.8

After students have filled out the first four pages of their journal, read the following scenario from page 5 of the journal:

Mr. Weathers has a problem. There is a stream running through his yard. The stream is getting wider every year. What should he do?

 (If you would like to project an actual photo of this scenario, you can find it here: *https://content.ces.ncsu.edu/media/images/Figure_2-highly_erosive.jpg*)

Ask

? Why is this a problem for Mr. Weathers? (He is losing his yard, and the water is getting closer to his house.)

> **SEP: Constructing Explanations and Designing Solutions**
> Compare multiple solutions to a problem.

Next, have students study the drawing, then answer questions 1–5:

1. How is this problem an example of erosion? (Students should be able to explain that soil is being carried away by the water in the stream.)

2. Think about the different erosion solutions in your journal. Which solution would be best for solving Mr. Weathers' erosion problem? (Answers will vary, but students should be able to name a reasonable solution from their Erosion Solutions Journal.)

3. Why did you choose that solution? (Answers will vary, but students should be able to describe an advantage of the solution or explain why it is a better choice than other solutions.)

4. What might be a disadvantage, or negative thing, about that solution? (Answers will vary, but students might cite the high cost or difficulty of installing the solution, risks to wildlife or the environment, how the solution looks, how long it would take to work, etc.)

5. Draw on the picture to show the solution being used.

A Local Erosion Problem

In order to give students an opportunity to apply what they have learned to a real-world local erosion issue, locate a place in your community that has an erosion problem. If you are unable to take the students to observe it firsthand, take photographs and/or video to share with your students in the classroom. You can use the questions from the Mr. Weathers scenario to guide the discussion. *Ask*

? Why is this a problem? (Answers will vary.)

? How is this problem an example of erosion? (Students should be able to explain how soil is being carried away by wind or water.)

? Think about the different erosion solutions in your journal. Which solution would be best for solving the erosion problem? (Answers will vary, but students should be able to name a reasonable solution from their Erosion Solutions Journal.)

A LOCAL EROSION PROBLEM

? Why did you choose that solution? (Answers will vary, but students should be able to describe an advantage of the solution or explain why it is a better choice than other solutions.)

? What might be a disadvantage, or negative thing, about that solution? (Answers will vary, but students might cite the high cost or difficulty of installing the solution, risks to wildlife or the environment, how the solution looks, how long it would take to work, etc.)

> **SEP: Constructing Explanations and Designing Solutions**
> Compare multiple solutions to a problem.

If the problem is on public property, you may want to have students write letters to the local soil and water conservation district describing the problem and their proposed solutions. Alternatively, invite someone from your soil and water conservation district to your classroom to evaluate their solutions.

STEM Everywhere

Give students the STEM Everywhere student page as a way to involve their families and extend their learning. They can do the activity with an adult helper and share their results with the class. If students do not have access to the internet at home,

Opportunities for Differentiated Instruction

This box lists questions and challenges related to the lesson that students may select to research, investigate, or innovate. Students may also use the questions as examples to help them generate their own questions. These questions can help you move your students from the teacher-directed investigation to engaging in the science and engineering practices in a more student-directed format.

Extra Support

For students who are struggling to meet the lesson objectives, provide a question and guide them in the process of collecting research or help them design procedures or solutions..

Extensions

For students with high interest or who have already met the lesson objectives, have them choose a question (or pose their own question), conduct their own research, and design their own procedures or solutions.

After selecting one of the questions in the box or formulating their own question, students can individually or collaboratively make predictions, design investigations or surveys to test their predictions, collect evidence, devise explanations, design solutions, or examine related resources. They can communicate their findings through a science notebook, at a poster session or gallery walk, or by producing a media project.

Research

Have students brainstorm researchable questions:

? What is topsoil and what is it made of?

? What was the Dust Bowl?

? What can farmers do to protect their topsoil from erosion?

Investigate

Have students brainstorm testable questions to be solved through science or math:

? What observations can you make of soil in your area?

? Can you change the course of a river using pebbles? Make a model.

? Does the slope of a hill affect the shape a river makes when running down it? Make two models using soil or sand and compare.

Innovate

Have students brainstorm problems to be solved through engineering:

? Can you build a model of a house located on a riverbank?

? Can you design and model a solution to protect the house you built from a flood?

? Can you design and model a solution to protect the house you built from a dust storm?

you may choose to have them complete this activity at school.

Websites

Websites are listed within lesson.

More Books to Read

Hyde, N. 2016. *Earthquakes, eruptions, and other events that change earth*. New York: Crabtree Publishing Company.
Summary: This book explains that although most of Earth's surface is changed slowly over hundreds or thousands of years, some changes happen quickly in a matter of minutes, hours, or days. These fast changes include earthquakes, landslides, volcanic eruptions, and tsunamis. Includes full-color photos, a glossary, an index, bold-print words, a hands-on activity, and diagrams showing the layers of Earth and how mountains are made.

Hyde, N. 2016. *Protecting Earth's surface*. New York: Crabtree Publishing Company.
Summary: This book reveals the ways Earth's surface is constantly being changed by wind, water, and human activity, and it describes how people can reduce the detrimental effects of these forces by planting trees and grass, installing plastic soil covers, and building levees. Includes full-color photos, a glossary, an index, bold-print words, and a hands-on activity.

Pattison, D. 2019. *Erosion: How Hugh Bennett saved America's soil and ended the Dust Bowl*. Little Rock, AR: Mims House.
Summary: Set in the 1930s during the Dust Bowl, this story of soil scientist Hugh Bennett describes how he used his vast knowledge of soil composition, erosion, and land management to convince politicians that the soil needed help. In the end, his hard work paid off and Congress passed a law establishing the Soil Conservation Service, the first government agency dedicated to protecting the land.

Storad, C. 2012. *Earth's changing surface*. Vero Beach, FL: Rourke Educational Media.
Summary: Simple, spare text and full-color photos describe both quick and slow changes to Earth's surface. Includes bold-print words, comprehension questions, a glossary, an index, and websites.

Name: _____

Wind and Water Cloze

1. Wind, water, and ice can break large landforms into small pieces. This is a slow process called _____.

2. Air that moves is called _____.

3. Moving material from one place to another is called _____.

4. Almost three-quarters of Earth is covered by _____.

5. _____ can make big changes to Earth's surface quickly by moving rocks and carving out new channels.

6. Rivers and streams can slowly carve out deep valleys with steep sides called _____.

7. When too much rain hits soil or sand, it can begin to slide away. This is called a _____.

8. Slowly moving rivers of ice are called _____.

landslide	floodwaters	erosion	glaciers
weathering	canyons	wind	water

National Science Teaching Association

Erosion Solutions Journal

What is erosion?

Wind and water can move Earth materials like sand or soil from one place to another. This is called erosion. Erosion can cause many problems. Let's explore some solutions!

Name: _____

Plants

Erosion Solution: Use plants to hold sand or soil in place.

What do you notice?	What do you wonder?

Fabric

Erosion Solution: Cover soil with fabric to hold it in place while plants grow through it.

What do you notice?	What do you wonder?

Rocks or Walls

Erosion Solution: Install rocks or build retaining walls to keep soil in place.

What do you notice?	What do you wonder?

National Science Teaching Association

Levees

Erosion Solution: Construct earthen or concrete levees on riverbanks to control flooding.

What do you notice?	What do you wonder?

Comparing Solutions

Mr. Weathers has a problem. There is a stream running through his yard. The stream is getting wider every year.

1. How is this problem an example of erosion? _____

_____

2. Think about the different erosion solutions in your journal. Which solution would be best for solving Mr. Weathers's erosion problem?

_____

3. Why did you choose that solution? _____

_____

4. What might be a disadvantage, or negative thing, about that solution?

_____

5. Draw on the picture above to show the solution being used.

National Science Teaching Association

Name: _____

STEM Everywhere

At school, we have been learning **how wind and water can change Earth's surface**. To find out more, ask your learner questions such as:

- What did you learn?
- What was your favorite part of the lesson?
- What are you still wondering?

At home, you can watch how a civil engineer studies the damaging effects of wind.

 www.pbslearningmedia.org/resource/b9199698-8a69-4468-b224-8bbcab0c7531/b9199698-8a69-4468-b224-8bbcab0c7531

Available in English and Spanish.

After watching the video, discuss the following questions:

1. How did the engineer model the effects of wind damage on a wall and a car door?

_____

_____

_____

2. What would be fun or interesting about this job?

_____

_____

_____

Our Blue Planet

Description

A famous photograph of Earth called "The Blue Marble" introduces the phenomenon that most of our planet is covered in water. By exploring with maps, globes, and satellite images of Earth and reading a book that shares names and descriptions of various bodies of water, students are able to identify both liquid and solid bodies of water (ice) on Earth. Students also use the Google Earth app to take virtual field trips to different places on the planet and to locate the bodies of water closest to their school.

Alignment with the *Next Generation Science Standards*

Performance Expectations

2-ESS2-2: Develop a model to represent the shapes and kinds of land and bodies of water in an area.

2-ESS2-3: Obtain information to identify where water is found on Earth and that it can be solid or liquid.

Science and Engineering Practices	Disciplinary Core Ideas	Crosscutting Concept
Developing and Using Models Develop and/or use a model to represent amounts, relationships, relative scales (bigger, smaller), and/or patterns in the natural and designed world(s).	**ESS2.B: Plate Tectonics and Large-Scale System Interactions** Maps show where things are located. One can map the shapes and kinds of land and water in any area.	**Scale, Proportion, and Quantity** Relative scales allow objects to be compared and described (e.g., bigger and smaller; hotter and colder; faster and slower).
Obtaining, Evaluating, and Communicating Information Read grade-appropriate texts and/ or use media to obtain scientific and/or technical information to determine patterns in and/or evidence about the natural and designed world(s).	**ESS2.C: The Roles of Water in Earth's Surface Processes** Water is found in the oceans, rivers, lakes, and ponds. Water exists as solid ice and in liquid form.	
	ETS2.A: Interdependence of Science, Engineering, and Technology Science and engineering involve the use of tools to observe and measure things.	

Note: The activities in this lesson will help students move toward the performance expectations listed, which is the goal after multiple activities. However, the activities will not by themselves be sufficient to reach the performance expectations.

Featured Picture Books

TITLE: **All the Water in the World**
AUTHOR: **George Ella Lyon**
ILLUSTRATOR: **Katherine Tillotson**
PUBLISHER: **Atheneum Books for Young Readers**
YEAR: **2011**
GENRE: **Narrative Information**
SUMMARY: *Rhythmic language and vibrant artwork describe why "all the water in the world is all the water in the world," which keeps cycling through various forms and places.*

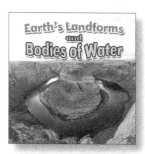

TITLE: **Earth's Landforms and Bodies of Water**
AUTHOR: **Natalie Hyde**
PUBLISHER: **Crabtree**
YEAR: **2015**
GENRE: **Non-Narrative Information**
SUMMARY: *Vivid photography and simple text introduce children to the different landforms and bodies of water that are found on Earth. The book includes ways that maps and globes are used to model Earth's features.*

Time Needed

This lesson will take several class periods. Suggested scheduling is as follows:

Session 1: **Engage** with *All the Water in the World* Read-Aloud and **Explore** with "The Blue Marble" and Google Earth Virtual Field Trip

Session 2: **Explain** with Comparing Bodies of Water and *Earth's Landforms and Bodies of Water* Read-Aloud

Session 3: **Elaborate** with Where's Our Water? and **Evaluate** with Our Blue Planet Place Map

Materials

For "The Blue Marble"

- "The Blue Marble" photograph from *Apollo 17* (see "Websites")
- Globe and world map

For Google Earth Virtual Field Trip

- Google Earth and Google Maps app

For Earth's Landforms and Bodies of Water *Read-Aloud*

- Scissors
- Globe and world map
- Tape or glue

SAFETY
Use caution when handling scissors to avoid puncturing skin.

For Where's Our Water?

- Google Earth and Google Maps apps

For Our Blue Planet Place Map (per student)

- Scissors
- Crayons or markers
- Bodies of Water Cards (uncut)
- Cutout strips of Ocean Cards
- 9 × 12 in. white card stock or construction paper
- Glue

Student Pages

- Google Earth Virtual Field Trip
- Bodies of Water
- Bodies of Water Cards
- Ocean Cards
- Our Blue Planet Place Map
- STEM Everywhere

Background for Teachers

In 1972, NASA took a photograph that changed the way we see our world. In fact, it is one of the most widely distributed photographs of all time. This photo of Earth, taken as the *Apollo 17* astronauts were heading to the Moon, gave us a new perspective on our planet. It reminded the astronauts of a swirly blue glass marble, so the photograph was aptly titled "The Blue Marble."

The blue color of our planet is due to the abundance of water, which gives off blue light upon reflection. Nearly three-fourths (about 71%) of the surface of Earth is covered in water, and most of that water (about 96.5%) is contained within the ocean as *salt water*. The greatest volume of *freshwater* on Earth is not located in rivers or lakes. It is located underground or frozen in *glaciers* and *polar ice caps*. In fact, only about 1% of all the water on Earth is accessible freshwater. Our water is precious—all that's here is all we have. Thus, understanding Earth's water is a key concept in K–12 science education.

An *ocean* is a large, deep body of salt water. There is really just one ocean that covers our planet, but explorers and oceanographers have divided the world ocean into five named regions: Atlantic, Pacific, Indian, Arctic, and Southern. All these ocean regions flow into one another (which is why

THE BLUE MARBLE

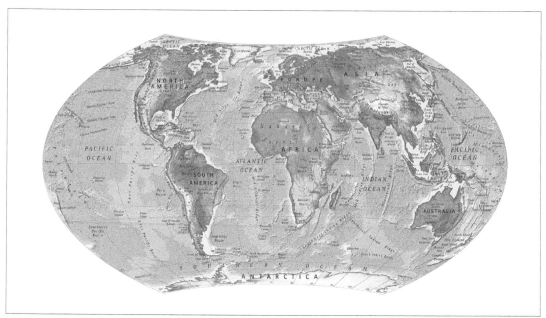

*O*CEAN REGIONS

there is truly only one ocean). There used to be only four named oceans, but since 2000, most countries recognize the Southern Ocean as the fifth ocean. (Note that older classroom maps and globes may not have the Southern Ocean labeled.). Also, many people use the words *ocean* and *sea* to mean the same thing, but geographically, a sea is a large body of salt water that is completely or partly surrounded by land (often part of an ocean).

This lesson also addresses several bodies of freshwater: lakes, ponds, rivers, streams, canals, and glaciers. A *lake* is a large body of (usually) freshwater surrounded on all sides by land, whereas a *pond* is a smaller body of still water. A *river* is a long, narrow body of water that flows into a lake or the ocean. A *stream* is a general term for a small body of moving water. Depending on its location or certain characteristics, a stream may be referred to as a river, branch, brook, creek, or other term. A *canal* is a humanmade waterway that connects two bodies of water. Canals can be either freshwater or salt water depending on the bodies of water they connect. A *glacier* is a dense layer of slow-flowing ice that forms over many years, sometimes centuries. A glacier differs from an iceberg, which is a huge body of ice that floats on water. Understanding how bodies of water are named can be tricky. For example, the Dead Sea is actually a saltwater lake, the Sea of Galilee is actually a freshwater lake, and there are many more exceptions to the naming conventions that people have used throughout history. For students, learning the names of bodies of water is not as important as their understanding that (1) water can be found as a liquid and a solid in a wide variety of bodies, (2) these bodies can be located on maps, and (3) technology can help us map our planet.

Since "The Blue Planet" photo was taken, there have been great advances in photographing and mapping our planet. Satellites orbiting Earth can take pictures, and global positioning systems (GPS) can locate us (or at least our smartphones) on maps. In this lesson, students are engaged in the science and engineering practice (SEP) of developing and using models as they use digital models, such as Google Earth and Google Maps, to locate and compare different bodies of water on Earth. The composite images on Google Earth are made using photographs taken by satellites orbiting our planet, airplanes that fly over Earth, and even Google cars that drive around and take "street view" footage. This technology allows us to explore our planet from the comfort of our classrooms. Finally, students make their own "place-map" model of our blue planet, showing the locations of the five named ocean regions. The SEP of obtaining, evaluating, and communicating information is used as students compare the ideas about bodies of water they put together from their experience with Google Earth to the information in a nonfiction book. The crosscutting concept (CCC) of scale, proportion, and quantity is incorporated as students compare the sizes of different bodies of water on Earth and how that relates to the way the body of water is classified (e.g., ocean, sea, lake, pond).

Using maps to locate different kinds of land and water in grades K–2 sets a foundation on which students can build in grades 3–5. In the upper elementary grades, students not only use maps to locate land and water features on Earth but also begin to explore the patterns of different landforms on Earth that are often formed along the boundaries between oceans and continents.

Learning Progressions

Below are the disciplinary core idea (DCI) grade band endpoints for grades K–2 and 3–5. These are provided to show how student understanding of the DCIs in this lesson will progress in future grade levels.

DCIs	Grades K–2	Grades 3–5
ESS1.C: The History of Planet Earth	• Some events happen very quickly; others occur very slowly, over a time period much longer than one can observe.	• Local, regional, and global patterns of rock formations reveal changes over time due to Earth forces such as earthquakes. The presence and location of certain fossil types indicate the order in which rock layers were formed.
ESS2.A: Earth Materials and Systems	• Wind and water can change the shape of the land..	• Rainfall helps to shape the land and affects the types of living things found in a region. Water, ice, wind, living organisms, and gravity break rocks, soils, and sediments into smaller particles and move them around.
ETS1.C: Optimizing the Design Solution	• Because there is always more than one possible solution to a problem, it is useful to compare and test designs.	• Different solutions need to be tested in order to determine which of them best solves the problem, given the criteria and the constraints.

Source: Willard, T., ed. 2015. *The NSTA quick-reference guide to the* NGSS: *Elementary school.* Arlington, VA: NSTA Press.

 engage

All the Water in the World Read-Aloud

 *Inferring*

> Connecting to the Common Core
> **Reading: Literature**
> KEY IDEAS AND DETAILS: 2.2

Show students the cover of *All the Water in the World* and introduce the author, George Ella Lyon, and the illustrator, Katherine Tillotson. Read the first line, which says, "All the water in the world is all the water in the world." *Ask*

? What do you think the author means by this? (Answers will vary.)

Continue reading the book aloud and stop after reading page 11, which says, "Water doesn't come. It goes. Around." *Ask*

? What do you think the author means by those lines? (Answers will vary.)

Have students listen for the answers to the two questions you've asked as you continue reading the book to the end. From the reading, they should recognize that all the water in the world has been here before in different places and different forms. There is no other supply of water—all the water in the world is all the water we have. After reading the book, *ask*

? Where is water found on Earth? (Answers will vary.)

Tell students that they will be learning all about all the water in the world!

explore

"The Blue Marble"

 *Inferring*

Project the famous NASA photograph titled "The Blue Marble" (see the "Websites" section). *Ask*

? What do you observe about this picture? (Answers will vary.)

? How do you think it was made? (Answers will vary.)

Explain that this photograph of Earth was taken in 1972 by the *Apollo 17* astronauts as they were traveling to the Moon. The photograph is famous because it was the first to show an almost fully illuminated Earth from the view of a spacecraft. This was achieved because the astronauts had the Sun behind them when they captured the image. The photograph also marks the first time the south polar ice cap was photographed from space. An interesting fact is that nobody knows for sure which astronaut actually took the picture! What we do know for sure is that the photograph had a powerful effect on people and changed the way they thought about Earth.

 *Questioning*

Ask

? What are you wondering about the photograph? (Answers will vary.)

? What makes the blue color on Earth? (water)

? What makes the brown and green colors on Earth? (land)

? What makes the white colors on Earth? (clouds and ice)

? Why do you think the photograph was titled "The Blue Marble?" (Earth's shape is similar to a marble, Earth is mostly blue, and the swirls of clouds look like the swirls on some marbles.)

? From looking at this photo, can you tell whether Earth is mostly land or mostly water?

(Answers will vary, but students should realize that the photo shows only one side of Earth, so it is impossible to tell by looking at it.)

To find out whether Earth is mostly land or mostly water, students will need to see the whole Earth, not just one side. Use a globe to show students a three-dimensional view of Earth. Tell students that a globe is a *model* of Earth. *Ask*

? How is a globe like the real Earth? (It is round, it spins, etc.)

? How is it different? (It is much smaller, it is on a stand, etc.)

Point out that some globes have an arrow somewhere that shows the direction Earth spins on its axis. If you are looking down on the North Pole, a globe should turn counterclockwise to represent how Earth spins in space. Spin the globe slowly in a counterclockwise direction, and *ask*

? How does this model of Earth compare with "The Blue Marble" photograph? (The globe is round, but the photo is flat; the globe is not a real picture, but the photo is a real picture; the globe does not show clouds, but the photo does show clouds; both the globe and the photo show that Earth has a round shape; etc.)

? On the globe, does it look like Earth is mostly land or mostly water? (Answers will vary, but by looking at a globe, it is more evident that Earth is mostly water.)

? Is it possible to travel by water all the way around the globe without crossing any land? (Yes. Have a volunteer demonstrate this by placing one finger on an ocean region and moving it completely around the globe without crossing any landforms.)

Students should notice by observing the globe that the amount of water on Earth greatly exceeds the amount of land. (They will learn from the reading in the explain phase of the lesson that water covers three-quarters of Earth's surface and that most of the water is in Earth's ocean.)

Google Earth Virtual Field Trip

(*Note:* Depending on the availability of technology, this activity could be done as a whole group with the application projected on a screen or in pairs on computers or handheld devices.)

Tell students that they are going on a field trip! This is not a real field trip; it is a "virtual" field trip to explore Earth's water using a computer application called Google Earth. Explain that the images on the Google Earth app are made with *satellite* cameras that orbit Earth, airplanes that fly above Earth, and even cars that drive around to take photographs. Engineers at Google put these photographs together to create this digital model so that we can "fly" around our planet and see what different places actually look like.

> **SEP: Developing and Using Models**
> Develop and/or use a model to represent amounts, relationships, relative scales, and/or patterns in the natural world.

The search feature on Google Earth allows students to enter the name of a place and "fly" there. Point out that sometimes the red placemark icon that shows up is not located exactly on the body

USING GOOGLE EARTH

of water they have entered in the search box, so they will need to zoom out or zoom in (using a two-finger pinch) to get a better view. Students will need to enter the country or city (found in parentheses) for rivers and ponds to more accurately locate those bodies of water.

Give each student a copy of the Google Earth Virtual Field Trip student pages. In pairs, groups, or as a whole class, use the Google Earth app to "fly" to all of the different bodies of water listed on the student pages. There are ocean regions, seas, lakes, rivers, canals, ponds, and glaciers to visit. Have students make observations of each type of body of water and note similarities and differences. Then have pairs of students develop a definition for each body of water based on the evidence they collected from the virtual field trip and write it in the "Our Definition" column. For example, "An ocean is ... a large body of water that connects to other bodies of water around Earth."

CCC: Scale, Proportion, and Quantity
Relative scales allow objects and events to be compared and described. (e.g. warmer, cooler)

---

explain

Comparing Bodies of Water

After students have had a chance to locate the various bodies of water and develop working definitions for them, ask the following questions:

Ocean Regions and Seas

? Based on the evidence from the virtual field trip, how did you define *ocean*? (Answers will vary.)

? How did you define *sea*? (Answers will vary.)

? Which is larger, an ocean or a sea? (An ocean is larger than a sea.)

? What is your evidence from the virtual field trip? (Answers will vary.)

? Have you been to an ocean or sea? (Answers will vary.) Could you see to the other side? (no) Why not? (It is too far, they are too big, and Earth's surface is curved.)

? How many oceans do you think there are on Earth? (Answers will vary, but in the reading that follows, they will learn that Earth has one ocean with five named regions.)

Lakes, Rivers, Canals, and Ponds

? How did you define *lake*? (Answers will vary.)

? How did you define *river*? (Answers will vary.)

? How is a river different from a lake? (A river is longer and thinner than most lakes. Rivers are connected to other bodies of water.)

? What is your evidence from the virtual field trip? (Answers will vary.)

? How did you define *canal*? (Answers will vary.)

? How is a canal different from a river? (A canal usually has straighter sides and goes in more of a straight line.)

? What is your evidence from the virtual field trip? (Answers will vary.)

? How did you define *pond*? (Answers will vary.)

? How is a pond different from a lake? (It is smaller.)

? What is your evidence from the virtual field trip? (Answers will vary.)

Glaciers

? How did you define *glacier*? (Answers will vary.)

? Why do you think a glacier is considered a body of water? (It is made of frozen water.)

? Does a glacier flow like a river? (Answers will vary, but students may have observed the grooves formed by the flowing ice. In the reading that follows, students will learn that glaciers are thick layers of slowly moving ice.)

Earth's Landforms and Bodies of Water Read-Aloud

Connecting to the Common Core
Language
VOCABULARY ACQUISITION AND USE: 2.4

Next, show students the cover of *Earth's Landforms and Bodies of Water*, and tell them that this book will help them learn more about some of the different bodies of water on Earth. Read pages 4–5 aloud. Point out the map of the world at the top of page 5. *Ask*

? How do you think this map was made? (using photographs taken by satellites)

> **SEP: Obtaining, Evaluating, and Communicating Information**
> Read grade-appropriate texts and/or use media to obtain scientific and/or technical information to determine patterns in and/or evidence about the natural world.

Skip pages 6–13, which are about rocks, soil, and landforms (you may want to revisit these pages later). Then explain that the rest of the book describes several bodies of water, but before you continue reading, you would like the class to try to match these different bodies of water to their descriptions.

Card Sort (Before Reading)

Give each student a copy of the Bodies of Water and the Bodies of Water Cards student pages. Have them cut out the cards and place each one next to the description they think matches. Encourage students to think of how some of these bodies of water looked on the virtual field trip. If they are

not sure, they can guess at this point. Let students know that they will have a chance to move their cards after you read the book aloud.

After students have placed their cards, read aloud page 14 of *Earth's Landforms and Bodies of Water*, which defines an ocean as a large, deep body of salt water and explains that most of the water in the world is located in the five ocean regions on Earth. Stop and look at a large map of the world. Have students locate all five ocean regions. Use a globe to show the same bodies of water, and point out that older globes and maps may not have the Southern Ocean labeled because that region wasn't named until the year 2000. Then have students observe how the Pacific Ocean appears on the globe versus on the map. Explain that it is hard to show on a map that the Pacific Ocean is actually in between Asia and the American continents. Then remind students that, although the names all include *ocean*, there is really only *one* ocean on Earth because all ocean water can flow freely around the globe and mix with other ocean water (which you demonstrated in the explore phase). *Ask*

? If there is really only one "world ocean," why do you think five oceans have been named? (It is convenient to separate the "world ocean" geographically by naming different parts of it; having only one named ocean would make it confusing for sailors, mapmakers, and people in general.)

Continue reading to the end of the book. After reading, *ask*

? Which two bodies of water on the Bodies of Water Cards were not described in the book? (seas and canals)

? Which description do you think goes with *sea*? (description 6)

Explain that sometimes people use the terms *ocean* and *sea* interchangeably, but there is a difference. Seas are smaller than oceans and are usually located where the land and the ocean meet. Seas are partly or totally enclosed by land. The terms

can get tricky, though. Some bodies of water, such as the Dead Sea, are actually salt water lakes! *Ask*

? Which description do you think goes with *canal*? (description 7)

? Can you think of other bodies of water that were not described in the book? (bays, gulfs, straits, wetlands, puddles, etc.)

Card Sort (After Reading)

After reading the book, go through the answers together and have students move their cards, if necessary. When students have all of the cards correctly placed, they can glue or tape them into the appropriate boxes. The answer key is in Table 17.1.

Table 17.1. Answer Key for Bodies of Water

Description	Card
1. A large, deep body of salt water	Ocean
2. A long, narrow body of moving water that flows into a lake or the ocean	River
3. A large body of (usually) freshwater surrounded by land on all sides	Lake
4. A small body of still water	Pond
5. A thick layer of moving ice	Glacier
6. A large body of salt water that is completely or partly surrounded by land; often part of the ocean	Sea
7. An artificial waterway that connects two bodies of water	Canal

 ### Questioning

Then *ask*

? Which bodies of water are salt water? (oceans and seas)

? Which bodies of water are freshwater? (streams, rivers, lakes, ponds, and glaciers)

? There are actually some salt water rivers and lakes on Earth. Do you know of any lakes that are salt water? (Some students may be familiar with Utah's Great Salt Lake or other saline lakes around the world.)

? Are canals made of salt water or freshwater? (It depends on the bodies of water they connect.)

? Do you think most of the water on Earth is salt water or freshwater? (salt water, because most of Earth's water is in the ocean)

? Do we drink freshwater or salt water? (freshwater)

Explain that it is important to conserve and protect our freshwater sources, because although Earth is three-fourths water, only a tiny fraction of it is drinkable! Our water is precious. All that's here is all we have. *Ask*

? What are some ways we can conserve, or save, our water? (Answers will vary but may include turning off the faucet when we brush our teeth, not leaving water running, being careful not to litter or pollute water, using less water on lawns by planting drought-resistant plants, etc.)

elaborate

Where's Our Water?

Students can apply their knowledge of different bodies of water by locating and identifying the nearest bodies of water to their school using the Google Maps app. For this activity, you will be using the map layer instead of the satellite layer. The bodies of water will be easier to see in the map view than in the satellite view. Demonstrate how to locate your school in Google Maps by following these steps:

1. Enter the school's address in the "search" field of Google Maps.

2. Make sure you are viewing the map layer.

3. Explain that, on this map, blue represents water.

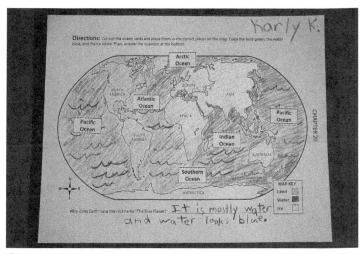

OUR BLUE PLANET PLACE MAP

SEP: Developing and Using Models

Develop and/or use a model to represent amounts, relationships, relative scales, and/or patterns in the natural world.

The following activity could be done as a class or with partners: Slowly zoom out and stop when you see a body of water. Determine what kind of body of water it is by its size, shape, and name. Keep zooming out, pausing to take note of all the bodies of water on the map. Together, see if you can locate which ocean, sea, stream, river, lake, pond, canal, and glacier is closest to the school.

evaluate

Our Blue Planet Place Map

*Synthesizing*

Give each student a copy of the Our Blue Planet Place Map student page and a strip of Ocean Cards to cut out. Have them refer to a classroom globe, map, or Google Earth to correctly place the names of all five of Earth's ocean regions. (Point out that Pacific Ocean will be used twice, and remind students that some maps and globes may not have the Southern Ocean labeled.) Then have students color the water blue, the land a different color, and the ice white. They can then fill in the map key showing the colors they used for areas of land, water, and ice. Finally, have them answer the question at the bottom, which asks, "Why does Earth have the nickname 'The Blue Planet'?" When students have completed their place maps, they can glue them onto a 9 × 12-inch piece of white card stock or construction paper. If possible, laminate the maps and then send them home with students to act as a daily visual reminder that "all the water in the world is all the water in the world"!

SEP: Developing and Using Models

Develop and/or use a model to represent amounts, relationships, relative scales, and/or patterns in the natural world.

STEM Everywhere

Give students the STEM Everywhere student page as a way to involve their families and extend their learning. They can do the activity with an adult helper and share their results with the class. If students do not have access to the internet at home, you may choose to have them complete this activity at school.

Chapter
17

Opportunities for Differentiated Instruction

This box lists questions and challenges related to the lesson that students may select to research, investigate, or innovate. Students may also use the questions as examples to help them generate their own questions. These questions can help you move your students from the teacher-directed investigation to engaging in the science and engineering practices in a more student-directed format.

Extra Support

For students who are struggling to meet the lesson objectives, provide a question and guide them in the process of collecting research or help them design procedures or solutions.

Extensions

For students with high interest or who have already met the lesson objectives, have them choose a question (or pose their own question), conduct their own research, and design their own procedures or solutions.

After selecting one of the questions in the box or formulating their own question, students can individually or collaboratively make predictions, design investigations or surveys to test their predictions, collect evidence, devise explanations, design solutions, or examine related resources. They can communicate their findings through a science notebook, at a poster session or gallery walk, or by producing a media project.

Research

Have students brainstorm researchable questions:

? How much of Earth's water is frozen?

? What was the first satellite in space? How many humanmade satellites are now orbiting Earth?

? What is the longest river in the world? Largest lake? Largest ocean?

Investigate

Have students brainstorm testable questions to be solved through science or math:

? Which is longer, the Nile River or the Amazon River? What is the difference in length?

? Locate the nearest ocean on a map. Find a city or town on the coast that might be fun to visit. Type your home address into Google Maps or another map program, and use the "Directions" feature. Type in the name of your coastal destination. How many miles away is it? How long would it take to get there by car? How much longer would it take to get there if you walked?

? Survey your friends and family: Would you rather live on the shore of a river, a lake, or an ocean? What would be the benefits and risks of your choice? Graph the results, then analyze your graph. What can you conclude?

Continued

Opportunities for Differentiated Instruction (*continued*)

Innovate

Have students brainstorm problems to be solved through engineering:

? Can you use Google Earth to plan your dream vacation?

? Can you design a model to show the shapes and kinds of land and bodies of water in your state or country?

? Can you design a way to keep a beach from eroding into the ocean?

Websites

 "The Blue Marble" From *Apollo 17* (1972)
https://earthobservatory.nasa.gov/ images/2181/the-blue-marble

 Google Earth
www.google.com/earth

 Google Maps
www.google.com/maps

More Books to Read

Dorros, A. 1991. *Follow the water from brook to ocean*. New York: HarperCollins.
Summary: This Let's-Read-and-Find-Out Science book explains how water flows from brooks, to streams, to rivers, over waterfalls, and through canyons and dams to eventually reach the ocean.

Lindstrom, C. 2020. *We are water protectors*. New York: Roaring Book Press.
Summary: Inspired by the many Indigenous-led movements across North America, poetic text and stunning illustrations express the importance of protecting and preserving Earth's water.

Olien, R. 2016. *Water sources*. Mankato, MN: Capstone Press.
Summary: This fact-filled book will introduce young readers to rivers, oceans, lakes, groundwater, and other bodies of water. Water on Earth in the form of ice is also covered.

Paul, M. 2015. *Water is water: A book about the water cycle*. New York: Roaring Brook Press.
Summary: Simple, poetic text and dreamy illustrations follow a group of children as they experience the different phases of the water cycle.

Chapter 17

Name: _____

Google Earth Virtual Field Trip

Directions: Use the Google Earth search feature to "fly" to the following bodies of water on Earth. Zoom in or zoom out with a two-finger pinch to get a good look! Put a check (✓) in the box after you have seen each one. Next, write a definition for each body of water that is based on your observations.

Body of Water	Our Definition
1. **Ocean Regions** ☐ Atlantic Ocean ☐ Pacific Ocean ☐ Arctic Ocean ☐ Indian Ocean ☐ Southern Ocean	An *ocean* is …
2. **Seas** ☐ Caribbean Sea ☐ Mediterranean Sea	A *sea* is …
3. **Lakes** ☐ Lake Superior ☐ Lake Victoria	A *lake* is …

308

National Science Teaching Association

Body of Water	Our Definition
4. **Rivers** ☐ Nile River (Cairo) ☐ Yangtze River (Wuhan)	**A *river* is …**
5. **Canals** ☐ Panama Canal ☐ Suez Canal	**A *canal* is …**
6. **Ponds** ☐ Walden Pond (Massachusetts) ☐ Antonelli Pond (California)	**A *pond* is …**
7. **Glaciers** ☐ Pine Island Glacier ☐ Bering Glacier	**A *glacier* is …**

Name: _____

Bodies of Water

Directions: Cut out the Bodies of Water Cards and match them to the correct description.

Description	Picture
1. A large, deep body of salt water	
2. A long, narrow body of moving water that flows into a lake or the ocean	
3. A large body of (usually) freshwater surrounded by land on all sides	

National Science Teaching Association

Description	Picture
4. A small body of still water	
5. A thick layer of moving ice	
6. A large body of salt water that is completely or partly surrounded by land; often part of the ocean	
7. An artificial waterway that connects two bodies of water	

Bodies of Water Cards

Sea

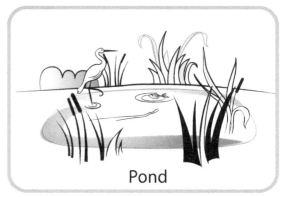

Pond

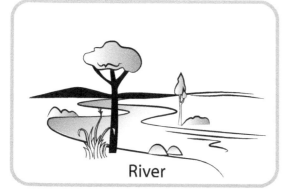

River

Lake

Ocean

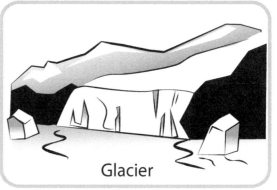

Glacier

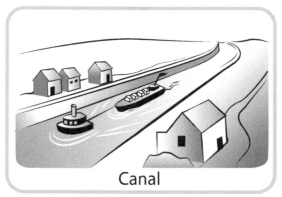

Canal

National Science Teaching Association

Ocean Cards

Arctic Ocean	Atlantic Ocean	Indian Ocean	Pacific Ocean	Pacific Ocean	Southern Ocean
Arctic Ocean	Atlantic Ocean	Indian Ocean	Pacific Ocean	Pacific Ocean	Southern Ocean
Arctic Ocean	Atlantic Ocean	Indian Ocean	Pacific Ocean	Pacific Ocean	Southern Ocean
Arctic Ocean	Atlantic Ocean	Indian Ocean	Pacific Ocean	Pacific Ocean	Southern Ocean
Arctic Ocean	Atlantic Ocean	Indian Ocean	Pacific Ocean	Pacific Ocean	Southern Ocean
Arctic Ocean	Atlantic Ocean	Indian Ocean	Pacific Ocean	Pacific Ocean	Southern Ocean
Arctic Ocean	Atlantic Ocean	Indian Ocean	Pacific Ocean	Pacific Ocean	Southern Ocean
Arctic Ocean	Atlantic Ocean	Indian Ocean	Pacific Ocean	Pacific Ocean	Southern Ocean

Our Blue Planet Place Map

Name: _____

Directions: Cut out the Ocean Cards and glue them in the correct places on the map. Color the water blue, the land a different color, and the ice white. Then answer the question at the bottom of the page.

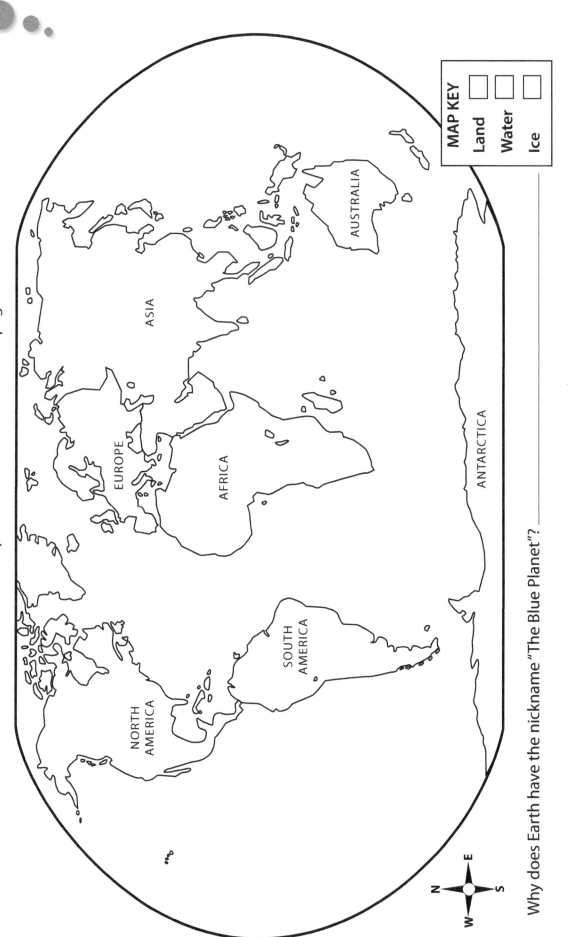

MAP KEY
☐ Land
☐ Water
☐ Ice

ASIA

EUROPE

AFRICA

AUSTRALIA

ANTARCTICA

NORTH AMERICA

SOUTH AMERICA

N
W — E
S

Why does Earth have the nickname "The Blue Planet"? _____

Name: _____

STEM Everywhere

Dear Families,

At school, we have been learning about how maps can be used to locate bodies of water on Earth. We used Google Earth to find different oceans, seas, lakes, ponds, and rivers on Earth. We used Google Maps to find the closest body of water to our school. To find out more, ask your learner questions such as:

- What did you learn?
- What was your favorite part of the lesson?
- What are you still wondering?

At home, you can read about how Google Street View technology works. First, read the passage below with an adult helper. Then begin exploring together by following the directions.

About Google Street View

Do you like to look at maps? One kind of map is the Google Street View map, which allows you to view places as if you were standing right there! The photographs you see on these maps are often taken by cameras mounted to the tops of special Google Maps camera cars. But cars can't go everywhere, so sometimes the photos are taken by cameras mounted on bikes, backpacks, boats, or even snowmobiles! The photos are then joined together to make the full 360° pictures you see.

Using this technology, you can relax in the comfort of your own home while you take a virtual walk through your neighborhood. Street View even offers views of national parks and other famous places. Let's take a look!

Continued

Name: _____

Using Google Street View

1. Go to *www.google.com/maps*.

2. Type your address into the box at the top that says, "Search Google Maps," and hit "enter."

3. Does a picture of your home appear below the search box? If so, click on the picture.

4. The picture will expand to full view. Click and drag the picture to explore the 360° view, if possible. What do you observe?

5. Click the back arrow to bring back the search bar. Then try typing a famous place into the search bar, such as Niagara Falls, Old Faithful, the Grand Canyon, or anywhere else you would like to visit! Click on the picture, then click on some of the pictures that may appear below the search bar.

6. Draw a picture of something you observed in the box below.

National Science Teaching Association

Index

Page numbers printed in **boldface type** indicate tables, figures, or photographs.

National Science Teaching Association